The Philippines and Japan in America's Shadow

The Philippines and Japan in America's Shadow

Edited by
Kiichi Fujiwara and Yoshiko Nagano

NUS PRESS
SINGAPORE

Published by:

NUS Press
National University of Singapore
AS3-01-02, 3 Arts Link
Singapore 117569

Fax: (65) 6774-0652
E-mail: nusbooks@nus.edu.sg
Website: http://www.nus.edu.sg/nuspress

ISBN 978-9971-69-469-2 (Paper)

National Library Board Singapore Cataloguing in Publication Data

The Philippines and Japan in America's shadow / edited by Kiichi Fujiwara and Yoshiko Nagano. – Singapore : NUS Press, c2010.
p. cm.
Includes bibliographical references and index.
ISBN-13 : 978-9971-69-469-2 (pbk.)

1. Philippines – Civilization – American influences. 2. Philippines – Colonial influence. 3. Japan – Civilization – American influences. 4. Japan – History – Allied occupation, 1945-1952. 5. Philippines – Foreign relations – United States. 6. United States – Foreign relations – Philippines. 7. Japan – Foreign relations – United States. 8. United States – Foreign relations – Japan. 9. United States – Territories and possessions – History.
I. Fujiwara, Kiichi, 1956- II. Nagano, Yoshiko, 1950-

DS821.5
952 – dc22 OCN667111790

Cover image: Fall of Panay (Diorama), c.1970s (Courtesy of the Ayala Museum)

Typeset by: International Typesetters Pte Ltd
Printed by: Mainland Press Pte Ltd

Contents

Abbreviations

CE	Clarence R. Edwards Papers, Massachusetts Historical Society
ERP	Elihu Root Papers. Library of Congress
MP	The Papers of William McKinley, Library of Congress
USCG	United States Consulate General, Hong Kong, USNA Microfilm
USMG	United States Major-General Commanding the Army
USNA	United States National Archives. Washington, DC
	BIA: Bureau of Insular Affairs RG: Record Group 350
USPC	United States Philippine Commission (Schurman)
USWD	United States War Department

Preface

This book is an outcome of the research project entitled "Under America's Shadow: A Comparative Study of American Perceptions and Social Formation in Japan and the Philippines," with the Grant-in-Aid for Scientific Research by the Japan Society for the Promotion of Science for the years 2005–2006. The aim of this research project was as follows:

The United States is an existence that loomed large in both Japan and the Philippines, not only in terms of world views per se, but also in such fields as political institutions, structure of economy, mass culture and consumption patterns. For both nations experienced a direct rule by the United States, a character that makes the two distinct from other Asian or European nations, though they have also received the tremendous impact from the United States.

In this study, a group of scholars including Japanese, Filipinos, and Americans, have for the first time, dealt with the magnitude of the American legacy in Japan and the Philippines. For this purpose, we got together three times in Japan and the Philippines. First, at the workshop at the Faculty of Law, University of Tokyo in November 2005 for brainstorming; and second, at the "The Philippines-Japan Relationship in an Evolving Paradigm" symposium held at the Yuchengco Center, De La Salle University in Manila in March 2006. This symposium marked the 50th anniversary of the normalization of diplomatic ties between the Philippines and Japan, under the co-sponsorship of the Embassy of Japan in the Philippines and the Japan Foundation in Manila. Then, at our third and final meeting, we participated in the First Philippine Studies Conference of Japan (PSCJ 2006) held at the Tokyo Green Palace Hotel in November 2006.

These three gatherings were made possible thanks to tremendous assistance and cooperation from various scholars and friends. For the symposium at the De La Salle University, we received the heartwarming support from Ambassador Ryuichiro Yamazaki at the Embassy of Japan, Trinidad Osteria of the Yuchengco Center and Tsutomu Suzuki of Japan Foundation, Manila. We also benefitted from the invaluable participation of scholars such as Maruja Asis, Maria Serena Diokno, Ricardo Jose, Yutaka Katayama, Julio Teehankee and Lydia Yu-Jose, aside from the members of our research group. The preliminary report of our research project, "Proceedings of the Symposium: The Philippines-Japan Relationship in an Evolving Paradigm" was published by Yuchengco Center, De La Salle University in 2006.

At the First Philippine Studies Conference of Japan (PSCJ 2006), the members of our research group got together again and presented their papers in various organized panels by the conference committee. This conference was prepared as the first of its sort in Japan, in conjunction with the International Conference of Philippine Studies (ICOPHIL), headed by Belinda A. Aquino of the University of Hawaii at Manoa. We are grateful to the Embassy of the Philippines in Japan for extending its sponsorship for PSCJ 2006 and to Ambassador Domingo L. Siazon who joined us as the guest of honor at the reception of the conference. We also received kind assistance and advice from Patricio N. Abinales, Donna J. Aromoso, Germelino M. Bautista, Leslie E. Bauzon, Caroline S. Hau, Vicente L. Rafael, and Michael Salman. We are happy to report here that this research project became a major part of PSCJ 2006, which saw the attendance of over 150 local and international scholars and students. Now the torch of this conference is being passed to our next generation.

Kiichi Fujiwara and Yoshiko Nagano
November 2010

Introduction

The Tale of Two Empires: Japan and the US as Latecomers in Colonialism

Kiichi Fujiwara

Comparing the United States and Japan as colonial empires must sound strange, or even bizarre. Japan was, after all, the power that annexed the Korean peninsula on a dubious basis that seemed "legal" only to the Japanese, violently took over Manchuria, and then further advanced her military forces to China and Southeast Asia. The United States, on the other hand, has shown far less interest in its territorial expansion. America was to give support to the freedom fighters, not to the oppressors; colonialism as practiced in 19th-century Europe had no room in a world that is "safe for democracies." After acquiring Cuba and the Philippines, the US gave up both territories, which may very well have been jealously kept as crown jewels by other empires, even though the power and influence of anti-colonial movements in both Cuba and the Philippines were limited. The Japanese aspired for colonial possession in spite of their relative lack of power, while America, in spite of its unprecedented power, promoted independence abroad.

Thus, there emerges a conventional wisdom that Japanese — and for that matter, Russians or Germans — may aspire for an empire, but not the United States. If an empire entails autocracy at home and territorial ambitions abroad, the United States promoted democracy both at home and abroad. Not only was the United States not an empire, it was the opposite, opening ways for a world free from tyranny and colonialism. Such seems to be the view among international relations students, as Japan — along with the Russians or the Germans — never fails to be included in the study of empires, while the US appears as the defender of freedom against such imperial aspirations.

I disagree. Historically, both the US and Japan were latecomers in the age of colonialism, way after the advances of British or French forces abroad, but that did not prevent them from seeking opportunities abroad that may expand their overseas territories. Moreover, both the US and Japan share distinct characteristics of what I will here call "latecomer-colonialism," sharing common traits not found in their predecessors, the British or French empires. Starting from the strong role of the state to the primacy of geopolitics, both empires, I argue, share enough similarities to allow comparative analysis between the two.

This is not to say they are the same. If the Americans pushed forward for an informal empire that relied less on territorial rule, Japan, through an expansionist reading of pan-nationalism, twisted the notion of self-determination for the sake of territorial expansion. Territorial rule was not central in the expansion of American power overseas, while the expansion of its territories was essential in the Japanese's pursuit of pan-nationalism.

Quests for informal empire and pan-nationalism, however, should not be taken as two opposites, but rather, as two models for latecomer-colonialism. Both the United States and Japan entered the period of colonialism when colonialism as such was difficult to defend; both informal empire and pan-nationalism were attempts to extend political influence overseas under a new framework that does not simply justify external rule by military fiat.

The argument will proceed as follows. First, I will try to establish the characteristics of latecomer imperialism as opposed to its more traditional European variants. Next, I will argue that the two models — informal empire and pan-nationalism — are the two answers to the post-First World War international order, and attempt to maintain and extend political control in an age that deprived colonialism of its legitimacy.

Finally, I will briefly discuss the aftermath of the two empires. When the American informal empire established itself as the prototype of world order after the Second World War, the Japanese empire collapsed as a consequence of a self-destructive war, reducing Japan to a *de facto* client state of the United States, who imposed a benevolent and reformist occupation that shared remarkable similarity to their previous rule in the Philippines. Japan, by a Faustian twist of fate, started from an empire and ended as a client.

Latecomers in Colonialism

What is latecomer-colonialism? The first point to be made, almost by definition, is the timing of which the annexation of overseas territories took place. And it goes without saying that the colonial expansion of both the Americans and the Japanese started in a far later period as compared to British or French expansion. Although American steamships had been sailing across the Pacific as early as the mid-19th century, there was little demand for expanding overseas territorial rule in the United States, as the nation was gifted with rich natural resources and market at home; pushing native Americans to the peripheral outlands was a higher priority than external engagements overseas, although advances into the Pacific had already been underway in late 19th century. The Japanese, way up until the turn of the century, had more reasons to fear being colonized by Western powers such as Britain, France, or Russia, than to expand and extend its forces to acquire colonies. It was only after the 1890s for the US and after 1905 for Japan that major advances in overseas territories become serious agendas.

When the US and Japan started their expansion abroad, the world had already been more or less carved up by the major

European powers. The only way to expand, therefore, was to occupy the remaining space that had yet to be gobbled up. The Japanese annexation of Taiwan, as well as American advances to island kingdoms in the Pacific such as Hawaii and Samoa, were the overtures to such expansion, that is, the expansion over regions that were left over from European colonialism.

The trouble, however, was that there was not much left on the globe that had yet to be colonized in late 19th century. The latecomers thus had to consider taking over territories that had been ruled by other powers. Some were acquired after relatively easy victories, such as the American rule of the Philippines after the Spanish-American War, or the Japanese annexation of the Korean peninsula after the Russo-Japanese War and Tsingtao after the First World War. Others proved to be heavily contested, the obvious case being the Japanese invasion of Manchuria. Latecomers could only build an empire at the cost of taking over territories governed by others, and such actions seriously challenged the balance of power and stability of international relations in the given region.

The timing of annexation also changed the major actors involved in the act of empire-building. Early empires had been built by individuals that received relatively limited support from formal institutions at home, for it was far more difficult to establish institutional ties with overseas territories in the days when sailing ships had no engine of their own and there was only limited medicine to face unknown diseases even when medical supplies were in order, which was rare. Under such conditions, only the brave, the ruthless and the committed would risk their lives in the barren lands far away from the comforts at home.

Thus, the Spanish conquest of Latin America was more the achievement of conquistadores than that of state-bureaucrats; more the act of individual missionaries than the act of the organized Church that brought Christendom to the New Continent; more the arbitrary exploitation conducted by ambitious and rogue merchants than the well-established companies listed in the London stock market that built up cotton industries in India. As Seeley lamented in 1885 in his *The Expansion of England*, the British Empire, without an overall governmental scheme for empire-building, was built through its back doors.

The development of regular steamship routes, as well as dramatic advances in medicine and healthcare, made it much safer to travel and stay abroad, and opened the way to a more institutional connection between the colonies and the mainland. Missionaries had become more closely tied to their churches, merchants integrated into corporate structures, and the loosely scattered official buildings were reshaped into a coherent administrative structure of the colonial state. Early colonialism was based on individual outlaws and the spiritually committed; colonialism in late 19th century was an act followed by institutions: the church, modern corporations and the state took over the acts of uncoordinated individual action.

The Primacy of the State

If such institutional buildup of colonial rule developed gradually and incrementally in the British and French empires, the latecomer empires, from the very beginning, involved strong initiatives offered by the state authorities at home. The colonies were important not only for the *conquistadores* but for the state itself. Colonialism was a paramount objective eagerly sought after by the state, which can be easily learned from the roster of the name of the people who were dispatched abroad. American rule in the Philippines involved many notable figures in early 20th-century US politics and military affairs, such as Taft, who would later become President; Forbes, a banking tycoon in Boston; Pershing, later a hero of the First World War; and last but not least, Leonard Wood, an unsuccessful candidate for presidency. The same goes for the Japanese: the first Governor-General of Japanese Korea was Hirobumi Ito, who ranks among the most prominent architects of the Meiji Restoration. It took two centuries for the British to send the likes of Cunning to India; the Americans and the Japanese had sent their best and brightest from the beginning of colonial rule, a clear indication that colonialism was, first and foremost, a state project.

Unlike the British, French or Dutch colonies, where the construction of resilient political institutions in the colonies took place only in the final decades of their rule, both the American and Japanese colonial administration, almost from the beginning of their colonial rule, engaged in costly projects that aimed at enforcing political surveillance upon their newly acquired territories. Among the first projects undertaken by the American colonial rule in the Philippines was a census. In the days when so many areas and islands were virtually inaccessible to the outside world, this endeavor implied a series of expeditions to the hinterlands, occasionally involving violent encounters with the "natives." In the Japanese case, the *Koseki* system, a resident registration system on an individual family basis, was introduced during the first decade of her rule in Korea. The name and address of each family, with the father figure as the head, were registered with the colonial administration without failure. Another case would be the *Tochi Chosa*, under which every strip of cultivated land in Korea was investigated, and land without legal titles was put under state, or Japanese ownership.

Both the census and the *Koseki* served similar objectives, that is, to provide basis for taxation and also to expand security measures to the hinterland. Similar public involvement can be found in the priority given over the construction of transportation networks and extensive education systems in the Philippines and Korea. The extent of public involvement and expenditure even gave a social democratic façade to these most undemocratic forms of governance. But the point here, of course, is not whether these policies served public benefit, which is dubious to say the least, but the extensive involvement of public administration in the daily lives of Filipinos and Koreans. Public education as offered by the American administration received a hostile reaction from the Muslim population in Southern Philippines, as its modern and reformist pragmatism ran against the more traditional Islamic schools. *Koseki*, for example, extended the Japanese notion of *Kafuchosei*, or the paternal household, more a natural unit of society in Japan than in Korea, and thus became a source of frustration among the Korean population, inviting strong resentment even to a greater extent than toward naked exploitation itself.

In British or French colonies, such a strong reach of the state was, if not unheard of, only brought about in the last days of the empire. Traditional colonialism started from fragmented actions taken on the individual basis, and such institutions as the Government of India or the Dutch *beambtenstaat* developed only gradually in India or the Dutch Indies, leaving the colonial rule over the hinterlands fragile and murky up till the end of their rule.

In contrast, both the American rule in the Philippines and Japanese rule over Korea started as state projects, with a strong interest in imposing political superstructure that was not only repressive but also highly institutionalized, equipped with bureaucratic gadgets that were even more "modern" than those practiced at home. For the latecomers, colonial rule was *ipso facto* territorial subordination and political surveillance, which could only be achieved through an extensive state apparatus. An early emergence of the colonial state, therefore, is a defining character of latecomer-colonialism.

Empire of Geopolitics

Another point that shows the role of the state in latecomer-colonialism is the primacy of geopolitics. Why the Americans had thought it necessary to subjugate the Philippines was already a question at the time of annexation, and remains a mystery up to this day. What remains clear, however, is the simple point that the US wanted no other nation (except itself) to rule the Philippines. That the annexation itself took place when the Navy was deep in dispute over who the potential enemy to American naval power may be is a clear indication of such strategic thinking. Whatever the economic value of the Philippines may have been, there was no question that it would provide a geopolitical asset to American foreign policy.

Imperial America was extremely guarded to the strategic aspirations of other empires. The Taft-Katsura agreement shows that Taft was more worried about Japanese advances over the Philippines than the possibility of independence. Most of the controversies over the Tydings-McDuffie Bill and Hare-Hawes-Cutting Act were spent on the measures that would keep the Philippines neutral and not allied to other powers, and especially not to Japan. Furthermore, the military bases were to be retained after independence, a clear indication of the predominance of geopolitics as against other economic interests: it was all right to withdraw from colonialism, but the bases had to stay. The primacy of geopolitics, although often neglected, was the defining character in the American Occupation of the Philippines.

Geopolitics played an even more pronounced role in Japanese advances to Korea. At the outset, Japanese territorial or geopolitical ambitions were all but concealed, evident only to the eyes of skeptics in the courts of the Lee dynasty. Japan had, after all, promised the Lee dynasty that it would protect Korea from Russian ambitions. The Koreans initially tried to play off both the Russians and the Japanese, and maintain their independence through such a balancing act. However, when that scheme broke down with Japanese victory over Russia (a Russian defeat rather than a Japanese victory, to be exact), the days of independent Korea were numbered.

Japanese attitudes toward Korea, however, were surprisingly dismissive. As a colony, Korea alone meant little to the Japanese, and we find remarkable indifference to the economic resources of the Korean peninsula. Korea was not an aim in itself; if anything, Korea provided a strategic token that would keep the Russians under control. The center of gravity of Japanese overseas action was in China, and Korea was used as a stepping stone to China, like the Philippines was for the Americans to China.

Moreover, China was important as a military-strategic asset rather than as an economic resource. The business sector had shown a consistent indifference toward territorial ambitions in China, for they could do business without turning the market into colonies. If we limit our attention to the business elite, it will be difficult to understand why the Japanese had territorial ambitions for China, because China had already become integrated into what Peter Duus called the "Japanese informal empire," or an economic sphere of influence since the 1920s.

For the military, however, a mere sphere of influence in the market was insufficient, and key officers continued to play with possible military advances to China. Their aim was purely geopolitical; if the Japanese did not secure Manchuria, the Soviet advance would be inevitable. The Japanese empire, therefore, was a military sphere of influence dominated by geopolitical concerns but only vaguely supported by economic needs or demands.

Latecomer-colonialism, both in terms of the construction of the colonial state and an excessive primacy of geopolitics, shows a remarkable contrast to traditional colonial empires. For the British or the Dutch, colonies meant wealth; naval stations in Singapore were necessary to keep the exploits from the colonies, and not vice versa. For the Americans and Japanese, colonies meant political rule and military assets, which may profit the homeland in the long run. This lopsided attention to control and geopolitics can only be understood when we see latecomer-colonialism as state projects, itself a consequence of the timing of colonial expansion.

Informal Empires and Pan-Nationalism

American and Japanese colonialism, however, show remarkable difference as well, most notably in the sphere of political ideologies. American rule in the Philippines is packed with seemingly universalistic ideals with little reference to nationalism or ethnicity. It was an encounter of the civilized and the uncivilized, as stated by Theodore Roosevelt: "peace has come through the last century to large sections of the earth because the civilized races have spread over the earth's dark places."

In this light, the ostensible objective of American rule in the Philippines was to educate Filipinos with the art of self-government. The American role, according to Roosevelt, was not to deprive, but provide liberty to the Filipinos — "such liberty as throughout their dark ages of their own history they have never known," and "such liberty they could never have under the rule of their own nationalist leaders" (Beale 1956).

White men's burden, indeed. The Americans, however, were less inclined to call their rule "colonialism," for theirs they saw as different from the tyranny practiced by the British, French, or Dutch. There is nothing new, of course, in justifying colonial rule through liberal patronage. What is interesting about the Americans is that they were ready to grant political independence to the "dark places" once the "dark" ceased to be dark and uncivilized; insofar as the non-European government obeyed the rules of civilization, there was no need for colonial rule.

This line of reasoning is almost identical to the idea of mandate in the League of Nations. Article 22 of the Charter of the League of Nations states that a mandate is required for colonies and territories from which former rulers have retreated, and where locals who are still incapable of governing themselves generally inhabit. In this sense, the universalistic rhetoric of American rule in the Philippines was a harbinger to the cosmetic makeover of traditional colonialism that took place after the First World War.

The Japanese, on the other hand, paid little attention to such universalistic creeds. Japan's drive for empire, after all, was ignited by the humiliating treaty settlements that had been imposed upon them during the 1850s when the country opened up to foreign relations. Ever since then, Japan had pursued the goal to become the economic, diplomatic, and strategic equal of Western countries. If the Japanese wished to face the West squarely, why should not other Asian nations as well? Thus, the Japanese rhetoric, in diametrical contrast to the universalistic ideas expressed by the Americans, was formed under the idea of "the East versus the West."

Examples abound. Japan was ruling Korea because only it could protect Korea from the hands of European powers; it was "natural" for Japan to "join hands" with China because both the Japanese and Chinese share common culture (*dobun*) and nationality (*doshu*). The actual stretch of the world under American and European influence, as Prince Konoe would later call "the Ameri-European centric world" (*beiei hon-i no sekai*), was the base for justifying such dubious reading of culture and nationality, at least in the eyes of the Japanese.

The Japanese were not alone in such cultural reinterpretation. The now infamous notion of *Hakko Ichiu*, the unity of eight nations, was but a modern revival of pan-nationalism that had rocked Europe through the late 19th century and beyond. The world, according to pan-nationalists, was composed of culturally distinct and mutually antagonistic nations, and if one wished to protect one's identity and lifestyle, one had to ally with nations that shared cultural heritage. Such was the claim of pan-Slavic movements in the mid- and late 19th century, as well as pan-Germanism, which first emerged as an ideological counterpart to pan-Slavism and eventually developed into the Nazi notion of *Lebensraum*.

If the Americans were liberal and universalistic, the Japanese were ethnic and particularistic. With the end of the First World War, it had become increasingly difficult to justify colonialism as such, making it all the more necessary to reconcile the demands of national self-determination and colonialism. The American notion of informal empire was a reconciliation through a liberal and universalistic interpretation of self-determination; the Japanese variant of reconciliation through an ethnic and expansionistic reading of self-determination. The US began its gradual retreat from formal colonial rule after the Great War, and instead expanded what later historians would call an "informal empire"; the Japanese, after a brief interval in the 1920s, resumed colonial aggression under the guise of pan-nationalism.

Conclusion

The winner of the two is painfully obvious. The informal empire, or imperialism without formal colonies, carried the day, and provided the key guideline for the world after the Second World War. Although the US constructed a far wider network of military bases than the British Empire at its height, this was achieved through minimal territorial rule, a liberal and also a very cost-effective way to manage overseas influence. Japanese pan-nationalism, along with her German variant, came to be categorically dismissed in the same world.

What makes it even more ironic is that Japan went through an occupation remarkably similar to the one conducted in the Philippines. Japan, in her retreat from pan-nationalism and latecomer-colonialism, had become a client state under American tutelage.

The failing of pan-nationalism need not be stated here; with all the nationalist rhetoric, some nations were more obviously equal than others, making pan-nationalism the least attractive in the eyes of the very Asian nations that the Japanese hoped to gain support from. What, then, about the liberal and informal empire? What legacies did it leave in the Philippines and Japan, both nations which were not only subject to American influence but also placed under direct American rule? Here we reach the agenda of our research. After the end of the Second World War, any comparison between the US and Japan as empires is futile; the remaining quest will be a comparison of the Philippines and Japan, both cast under the shadow of the liberal and informal empire that the Americans have created and sustained.

Part I:
Empires and Nation-Building

chapter 1

The Philippines and US Imperial Identity

Julian Go

Introduction

Traditional exceptionalist thought in American historiography insists that the United States has never been an "empire," not least because of America's anti-colonial origins and its attendant liberal-democratic traditions. But by now, this traditional denial of empire has been complexified in new ways. On the one hand, scholars and media commentators alike agree that the United States is and has always been an empire. It has almost become "cliché," as one commentator noted in the *Atlantic Monthly* in 2003, to say that the United States is an "empire." On the other hand, even as the word "empire" has gained entry to the popular lexicon, a certain strand of exceptionalist thought has been simultaneously reinscribed. This strand of exceptionalism might be called *liberal exceptionalism*. It admits that the United States has been an empire, but insists that the empire has been unique. While European empires were tyrannical and exploitative, American empire has been beneficent and selfless (Ikenberry 2002: 59). While European empires suppressed liberty, rights, and democracy, America's empire has been aimed at spreading them. "American imperialists usually moved much more quickly than their European counterparts to transfer power to democratically elected local rulers — as they are attempting to do in Iraq" (Boot 2003: 363). While traditional exceptionalism represses the word "empire," liberal exceptionalism proclaims a distinctly American imperialism — a unique "liberal imperialism" that manifests America's exceptional traditions, values, and political culture (Boot 2002; Ferguson 2004).

To demonstrate America's presumably exceptional empire, statesmen and scholars alike have pointed to American colonialism in the Philippines. They stress that while the United States seized the Philippines as a colony, it then proceeded to provide it with a liberal colonial state aimed at preparing Filipinos for American-style democratic self-government. America's so-called "mission" of "democratic tutelage" in the Philippines thus stands as a key feature distinguishing American empire from the "tyrannical" empires of European powers; proof that the United States' empire has been distinct and that this distinctiveness flows from America's exceptional political institutions, traditions, and values (Wheeler-Bennett 1929: 506; Moses 1905: 18). America's self-proclaimed identity as an exceptional empire is thus inextricably linked to the Philippines.

In the first part of this chapter, I will further explore this linkage. We will see how scholars and statesmen have appropriated the history of American colonialism in the Philippines to provide proof of America's imperial distinction. In the second part of the paper, however, I will take a closer look at the *origins* of the US colonial state and its special mission of democratic tutelage to register a critique of this appropriation. I show that America's so-called mission in the Philippines was itself the result of a prior appropriation by colonial state-builders for the purposes of cultivating and sustaining colonial power.

Liberal Exceptionalism and the Philippines

"Ever since the annexation of Texas and invasion of the Philippines," declared Niall Ferguson, "the US has systematically pursued an imperial policy" (quoted in Dowd 2003: 27). Here, America's annexation of the Philippines has been rightly used to critique conventional exceptionalism. The United States *has been* an empire; the fact that it seized the Philippines as a formal colony (officially in 1899) is undeniable proof. At the same time, however, America's subsequent brand of rule in the archipelago has been used as undeniable proof for America's *exceptional* imperialism. The writings of Bernard Moses (who served in the Philippines) are exemplary. Moses contended that America's new empire was a necessary historical development. The world would see more and more imperialism, and so it was "utopian" to suggest that the "lesser races" could go without intervention by the "superior races" (Moses 1905: 5). But Moses also carved a distinct niche for the United States. After reviewing the history of British colonialism in Asia and Africa, Moses claimed that it had been "reckless and tyrannical." Due to England's monarchical tradition, it had failed to live up to the promise of developing the "lesser races." The United States was special in contrast. Because of its unique democratic history, Americans were endowed with a liberal character unmatched by any other. Thus, only the United States would be able to construct a "wise and beneficent governmental authority over a rude people" and offer its imperial subjects an "impulse and guidance toward the attainment of a higher form of life and larger liberty." Referring to the Philippines explicitly, Moses concluded: "If America has any mission outside of her continental limits, it is not to preserve among less developed peoples such institutions and customs as make for bondage and social stagnation, but to put in their place the ideas that have made for freedom, and the laws by which this nation has been enabled to preserve its freedom" (Moses 1905: 7, 18).

A look at the American regime in the Philippines reveals that it was indeed aimed at pursuing the "mission" that Moses saw as distinctly American. Elihu Root's 1899 report as Secretary of War sketched the overarching idea. "[I]t is our unquestioned duty to make the interests of the people over whom we assert sovereignty the first and controlling consideration in all legislation and administration which concerns them, and to give them, to the greatest possible extent, individual freedom, self-government in accordance with their capacity, just and equal laws, and opportunity for education, for profitable industry, and for development in civilization" (USWD 1899: 24). President McKinley's first instructions to the Philippine Commission — inaugurating civil rule in the archipelago — expressed the same idea. McKinley urged the Commission to institute policies that would aid in the Filipinos' political "development" according to the "traditions" and political ideas "from which we have benefited" (Forbes 1928: II, 443).

On colonial ground, authorities put these guidelines to work. They insisted that theirs would be a tutelary government whereby the colonized would receive an "education" in the ways of American-styled political ideas, institutions, and values under America's "strong and guiding hand" (USWD 1899: 24; USPC 1900: I, 83–5). In part, this involved building a public school system that would offer civics classes for the "ignorant" and "credulous" masses (Taft 1908: 24). Schoolbooks preached about everything from the Bill of Rights to voting (Jernegen 1910; Margold 1995). Another part of the project was not education for the "masses" but a "practical political education" for the more powerful strata of society. Governor Taft (1908: 24) declared that the Filipino elite needed "as much education in practical civil liberty as their more ignorant fellow-countrymen in reading, writing, and arithmetic." "Practical political education" would fill the presumed gap, giving the elite the civilizing influences that Spanish rule had supposedly not provided.

The colonial state itself was to serve the educating process. At the local level, authorities first constructed elective offices and various other posts filled by Filipinos (Cullinane 1971). They also constructed a civil service to give native bureaucrats "a political education which will show them the possibility of the honest administration of government" (Taft to Hoyt, Sept. 8, 1900, CE, I). Then, in 1907, the Commission established a national legislative assembly manned by elected Filipino officials. This was to allow Filipino legislators to "receive instruction in the principles and methods of government … in the practical school of experience" and learn such "lessons" as the "American method of a strong executive separate from the assembly" (USPC 1900: 92–3). Governor Taft (1908: 42) claimed that the Philippine Assembly was a "school of politics" for "educating the Filipinos in the science and practice of popular representative government." Elections with an initially restricted but later expanded suffrage were to aid the curriculum. Authorities established electoral rules and ballot systems — advanced by Progressive-era reformers at home — to induce and ensure "purity" in elections. As American officials bragged: "those features that the experience of the United States has shown to be most conducive to the purity of the ballot and the honesty of elections have been embodied in the election law for the Philippine Islands" (Act 1582, RG 350, 10265-18, USNA).

In light of this tutelage regime, it is not surprising that contemporaries heralded it as exemplary of a uniquely benign imperialism. Officials and observers alike bragged that tutelage in the Philippines was "the greatest political experiment the world has ever seen" — something "unprecedented" in the world's history (*Manila Times*, October 15, 1907, p. 4). Cameron Forbes, an early official, later claimed that while European colonialisms had been driven by "the profit motive," American rule in the Philippines had been guided by different lights. "In the instructions of President McKinley [to the first colonial officials] ... a high note of altruism is maintained. They are enjoined to remember that the government is designed solely for the welfare of the Philippine people." Forbes even claimed that when European rulers later engaged in civilizing missions, they simply "followed the example set by the United States" (Forbes 1928: II, 391–2, 394–5). In the 1930s, historian Pratt added: "Probably no group of men in history ever took so seriously the task of administering colonies in the interest of their inhabitants as the best of the American officials … [who] worked to bring the Filipinos to a higher level of health, prosperity, education, and political capacity." "The Philippines," he concluded, "constitute Exhibit A among projects of benevolent imperialism" (Pratt 1934: 277–8).

As the United States emerged as a world power after the Second World War, the theme continued. It is well known, for example, that Franklin D. Roosevelt during the War was insistent on dismantling the European empires. Roosevelt, along with his Secretary of State Cordell Hull, envisioned a post-war world based upon America's special values of self-determination and liberal democracy. Throughout the pursuit, the Philippines remained a key referent. Cordell Hull referred to the Philippines in his famous 1942 radio address laying out America's vision of what the post-war world should look like. The United States, unlike European powers, "have always believed ... that all peoples, without distinction of race, color, or religion, who are prepared and willing to accept the responsibilities of liberty, are entitled to this enjoyment [...] We have striven to meet squarely our own responsibility in this respect ... in the Philippines and wherever else it has developed upon us" (Holborn 1943: I, 101). Later, when Roosevelt and Hull meet with European leaders to convince them to shift their colonial policies in a more liberal direction — and hence to help fulfill their post-war vision — they explicitly referred to the Philippines as the "model." As Hull later recorded about the meetings: "Our course in dealing with the Philippines offered, I thought, a perfect example of how a nation should treat a colony or dependency in cooperating with it to make all necessary preparations for freedom. We offered this as a strong example to all other countries and their dependencies" (Dulles 1955: 9).

While the Philippines has been used to forge America's special identity, a number of scholars have taken aim at the notion that American rule in the archipelago was especially benign. Salman (1991), Rafael (1993) and others, for example, highlight the violence attendant with the Philippine-American war and the racial discourses behind "white love" to reveal the underside of America's presumably benevolent project. Others show that America's health and sanitation projects — heralded as key examples of America's benevolent developmentalism

— were not as benign as they might first appear. Ileto (1988) suggests that such projects, rather than devoid of power's exercise, were but insidious forms of disciplinary power in their own right.

Still, there are key features of America's colonial regime that need to be further probed in order to cut to the heart of liberal exceptionalism's claims. After all, the American regime *was* tutelary; American authorities granted a comparatively wide amount of native participation in local governments, elections, and the national assembly. Without challenging the fact that the American officials indeed constructed such a tutelage regime — which was comparably liberal when considering European colonialisms — the general line of exceptionalist reasoning has been left intact. To register the idea that America's distinct "mission" is and has been intended to "export democracy" to the world, for example, recent scholarship repeatedly refers to the fact that the Americans' constructed a "modern government, from parties and elections to centralized governing institutions with a division of power" (Smith 1994: 45). In his Pulitzer Prize winning book on America's relationship with the Philippines, Karnow (1989: 13) asserts: "Compared to the Europeans, the Americans were far more liberal politically ... [they] encouraged elections soon after their arrival, so that the Filipinos had a national legislature, the first in Asia, as early as 1907 [...] This was a time when the British, despite their own democratic creed, were detaining Indian dissidents without trial and the French, for all their dedication to the principles of liberty, equality, and fraternity, were summarily executing Vietnamese nationalists." More recently, Boot (2003: 361) refers to tutelage in the Philippines to make his exceptionalist claim: "compared with the grasping old imperialism of the past, America's 'liberal imperialism' pursues far different, and more ambitious, goals. It aims to instill democracy in lands that have known tyranny." And while Philippine historians have attacked Boot on several grounds, they do not refute his factual fodder. One critic concedes to Boot: "As for the claims [of Boot] that Filipinos fared much better under US imperialism than their counterparts-elsewhere did under European colonialism, and that the Philippines was the first Asian state to establish a national legislature (1907), all are true" (Bankoff 2002: 180).

How does one confront this seemingly indisputable series of facts? Underlying the claims about America's liberal colonial regime is an assumption of cause and origin. Liberal exceptionalism's logic states that the reason why America instituted its democratizing project is that America had a special and unique political culture; an anti-colonial tradition and liberal-democratic past. In other words, American colonial rule in the Philippines was exceptional because Americans were themselves exceptional; the United States had a distinct "national character" that differentiated from European countries and which in turn determined the tutelage project. Thus, Woodrow Wilson (1901: 298) claimed that what Filipinos would acquire from American tutelage is "the aid of *our* character" (emphasis added). Glenn May's (1980: 17) seminal study similarly asserts that the tutelage project was distinct in comparison with European colonialisms because of the American officials' unique "American past." Gleeck (1976: 20) insisted that "the Americans [in the Philippines] ... put democracy, whether in its political, social, economic, or religious form, at the apex of their value system, and every official instinctively conceived of it perhaps the most self-evident of the principles enunciated by the McKinley instructions." As Carruthers (2003: 10) observes of exceptionalist thought, "If the US was uniquely virtuous ... then it stood to reason that American modes of imperial governance must be reflective of that virtuosity, both in the uplifting ends to which US interventions aspired, and the lightness of touch with which American agents pursued them."

But do the origins of America's democratic tutelage project actually lie in America's own exceptional "values" and "traditions"? This is a question that even critical scholarship has not fully addressed. Seminal work on "patron-clientelism" between American officials and Filipino elites, for example, revealed how the *practice* of the tutelage project was betrayed by the reality of collaboration and patron-clientelism, but that scholarship never questioned *why* the tutelage project was enacted in the first place (Paredes 1988). We are left to assume that tutelage — even though it failed to live up to its own ideals — nonetheless reflected America's distinct liberal-democratic values and traditions. This critical issue of origins demands deeper attention.

The Provincial Origins of American Empire

Understanding the origins of the tutelage project first demands an understanding of colonial states in general. How do colonial states insinuate themselves? How do they cultivate their power to rule? Traditional scholarship treats colonial states as mechanisms of coercion that maintained their "dominance without hegemony" (Guha 1997). This scholarship insists that force and force alone is the rule of colonial rule. But various studies on colonialism around the world have revealed that, in fact, colonial rulers did not always resort to guns, bullets, and swords. While colonial regimes surely resorted to brute force, they did not always have the resources to do so, nor did they prefer to. Working on the cheap and on the spot, their preferred aim was to cultivate collaborators and cooperation, win consent and create compliance. Accordingly, rulers often tried to represent rule as meeting the colonized's own interests, using signs and symbols to articulate the local demands and desires as their own. And they often granted material and political concessions to win hearts and minds or at least shore up compliance. In this sense, rulers strove to legitimate their occupation. They *had* to (Engels and Marks 1994: 3).

American authorities were no exception to this. Their internal correspondence reveals stark concerns over the legitimacy of their rule and how local inhabitants perceived it. The first Philippine Commission, for example, insisted that American rule should not and cannot depend upon coercion alone. It would fare better to demonstrate benevolence. To quell resistance, the fledgling colonial regime had "to create a situation where those in favor of peace can safely say so, and can argue with their brethren in the field not only that our intentions are good but, by pointing to accomplished facts, show the advantage of accepting our authority" (Williams 1913: 60–1). Jacob Schurman, head of the Commission, thus suggested that replacing the existing military government with civil government "would do more than any other single occurrence to reconcile the Filipinos to American sovereignty" (USPC 1900: 90). In addition, policymakers like Schurman not only claimed that winning hearts and minds would help to quell resistance and *establish* American rule, they likewise insisted that it would also help to *sustain* it in the long run. "Americans and Filipinos will have to trust each other," Schurman wrote to State Secretary John Hay in Washington, "... while the Filipino stops at nothing nor thinks of death when influenced by hatred, resentment or revenge, he is much moved by sympathy and generosity of powerful superior, whose power he has felt. Believe magnanimity our safest, cheapest, and best policy with Filipinos" (Schurman to Hay, June 3, 1899, MP ser. 1, r. 7).

Recognizing this overarching imperative of legitimacy is the first step toward explaining US colonialism's form. The logic of legitimation was twofold. First, the fledgling colonial regimes had to determine the needs, desires, and interests of the inhabitants. If authorities hoped to "persuade" the colonized, this necessitated understanding what exactly what would best persuade them. If authorities aimed to secure "cooperation," "confidence" and "trust," this demanded ascertaining what the colonized would cooperate with and what exactly they would trust. "To secure the confidence and affection of the Filipinos," the Schurman Commission wrote to Washington, "it is necessary not only to study their interests, but to consult their wishes, to sympathize with their ideals and prejudices even" (USPC 1900: 90). Second, and most critically, authorities had to incorporate what they learned into their ruling practices. They had to signify their rule as meeting local demands and incorporate at least some of those demands into their policies and programs. To achieve a successful occupation without the use of force, colonial rulers had to construct accommodating states — ruling regimes that would partially shape themselves to perceived local molds.

This logic took hold long before the tutelage policy was instituted. The Schurman Commission, responsible for recommending what type of colonial government the United States should institute, stated that its first task was to discern the "wishes" and "ideals" of the people. It therefore devoted much of its time to learning about them. It held hearings and conducted interviews in Manila with "eminent Filipinos." Commissioners also collected information from their commanders in the field, and dug into documents from the Philippine Republic, the revolution, and "pacific organizations of other Filipinos" (USPC 1900: I, 83). Even before this commission's work, the Hong Kong Consulate General had met with exiled leaders of the Philippine revolution. Then, as they began devising their colonial policy, they did try to incorporate perceived local demands and desires into their own discourse, policies, and ruling forms.

Consider the first public proclamations issued by American authorities in the Philippines. One of them was McKinley's "Proclamation to the Philippine People" issued in late December 1898. This was McKinley's "benevolent assimilation" proclamation, the earliest public issuance articulating tutelary ideals. Existing scholarship has referred to the proclamation as evidence for America's uniquely benign goals, but the references elide an important fact: the proclamation came six months after Washington had already received reports on the Philippines from R. Wildman, the US Consulate General in Hong Kong. Wildman had met with exiled revolutionary leaders. His subsequent report titled "The Policy and Hopes of the Insurgent Government of the Philippine Islands" was telling. It first contended that the Filipinos "cannot be dealt with as though they were North American Indians willing to be removed from one reservation to another at the whim of their masters." The Filipinos were far too westernized: insurgent leaders like Aguinaldo, Agoncillo and Sandiko "are all men who would all be leaders in their separate departments in any country"; their supporters were wealthy and educated families who "would hold their own bankers and lawyers everywhere." Wildman then noted that the insurgents wanted "annexation to the United States first, and for independence secondly." And they were not driven by primitive instincts but "are fighting for freedom from the Spanish rule and rely upon the well known sense of justice that controls all the actions of our Government as to their future" (Wildman to State Dept., July 18, 1898, USCG 19).

Note, then, the content of McKinley's proclamation. The proclamation portrayed Spanish rule as tyrannical and American rule as benign, referring to concepts like freedom and justice: "we come, not as invaders or conquerors, but as friends ... the earnest wish and paramount aim of the military administration to win the confidence, respect, and affection of the inhabitants of the Philippines by assuring them in every possible way that full measure of individual rights and liberties which is the heritage of free peoples, and by proving to them that the mission of the United States is one of benevolent assimilation, substituting the mild sway of justice and right for arbitrary rule" (Forbes 1928: II, 438). It is as if McKinley's discourse had been directly shaped by Wildman's report. To be sure, previous proclamations — before Wildman's report — did not contain tutelary rhetoric. They simply announced American sovereignty and demanded compliance from the population.[1] In turn, Wildman's report was based not on American values but upon what he perceived the Filipino leaders to be like, what they demanded, and what their interests were. McKinley's proclamation was thus aimed at incorporating those characteristics and demands. His proclamation reflected a strategic attempt not to transport American benevolence to the Philippines, but to appropriate local interests for the purposes of winning consent.

The appropriation of local demands is also seen in the recommendations for colonial policy in the longer run. Return to the activities of the Schurman commission, whose recommendations on policy were determinant for later developments. As noted earlier, the commission had spent much time trying to ascertain local interests, meeting with prominent Filipinos in

Manila and emissaries from the Malolos government, studying the constitution of the Philippine Republic, speeches of ilustrado leaders, and a host of other documents — all of which the commissioners deemed "of the most vital significance" for crafting colonial policy. From their investigations, the commissioners concluded that the majority of Filipinos wanted "the tutelage and protection of the United States" rather than independence. Consulting Manila-based ilustrados like Pardo de Tavera (who indeed stated a desire for American rule), the commissioners argued that the people wanted a more liberal form of colonial government than Spain had provided. The commissioners also concluded that the Filipinos who had rebelled against American sovereignty wanted the same thing. Referring to documents from the revolution, they concluded: "What the people want above every other thing, is a guarantee of those fundamental human rights which Americans hold to be the natural and inalienable birthright of the individual but which under Spanish domination in the Philippines were shamefully invaded and ruthlessly trampled upon" (USPC 1900: I, 82–3).

The commissioner's recommendations for US colonial government were guided by these revelations. "If these abuses [from Spanish rule] are remedied," they reported, "if a capable and honest government is instituted, if the Filipinos are permitted to the full extent of their ability to participate in it ... if church is separated from state, if public revenues are used solely to defray the legitimate expense of government ... if, in a word, government is administered in the Philippines in the spirit in which it is administered in the United States, the people of that archipelago will, as already a few of them foresee, enjoy more benefits than they dreamed of when they took up arms against the corrupt and oppressive domination of Spain" (USPC 1900: I, 82). The commissioners' final conclusion was that a liberal tutelage government was necessary. Such a government should give Filipinos a place in the colonial state, attend to public education, and point to the possibility of self-rule in the future (either in the form of statehood or national independence). More specifically, the commissioners recommended the very governmental form which colonial rule finally took — control by American authorities in the central branch but with native participation, an elective national legislative assembly, and elective local posts. Such a government would put the colonized upon "a course of development under American training [and] eventually reach the goal of complete local self-government" and eventual "contentment, prosperity, education, and political enlightenment" (USPC 1900: I, 109, 120).[2] But it would also be predicated upon local demands and interests. "It has been a leading motive with the commission in devising a form of government for the Philippines," Schurman later reported, "to frame one which, to the utmost extent possible, shall satisfy the views and aspirations of the educated Filipinos" (Schurman 1902: 49). Finally, and by the very same token, a tutelage government would realize the Americans' own interests in sustaining a successful occupation. As the commissioners wrote when registering their recommendations, "The United States can succeed in governing the Philippines only by understanding the character and circumstances of the people and realizing sympathetically their aspirations and ideals. A government to stand must be firmly rooted in the needs, interests, judgment and devotion of the people, and this support is secured by the adaptation of government to the character and possibilities of the governed — what they are, what they have it in them to become, what they want, and, not least, what they think they are entitled to have and enjoy" (USPC 1900: I, 82).

Return, finally, to President McKinley's instructions to the first civil commission. As with McKinley's "benevolent assimilation" proclamation, existing studies have pointed to the instructions — which insisted that civil rule should offer political education along American political lines — as exemplary of America's exceptional form of rule. William Taft took them as among "the greatest state papers ever issued," and as seen earlier, Cameron Forbes pointed to the instructions as exemplary of America's exceptional approach to empire (Taft to Root, November 30, 1900, ERP; Forbes 1928: II, 443). But the instructions came only after initial reports on the Filipinos' political desire for political autonomy and their discourse of rights, liberty, and freedom. And they came after Schurman Commission's report that had proposed the tutelage policy in the first place. In fact, McKinley's instructions simply reproduced these earlier suggestions — all of which insisted that the legitimacy and sustenance of rule would be obtained if local demands for rights, autonomy, and eventual self-rule were incorporated into colonial form.

McKinley himself alluded to this process of incorporation in his instructions. On the one hand, the instructions dictated that the commission's work should be guided by America's political traditions and ideals, and that colonial rule should try to implant them. "There are certain great principles of government which have been made the basis of our governmental system ... of which [the Filipinos] have, unfortunately, been denied the experience possessed by us ... there are also certain practical rules of government which we have found to be essential to the preservation of these great principles of liberty and law, and that these principles and these rules of government must be established and maintained in their islands for the sake of their liberty and happiness." On the other hand, McKinley was fully cognizant that these principles, and the form of tutelary rule that was to follow from them, would be understood by and resonate strongly with the Filipino elite. "It is evident that *the most enlightened thought of the Philippine Islands fully appreciates the importance of these principles and rules,* and they will inevitably within a short time command universal assent. Upon every division and branch of the Government of the Philippines, therefore, must be imposed these inviolable rules" (Forbes 1928: II, 443, emphasis added). While McKinley's instructions have been typically taken in extant historiography as evidence of America's virtuous character, they here suggest a different point altogether: McKinley and subsequent authorities called for a liberal and hence "exceptional" colonial rule, but they did so because they tried to secure colonial power by articulating the colonized's unique demands and desires as their own.

Conclusion: Imperial Identity and Appropriation

American colonial rule in the Philippines has been the basis for America's self-fashioned identity as a unique, exceptional, and benign empire. The United States seized the Philippines but treated it according to its own exceptional political values of self-determination and democracy. Yet, as we have seen, the origins of America's presumably exceptional project do not lie in America's "values" or unique national character. They do not lie in America's special anti-colonial past or liberal institutions. Rather, they lie in what the American officials found in the Philippines: a people who had been long demanding liberty, democracy, and self-government. Thus, American officials appropriated the Filipinos' longstanding discourse for their own purposes. In order to effectively sustain their rule, American authorities incorporated the Filipinos' own desires and demands into the very structure of their colonial state. American rulers did not impose themselves and their presumed values upon foreign societies to then produce colonial states reflecting those values. Instead, as they strove to cultivate consent and compliance like any colonial power, authorities worked the other way around. They made for a regime that ultimately went native, shaping itself to local conditions and incorporating what they found there. In this sense, America's presumably exceptional empire was the product of historical and geographical accident. In other words, if America's colonialism was exceptional at all, this only had to do with the particular features and history of the people it aimed to rule, *not* the presumably exceptional features and history of the United States.

None of this is to sneak exceptionalism through the back door and imply that American authorities were uniquely benign for attempting to meet perceived local conditions and accommodate local demands. As seen, a large part of their incorporating efforts was driven by the desire to establish and sustain their rule, hence to realize their own interests as colonial rulers. Nor was the tutelage project a gracious gesture in giving the colonized what they wanted. Authorities reckoned local discourses but did not respect them, instead insisting that they themselves knew best. "While they deal in high-sounding phrases concerning liberty and free government," asserted Taft on the Filipinos, "they have no conception of what that means" (Taft to Root, August 18, 1900, ERP). The very logic of tutelage therefore dictated a subtle project in power: tutelage aimed to partially concede to local demands as American authorities perceived them but then reshape them on the authorities' own terms. In this sense, American rule was like European colonialisms elsewhere — rulers aimed to incorporate local needs, desires, and demands while refashioning, redirecting, or otherwise disciplining them (Salman 1991; Scott 1995).[3]

Dipesh Chakrabarty, one of the founders of subaltern studies, has offered a novel strategy for challenging traditional historiography. While traditional discourses work from linear and presumably universal narratives that privilege Europe as the center of "progress," Chakrabarty (2000) suggests that historians might fare better to "provincialize Europe." As I read it, this strategy does not mean wishing traditional European narratives away but rather disclosing how those narratives — and "Europe" itself — have always been shaped and reshaped in relation to peripheralized spaces and peoples. "Europe" was never a privileged center that was then extended to the imperial provinces; its very identity and narratives were constituted in the first place through complex interactions *with* and *in* empire's "provinces." My analysis suggests that this same strategy might be fruitfully extended to better understand American imperial exceptionalism. According to the exceptionalism narrative, the United States has been bestowed with a unique liberal democratic culture and virtuous character which is then embodied, reflected, and manifested in its imperial forms and practices overseas. The larger assumption is that imperial exercises of power abroad are simple expressions of the presumed national character of the metropole. Understanding the provinciality of American empire offers a critical transcendence. It shows that the character of the American empire in the early 20th century was molded by the perceived particularities of the peoples and spaces it aimed to rule, rather than by the national character at home. Thus, America's imperial identity, the very identity that it currently projects as it rules Iraq and Afghanistan, has been dependent upon the special history of the Philippines — even if it necessarily obscures that history in order to achieve its identity in the first place.

Notes

1. For example, the phrase "benevolent assimilation" was reproduced again in a proclamation by General Otis of January 4, 1899 but earlier proclamations by Otis (August 14, 1898) did not contain the tutelage rhetoric. It only declared the establishment of military rule (Forbes 1928: II, 429–30, 437–8).
2. See also the Schurman Commission to Elihu Root, Aug. 21, 1900 (MP 31–3). In proposing the specific form of tutelary government, the commissioners in part drew from models of territorial government in the frontier (USPC 1900: I, 106), but as seen, the Schurman Commission turned to the territorial model only after concluding that the model would help meet local demands.
3. If this argument is correct, then we would expect different local conditions to lead to a different type of US colonialism (i.e., non-tutelary colonialism). A look at US rule in Guam and Samoa shows this to be the case. I discuss this in Go (2007). For more on US tutelage in the Philippines compared with Puerto Rico, see Go (2008).

chapter 2

Wars with the US and Japan, and the Politics of History in the Philippines

Reynaldo C. Ileto

The Filipino-American War (1899–1902) and the Filipino-Japanese War (1942–1945) are two crucial events in Philippine history. Although they occurred just 42 years apart, they have been treated very differently in political discourse and the construction of histories for nation-building purposes. The former tends to be forgotten, the latter remembered. The former is downplayed as a great misunderstanding, while the latter is held up as an exemplary war against an evil enemy. A closer look at both events, however, suggests that they are really quite similar. What accounts for their disparate treatments? And how are they connected with some of the most heated political controversies in the post-war period?

Theodore Friend, in his influential book, *Between Two Empires,* written at the height of the Cold War in 1965 acknowledges the Filipino-American War for what it was — a destructive and cruel event: "If American occupation of the Philippines had ended in 1901 with military rule," he says, "the United States would be remembered more for cruelty than for generosity, even though Arthur MacArthur had begun the work of reconstruction." But "the civil government that followed, designed for 'the happiness, peace, and prosperity of the people,' and lasting for over forty years, erased cruel memories and won the friendship of most Filipinos"(Friend 1965: 264). The period of US colonial rule or "civil government" has made all the difference, turning "cruel memories" into sentiments of "friendship."

Establishing a theme that would be picked up and recirculated two decades later by the even more influential writer, Stanley Karnow (1989), Friend dwells on the crucial moment when Elihu Root "directed that the government conform as far as practical 'to [Filipino] customs, their habits, and even their prejudices,' and so it was done. The policy of permissiveness, with few exceptions, won over the most ardent Filipino nationalists." Root's policy not only won "Filipino loyalty" but it also made Filipinos "the envy of nationalists elsewhere in Southeast Asia and in the wide colonial world" (Friend 1965: 264).

As Friend puts it in so many words, in weaning Filipino memories away from the cruelties inflicted by the Americans in the war of 1899–1901, the Americans had to adopt the position of a stern father who eventually relents and adopts a "permissive" attitude toward his wards. The painful past can then be turned into a necessary stage in a disciplinary process, i.e., political tutelage, and eventually forgotten. But forgetting becomes possible when the relationship between colonizer and colonized is subsumed into a "familial polity" — the fundamental mode, argues Friend, through which Filipinos establish meaningful relationships with one another. Thus, while "reconciling Philippine customs with American requisites" was never going to be simple or easy, it could still be accomplished within the context of tension-fraught relationships, "misunderstandings," "scandals," "humiliations" and "recriminations" among fictive kin.

That the cruelties of the Filipino-American War were generally forgotten by Filipinos does not mean, however, that memories of the war no longer mattered in politics. In another section of his book, Friend astutely observes that many Americans in official positions — specifically, Hoover's Secretary of War, Patrick Hurley during his visit to the Philippines in 1931 — "forgot" that "the Filipino leaders of his time had all lived through the most militant period of nationalism in the history of their country. The era of glory and terror at the turn of the century had profoundly affected each of them, although their own views might have become more moderate since then." Friend reminds the reader that Rafael Palma and Sergio Osmeña had been revolutionary journalists, Manuel Quezon a guerrilla leader who did not surrender to the Americans until 1901, and that "Americans in 1901 tortured Jose Laurel's father in a Batangas concentration camp." Even the staunchly pro-American Carlos Romulo at the age of three "saw a beloved neighbor hanged by the Americans in the village square." Of course, Romulo and others would learn their ABCs from American soldiers, "and the fear would turn to affection," but "even American kindliness would not erase the recollected thrill of fighting to be free, or submerge the anticipated pride of leading an independent nation"(ibid.: 45–6).

Theodore Friend in fact recognizes that memories of the past revolution and war with the United States were suppressed but not erased, and could be rekindled by politicians seeking to mobilize followers and votes. A glance at the Constabulary reports from 1908–1914, discovered in the Bandholtz collection of the University of Michigan, reveals war memories to be very much alive through this period.[1] This dimension of Philippine politics is not pursued in Friend's book, however. Instead, his indebtedness to Carl Lande's patron-client, kinship-based model of Filipino politics is evident throughout and profusely acknowledged in the preface. This overarching framework enables him to state that American rule "erased cruel memories" because the conquerors bent over backwards to accommodate the familial (and, hence, pre-modern) mode of relationships that Filipinos were accustomed to. This "forgetting," however, can just as well be understood as an effect of ongoing hegemony and contestation at the level of historiography, textbook construction, and the promotion of heroes.

Liberation of Manila, 1945 and 1898

At the ceremony in early 2006 marking the 61st Anniversary of the Battle for the Liberation of Manila, Ryuichiro Yamazaki, Japan's ambassador to the Philippines, alluded to a "historical fact" — a battle in which the city was totally destroyed and about 100,000 Filipino civilians were killed, "most of whom suffered the atrocities by the Japanese military, and some caught in friendly fire. The terror that each Filipino man, woman, and child must have experienced in Manila 61 years ago is beyond the imagination of any sane human being." The Ambassador ended his brief speech by expressing his "heartfelt apologies and deep sense of remorse over the tragic fate of Manila."[2]

Mr Yamazaki's allusion to *"friendly* fire" conjures up an image of Filipinos caught in a crossfire between two warring superpowers. But they are not morally equivalent, since one power — Japan — is assigned to the axis of evil, while the other power — the United States — is the origin of "friendly fire." Although the latter is responsible for around 30 percent of Filipino casualties, the terminology suggests that we would rather forget the manner in which those 30 percent perished because the outcome is what determines the meaning of their deaths. This outcome is the liberation of Manila in February 1945. Because the American tank commanders, soldiers and bomber pilots were Liberators, whatever destruction they wrought amongst the liberated was for a greater good; thus, "friendly fire," or in today's parlance, "collateral damage."

The "Battle for Manila" in 1945 was not the first of its kind. In 1898, something similar took place when American forces arrived to liberate Manila from Spanish occupation. Parallels between those two events have been noted by various commentators, the most prominent among them being President Osmeña in a speech marking the restoration of the Commonwealth government on February 27, 1945.[3]

Osmeña first of all thanked President Roosevelt and General MacArthur for rescuing the country from the hands of the Japanese "vandals" and "savages." MacArthur, he said, was being "faithful in his role as liberator in the truest American tradition." Then the startling parallel: This tradition, Osmeña pointed out, was started by no less than Douglas' father, Arthur. "In this crusade, [Douglas MacArthur] is finishing the noble work begun by his illustrious father, General Arthur MacArthur who, on August 13, 1898, successfully led another American army to free Manila from a European power."

August 13, 1898 was an important event celebrated during the American era, when it used to be called "Occupation Day." Today, "Occupation" (with a capital "O") is still memorialized but the historical referent is the Japanese Occupation, portrayed as a dark and harsh period. In stark contrast, "American Occupation" meant the obverse; in fact, as "Japanese Occupation" displaced this term in the post-war period, the American Occupation came to be referred to as "Peacetime."

Osmeña assumed that Occupation Day 1898 was a positive and even liberating event. In his speech, he even suggested that Independence Day should be advanced to August 13, 1945, to coincide with the 47th anniversary of the original American landing in Manila in 1898. Thus, he concluded, "Occupation Day will become the Philippine Independence Day." He seems to have forgotten that August 13, 1898 was the prelude to the Filipino-American War.

When the elder MacArthur came, it was eventually to do battle not with Spain but with a Filipino army led by Aguinaldo. The ensuing war raged for three and a half years — approximately the same duration as the Japanese War and Occupation. It took another ten years, at least, for the "pacification" of the islands to be completed by the US Army and Philippine Constabulary forces. This event, however, is not officially acknowledged as a bad thing by the United States. To be sure, there were American voices in opposition to that war, but in the end, such voices were silenced and the event was marginalized as a peripheral disturbance in the greater Spanish-American War.

In contrast to the American Occupation, the Japanese Occupation was a dark event, and its perpetrators have acknowledged it. Mr. Yamazaki reiterated his government's "determination not to allow the lessons of that horrible Second World War to erode, and to contribute to the peace and prosperity of the world without ever waging a war." Here we have not only the admission of a terrible crime, but also a determination to remember this event and never again allow war to be a means of change. The United States, in contrast, has sought to transform parts of the world today precisely by waging war. In October 2003, President George Bush told the Philippine Congress that the US liberation of Iraq from tyranny was a repeat of the American liberation of the Philippines in 1945 (although he diplomatically did not mention the Japanese as the old enemy). Totally absent in his discourse was the forcible US Occupation of the Philippines in 1899–1902 — the true precursor to the Iraq War.[4]

Forgetting the Filipino-American War

For Filipinos, the Filipino-American War is still generally a forgotten war. After the United States had pronounced victory on July 4, 1902, it proceeded to reshape the collective memory of those continuous years of war from 1896 to 1902. The aim was, first, to encourage Filipinos to remember the war against Spain from 1896 to 1898; and second, to forget as much as possible the war against the United States. This politics of remembering and forgetting was conducted through censorship in the press, civic rituals, and above all, the school system. Filipinos were taught to "remember" above all that the US army had come as liberators to help free the country from oppressive Spanish rule.

School textbooks cannot avoid mentioning the formation of a government by Aguinaldo, which the liberators refused to recognize. The coming of the Americans was, in fact, prone to be interpreted as an invasion under false pretences. In order to combat such negative meanings and to establish the official memory of the two wars, the US administration did the following: it recognized the liberal aspirations of the leaders of the revolution. But the Americans insisted that Filipinos as a whole were not prepared for democracy and self-rule. As "proof" of this lack of readiness, a flood of writings appeared picturing Aguinaldo no longer as an ally but as a ruthless dictator, and the masses of the people as blind followers of their local caciques and bosses. There is a fascinating story, which I cannot go into here, of the process through which Philippine history was rewritten, and even historical sources tampered with — as in the monumental compilation of records by Blair and Robertson — in order to justify the US invasion and occupation as the liberation of the masses from their despotic leaders — the likes of Aguinaldo and Malvar included — who were termed "caciques" (a term not identified with Filipino elites prior to US rule) in order to identify them with the "dark age" of Spanish rule.[5]

At the end of the day, a new generation of Filipinos studying in public schools learned to remember the coming of the Americans in 1898 as an act of liberation and "benevolent assimilation." Their 1898 Republic was a worthy attempt but it was flawed and lacking. It needed the Americans, so the argument went, to prepare a backward people for democracy and responsible self-government. David Barrows, the superintendent of schools, used the term "great misunderstanding" in his high school Philippine history textbook to describe the Filipino-American War. If only the Filipinos had fully understood the noble motives of the United States, they would not have resisted the US Occupation, and the disastrous war would not have taken place (Barrows 1905: 295). If it was just a great misunderstanding, then why bother to remember the event?

Words had to be matched by firm action to make Filipinos take these directives from a new colonial ruler seriously. The government decreed in 1902 that anyone who continued to oppose the American presence would be arrested for sedition. Armed groups that attacked government forces would be treated as bandit gangs, religious fanatics, and remnants of the defeated guerrilla armies. They would be treated as plain criminals and terrorists. From this time on, any further opposition to the US would be dealt with as banditry, fanaticism, criminality, or even mental disturbance.

The new generation of Filipinos in the schools largely went along with the official view of the past. This was the logical thing to do in order to succeed in school, and to be employed in the colonial civil service. It helped in dealing successfully with the new American order. One effect of the institutional power of this history was that, on the eve of the Japanese invasion, the vast majority of Filipinos had forgotten the Filipino-American War. They saw their fate and that of the United States as intertwined. So when the Japanese forces arrived, they were resisted with great persistence, particularly in Bataan and Corregidor. After the surrender of the Filipino-American forces, a guerrilla war of resistance continued to be waged, inspired by expectations of MacArthur's return. Nowhere else in Southeast Asia did the local population fight so hard, and suffer so much, on behalf of their colonial rulers.

A Tale of Two Wars: Against Japan *and* America

The conventional narrative of Philippine history consists of the familiar saga of the revolution, the Republic of 1898, the American Occupation and tutelage, the semi-independent Commonwealth, Japanese invasion, the Liberation, and finally, independence in 1946. But the story is complicated by the fact that the Filipino-American War was only *partly* erased from the collective memory. The reason that President Quezon could rise to the occasion and capture the crowd's imagination in his political speeches, was in fact because he was a veteran of the Filipino-American War, fighting for independence then as now. Like Presidents Marcos and Magsaysay, who made political capital out of their heroic exploits in the war against Japan,

Quezon did likewise. But the war in which he had fought was against the United States. He was arguably pro-American, but he was also an icon of the war against the Americans.

One of Quezon's most potent political rivals was also a veteran of the Filipino-American War, General Artemio Ricarte. When the war ended in 1902, Ricarte refused to take the oath of allegiance to the United States and was imprisoned. But he managed to escape, first to Hong Kong, where he allied himself with Sun Yat Sen, and then to Yokohama. From these locations elsewhere in Asia, Ricarte gave inspiration to Filipino anti-colonial nationalists ranging from party politicians to leaders of various secret societies and peasant movements (Terami-Wada 1999: 61–5).

It is well known that anti-colonial nationalists worldwide found inspiration in the fact that Russia's eastward advance was thwarted by Japan in 1905 — the first such accomplishment by an Asian power. Less acknowledged is the fact that Japan's victory over Russia was a source of pride to veterans of the Filipino-American War, since Japan had been an ally — albeit a hesitant one — in that war and the previous one against Spain. Japan's victory in 1905 was hailed even by some of the new generation of Filipinos learning English in the American schools. Japan soon became an alternative model for Filipino nationalists. Its *bushido* tradition fascinated those seeking alternative models for nation-building in the 1930s (Gonzalez 1980: 78). The idea of the Philippines belonging to Asia or the Orient rather than the "West" is an old one dating from Rizal's time, but it was given a new twist by Japan's rise as a possible regional leader. This is the "other side" to the dominant picture of Americanization in the Philippines.

Bolstered by Japan's rise, Ricarte was a voice from faraway Yokohama that announced to the Filipino people: *I shall return, with Japan's help*. The Philippine Constabulary reports from 1908 to 1914, alluded to earlier, reveal to us how powerful Ricarte's appeal was. Secret societies, Katipunan revivals, veterans associations, local militias, congregations of the *Iglesia Filipina Independiente*, patriotic religious sects — the US administration up to 1914 had to deal with hundreds of such attempts to challenge it. The Tanggulan and Colorum movements in the 1920s, and the Sakdalistas in the 1930s, continued this tradition. In most cases, these demonstrations, mutinies, and revolts were inspired by Ricarte's promise to come with Japanese help.[6] The way people imagined Ricarte and the "Mikado's navy" that would carry him back, prefigures the more familiar expectations of MacArthur returning as the head of a mighty American armada.

Quezon understood Ricarte's position perfectly. That is why, as Resident Commissioner in the US, he worked hard to have the Jones Law passed so that he could in 1916 announce his return to the Philippines with a promise of independence from the US Congress. That took the bite out of Ricarte for a while. In the meantime, the Philippine Constabulary intelligence service had begun to understand the workings of the Filipino messianic complex. Clear evidence of this is seen in their advice to Douglas MacArthur in 1942 to make this promise: *"I shall return!"* And it worked like magic. The majority of Filipinos continued to resist Japanese occupation to the bitter end because they believed the Savior-General MacArthur would surely return to redeem the country.

The history of US colonial rule and the Commonwealth era cannot be understood fully without recognizing the competition and synergy between those two veterans of the Filipino-American War: Quezon and Ricarte. Up to the very end, Quezon held Ricarte in high regard and remained in touch with him. On the eve of the Pacific War, he secretly journeyed to Yokohama to seek Ricarte's advice. Upon his return, he proposed to the Americans that if the Japanese invaded, the Philippines should be neutral. Of course, the response from Washington was thoroughly hostile. Ricarte, on his part, reciprocated the respect coming from his fellow *veterano*. When he returned to the Philippines on December 19, 1941, he wrote to Quezon, urging him to stay in Manila in order to avert further bloodshed. I think Quezon would seriously have considered this offer, but it was too late. He was already at Corregidor when Ricarte's letter arrived.

The Americans were always on the lookout lest Quezon tried to make a deal with the Japanese. No deal could possibly have been made with the Japanese enemy, but this did not stop Quezon from asking Roosevelt, on February 8, 1942, to give the Filipinos independence immediately, to allow them to be neutral in a war between the United States and Japan. But predictably, Roosevelt refused. Filipinos and Americans, he insisted, must stand beside each other and fight to the end. Quezon, politically powerless and consumed by tuberculosis, had no choice but to stick by his *compadre* MacArthur. Thus, more Filipinos were martyred at Bataan and Corregidor while waiting for reinforcements that never arrived because the US priority was to liberate Europeans from the other pole of the axis of evil, Hitler's Germany.

Ricarte: Voice from a Forgotten War

What I have said about Ricarte's influence applies mainly up to the first 15 years of American rule. Over time, as Quezon gained the upper hand and as more and more Filipinos who went through the American educational system were trained to remember the Filipino-American War as a great misunderstanding, Ricarte's appeal was effective only among secret societies and rural-based movements such as the Tanggulan and Sakdal. It comes as no surprise, therefore, that Ricarte had little or no popular influence after he returned to the Philippines in December 1941. No doubt he still held the respect of his countrymen, particularly the older generation that had experienced the war against the Americans or at least the decade of "pacification" that followed it. But according to Agoncillo, Ricarte "could not, with his past heroic deeds, talk the Filipinos into collaborating wholeheartedly with the Japanese." He chides Ricarte for being "naive, for he sincerely believed that the redemption of the Philippines lay in a close partnership with Japan." In the end, Agoncillo concludes that "Ricarte was a political non-entity" (Agoncillo 1965, vol. 1: 388–9).

Why was Ricarte a political non-entity by 1942? As I have argued, this is related to a collective forgetting of certain features of the revolutionary past, an effect of colonial politics. Ricarte himself was aware of the memory gap that existed between the youth of 1942 and his own 1890s generation, and expressed his concern immediately through his arrival speech in 1942, *Mahal Na Kabataan Ng Aking Bayan* (Beloved Youth of my Country).[7] Listen to what he says in the first few paragraphs (my English translation):

> It was about forty years ago when your fathers and elders were young people like you. I was together with them in the war against the Americans. In the end we were defeated in battle, not because we lacked bravery or inner strength (*lakas ng loob*), but because we lacked weapons. They surrendered against their will to the American army.
>
> When this country, Filipinas, was occupied at that time, they burned our houses; they destroyed our towns; and they behaved towards us with such cruelty that had never before been seen in the history of Mankind.
>
> Our past experience is the stark witness of the extent of the suffering we went through during that violent era. Most of our talented and dashing leaders, and the heroes of the land during that time of turmoil, were thrown in prison. Others were carried off to different parts of the world. I was dumped, together with Mabini and 80 other compatriots, on Guam, the island that was occupied by the Japanese during the initial days of this present war. I was a prisoner there for two years, during which time some of my companions died of hunger.
>
> Such was also the fate of Mabini. He eventually returned here but was in such a weak condition that he died after a few days. When our countrymen learned about our inhuman (*malahayop*) treatment by the Americans, this brought deep pain to their hearts and they were overcome with sorrow. They protested against the inhuman methods of the westerners, to no avail.

One thing we immediately notice is that the Americans during the Filipino-American War are portrayed as cruel and inhuman conquerors. This is exactly how the Japanese conquerors would be portrayed in the course of the Filipino-American-Japanese

War. This is what I mean by the two wars being similar. Ricarte was not inventing that image of the American army. Archival research can back him up readily, and we can also read about similar happenings at My Lai (Vietnam), Fallujah (Iraq), and other such places. What is significant here is Ricarte's move to reinstate the narrative of a harsh American invasion, even though at this point, few of his countrymen were listening. As he puts it, "I have long been waiting for this opportunity **to narrate to you a true rendering** [*maisalaysay sa inyo ang matapat na pagkilala*] of the heroic deeds that were performed by your parents." Ricarte is saying that the youth have been imbued with a false memory of the past that needs to be set right by his retelling of the story.

Ricarte continues: "From the time I set foot on our country, I traveled to all parts of the Philippines, and I observed what the Americans had taught and left behind for us. We were deceived by them [*tayo ay kanilang dinaya*]. We were exploited as we progressed, because they were lacking in conduct and behavior [*walang mabuting kaugalian*]. Their oppressive aims were deviously kept from our view ..."

Here, Ricarte's frames the US intervention in the Philippines in terms of familiar tropes in Tagalog literature of *ningning* versus *liwanag*, seductive appearance versus reality, the rhetoric of freedom and democracy concealing selfish, exploitative aims. The failure to see the real and destructive effects of American intervention is caused, he implies, by a defective study of history. "The fact is," says Ricarte, "that America taught our youth to remember the past through the lives of men like Lincoln and Washington in order to make us forget in our hearts the shining accomplishments of the great heroes of our country here in the east." He exhorts the youth to respect their elders and their teachers as sources of knowledge, but above all, to "Honor the heroes and martyrs of their country [i.e., not of America]. This is clear to everyone and this needs to be carried out always."

There is no doubt that Ricarte was also calling on the youth to observe the dictates of the Japanese New Order. He makes reference to Japanese history and policies, and says in conclusion: "We shall take this road [that is, the New Order] firmly and without hesitation, prepared for the final journey that will take us to the joyful conclusion of everything we have striven for in history: the sacred dream of our parents — freedom (*kalayaan*) and independence (*pagsasarili*)."

It is easy enough to dismiss this as "propaganda." But if we focus excessively on how Ricarte was harnessed to serve Japanese policy, we lose sight of another even more important agenda in his speech: the transmission to the youth of a story of the past that had up to then been kept in darkness by muted "elders" and forgotten heroes. The public may have resisted the implementation of Japanese policies, since ideals were not matched by practice, but the attempt to transform historical consciousness would have far-reaching effects. To move this discussion further, we need to examine the career of Jose P. Laurel and his government's handling of Philippine history.

Independence — October 14, 1943

The trajectory of Philippine national history from the Katipunan revolt of 1896 onward was to obtain independence. The people would then get to enjoy a life of *kalayaan*, whose range of meanings cannot be captured in the English translation, "liberty." Whether the path was through continued armed struggle, joining secret societies and religious sects, popular elections, or collaborating with the colonial state, the objective of most political and social movements since 1896 was to gain independence of sorts for *Inang Bayan*, the suffering motherland.

We saw how Quezon and Ricarte vied with each other for the glory of returning home to the Philippines with independence as a present for the masses. This rivalry resurfaced in a different, almost ludicrous, form during the early part of the war when both the United States and Japan engaged in a rhetorical contest over who would grant independence to the Philippines sooner. We can view the vigorous alternation of "promises" by Tokyo and Washington as two series of events, one culminating on October 14, 1943 and the other on July 4, 1946.

Despite the fact that Laurel's government has been officially recognized as the "Second Republic" following the First Republic at Malolos, it nevertheless cannot shake off the stigma of being a "puppet government." The assumption of independence in October 1943 has been viewed as a sham, and the second republic, fiction. Nonetheless, there are those who have argued that the July 1946 event was no less a charade, since the US continued to be in control of key areas in the Republic. If there continues to be nagging doubts about the reality of independence "granted" by the United States in July 1946, perhaps it is more comparable with October 1943 than what we have admitted thus far.

Let us postpone judgment for now and take a closer look at the event that is prone to being forgotten: Independence Day, October 14, 1943. Unlike July 4, 1946, which was framed by the victory over the Japanese and the preceding decades of American tutelage, October 14, 1943 had to be linked directly to the events of the Philippine Revolution and to early Japanese support for it. Rizal was the dominant symbol of this event, just as he was for independence in 1946. As the newspapers in 1943 repeated over and over, Rizal had died without seeing his country's independence, and now it was finally arriving, thanks to Japanese help. On Rizal's birth anniversary in 1943, it was said that Ricarte even went to Calamba to "report to the spirit of Rizal" that the hope of independence would soon be fulfilled.[8]

Independence in 1943 was also portrayed as a culmination of Bonifacio's armed struggle. Here we see a departure from the treatment of Bonifacio in 1946, where he is less the militant revolutionary than a "founding father" of the nation alongside Rizal — a continuation of the way Bonifacio was portrayed under the Americans. Under Japanese rule, the founder of the Katipunan secret society was proclaimed as the "militant exponent of Oriental liberation from the West."[9] Japanese and Filipino officials preparing the stage for the independence ceremony at the Luneta took time out to pay a visit to Rizal's death cell in Fort Santiago as well as to the Bonifacio monument in Balintawak (Martin 1952: 178).

Half a million people attended the independence ceremony, a significant number at that time. Here is Teodoro Agoncillo's account of this momentous event:

> As General Emilio Aguinaldo, assisted by General Artemio Ricarte, hoisted the Filipino flag in front of the inaugural stand, to the tune of the Philippine National Anthem, many in the crowd shed tears of joy. It was the first time since the Japanese Occupation that the Filipino flag was displayed in public and the Anthem played. Loud and prolonged cheers rent the air as the old flag fluttered in the breeze, alone (Agoncillo 1965, vol. 1: 394).

What strikes me about Agoncillo's account is the detail about the crowd shedding tears of joy. Vicente Guzman of the Tribune staff indeed reported that there were tears in the eyes of the throng "when the magic words that announced the birth of a new Republic were pronounced at 9:44." Another Tribune columnist confessed that tears rolled down his cheek and that many around him had that same experience. "Not a few were moved to tears," he said, when the flag was hoisted by Aguinaldo and Ricarte. The anonymous columnist explained further "that the people present at the ceremony, while having no illusions about the farce that was Philippine independence, were sincerely touched by the sight — for the first time in the life of most of them — of the Philippine national flag being hoisted alone in the breeze."[10]

A significant proportion, it seems, of the half-million strong that attended the rituals of October 14 recognized the connection that was being made between Independence Day and the events of the Revolution, including the dreams of Ricarte's generation. That is why tears began to flow. Laurel added to this process of reconnecting with the past when he spoke of independence as a fulfillment of the dreams of the heroes of 1896 and of the new Republic as a successor to Aguinaldo's Republic of 1898.

Although the Second Republic enjoyed a short lifespan — October 14, 1943 to August 17, 1945 — it pursued many initiatives that would bear fruit after 1946. The Laurel government took advantage of the opportunities offered by the Japanese policy of de-Americanization and the search for Oriental roots. It pursued its own nationalist agendas in the areas of foreign policy, language, national history, and character building, even though the return of the Americans prevented much from actually being implemented.

Laurel's "Forces that Made a Nation Great"

In his public speeches, President Laurel spoke to the crowd in the language of the past, or history — a permissible discourse in the climate of de-Americanization and its complement, Asianization. This discourse cushioned him and his audience from the full force of Japanese power. Historical discourse here should be seen as an autonomous domain that enabled Filipinos to pursue their own agenda of nation-building within the constraints of foreign occupation. Filipino historians and writers were, in fact, encouraged by their new rulers to explore the pre-Hispanic and late 19th-century nationalist roots of their identity.

Not surprisingly, then, history was a crucial policy area of the second Republic and its Japanese patrons. Laurel himself authored a group of essays that originally appeared in the newspaper *Tribune* in 1943, collectively titled "Forces that Make a Nation Great."[11] This work is arguably the best statement of the ideology of the 1943 Republic.

In the initial pages of the book, Laurel states: "Under the new order in our country all impediments to frequent and devout communion with our glorious past have been removed." This will enable access to the "founts of inspiration issuing forth from the valiant deeds of Soliman and Lapu-Lapu, from the achievements of Kalantiao and the unknown builder of the Benguet terraces, from the supreme sacrifice of Rizal and Bonifacio and countless other heroes of the race." This access to power in the past "should refresh our energies, wash away any trace of inferiority we might still feel, and nourish us into greater strength."

Laurel suggests that the American colonial order had repressed much of the knowledge of the past that Filipinos could have tapped as a source of power. In fact, the teaching of Philippine history in the American period tended to take the backseat to American and European history. And especially in the Catholic schools and colleges, students were discouraged or even prohibited from accessing the writings of revolutionary heroes such as Jose Rizal, Marcelo del Pilar, Graciano Lopez-Jaena and Andres Bonifacio. At one level, what Laurel meant by impediments to communion with the past being lifted now, was that finally, the lives and works of *all* the heroes of the revolution and the Filipino-American War could be taught to Filipino students. Laurel's goal of harnessing the creative forces of the past, particularly the patriots and heroes of the Revolution, in effect takes up Ricarte's call for the experience of the veterans of past wars to be relived by the youth of the 1940s.

What enabled the visions of Laurel and Ricarte to intersect in spite of the generation gap between the two? In exploring Laurel's family background, we cannot help but be struck by the involvement of his clan in the Filipino-American War. His father, Sotero, perished in the concentration camp which his hometown, Tanauan, in Batangas province, had been turned into during the period of "scorched-earth" tactics employed by the US army from December 1901 to March 1902. A first cousin, Captain Maximiano Laurel, was killed in an encounter with American troops in March 1902. Jose's aunt, Marcella, filed an unsuccessful claim for compensation for the US army's destruction of their property in 1901 (Laurel and Carandang, ca. 1991).[12] Jose Laurel was only ten years old when these events occurred, but he remembered them vividly.

Laurel's closest associate, Claro M. Recto, was also ten years old when the US army captured his mother and schoolteacher uncle who were supporting the guerrilla resistance. He wrote in his diary about hearing his mother crying as American officers were interrogating her concerning the whereabouts of another brother, guerrilla Colonel Norberto Mayo, whose unit was protecting General Miguel Malvar. He remembered the destruction that this war brought to his hometown of Tiaong, in present-day Quezon province, whose municipal center was turned into a gigantic "protected zone" (as the Americans termed it)[13] while most of its barrios were razed by the US cavalry.[14]

Both Laurel and Recto grew up coming to terms with the American Occupation and gaining high office in the colonial establishment. But the past would always haunt them, or at least render intelligible some of the more controversial things they did as leaders of the 1943 Republic and as Senators in the 1950s.

Revisiting the Filipino-American War

Laurel's government enjoyed the blessing of the Japanese administration when it continued the Commonwealth policy of teaching the youth to emulate Filipino heroes. But things were a bit different from the Commonwealth era: with the Americans gone, no longer was it considered taboo to excavate memories of the Filipino-American War itself. Veterans and descendants of these two wars who had never forgotten that the Americans had come as invaders were encouraged to speak freely about the past and to play leading roles in organizations supportive of the Japanese administration.[15]

As we saw earlier, August 13 had always been observed as American Occupation Day — the anniversary of the American entry into Manila in 1898. Not surprisingly, this "Day" was treated very differently by both Japanese and Filipino writers, radio broadcasters and public speakers: it now meant the beginning of national enslavement for the Philippines. As the *Tribune* stated in August 1944: "Against the perspective of history, particularly those events in it which mark our bloody and peaceful struggles for freedom, August 13 stands out as a black day of weeping."[16]

Instead of General Arthur MacArthur, the limelight was now held by Filipino General Pio del Pilar. Eufronio Alip and Antonio Abad, writing in the *Sunday Tribune Magazine* of August 13, 1943 focused on Del Pilar besieging Manila from the landside while Dewey's fleet was attacking from the sea. It was this very same General, they said, who challenged General Anderson and his soldiers to a fight in a San Pedro Makati cemetery sometime in January 1899, in retaliation for the Americans' insincerity, duplicity, and arrogant attitude. "So firm was [Pio del Pilar's] stand against the Americans," said Alip and Abad, "that the more diplomatic Aguinaldo, who wanted to preserve their 'friendship,' sent Gen. del Pilar away to La Union."[17]

Benigno Aquino Sr., Director-General of the KALIBAPI (Kapisanan sa Paglilingkod sa Bagong Pilipinas) said that August 13 is a day of "national humiliation ... not a day of jubilation." "On that day 46 years ago," he explained, "the Philippines entered upon a phase of history characterized by American rapacity and Filipino vassalage to American imperialism and imperialistic aggrandizement." "Aquino's was a more controversial stand," wrote Manuel Buenafe in 1950. "The people up to the end did not know whether to praise or despise him. There were many who admired his courage and condemned him" (Buenafe 1950: 137–8; Martin 1952: 194). Note that Aquino's denunciation of Occupation Day was met with mixed reactions. What is surprising is that there were those who "admired his courage." Perhaps Aquino's assertions carried authority because he was the son of General Servillano Aquino, who had fought against the Americans.

The Japanese Occupation was, in fact, the time to resurrect and dwell upon the battles and other events of the Filipino-American War. Here, Generals Aguinaldo and Ricarte played leading roles. Aguinaldo made the headlines in February 1942 by writing to General MacArthur "to stop the useless resistance against the Japanese Army." Later that year, he proudly presented General Homma with a copy of his still-unfinished biography (Martin 1952: 190). After the war, it was predictably argued that Aguinaldo had unwittingly been "used" by the Japanese, but there is another logic that makes Aguinaldo's behavior, like Ricarte's, completely intelligible on its own terms.

Another hero of the Revolution who rose in stature during this period was General Gregorio del Pilar of Tirad Pass fame, who gave his life in 1899 to protect Aguinaldo from pursuing American forces. Del Pilar was especially honored by the Republic with the creation by President Laurel of the military: "Order of Tirad Pass." The award was considered an "appropriate symbol of what the youth who love their country can do." The first recipients were given their decorations posthumously at a solemn rite at the Luneta on May 4, 1944.[18] Such rituals, in addition to the stories that circulated about the Revolution and the war against the Americans, became vehicles for public reflection about the past and the present, making possible the resurrection of collective memories suppressed under US colonial rule.

Liberation and Independence, 1946

We can speculate that had the Japanese really won the war and ruled the Philippines for 40 years as the Americans did, there would have occurred a reshaping of the collective memory similar to what the Americans had accomplished. The Filipino-American War would have been resurrected from oblivion, and the Americans remembered as invaders, while the Japanese would perhaps have come to be perceived as liberators. But it is fruitless to talk about what might have happened. For General MacArthur kept true to his promise and returned in 1945. This moment in Philippine history is called "the Liberation."

As soon as the Commonwealth government was reinstalled in Manila by the Liberators, it proceeded to restore those collective memories of a shared Filipino-American past that the wartime period had begun to erode. This is the context of President Osmeña's 1945 speech I mentioned earlier comparing Douglas MacArthur favorably to his father Arthur, both father and son having liberated Manila from tyrants: first the Spanish, then the Japanese. Osmeña's speech marks the beginning of an intense effort to reestablish some of the institutionalized memories or amnesia of the past that Laurel's government had begun to challenge and dismantle.

Since the final months of the war against Japan were bloody and traumatic for many Filipinos, Presidents Roxas and Quirino had no trouble establishing an official historical discourse in which the American colonial period was seen as a "Golden Age," following upon which was a "Dark Age" of Japanese Occupation in 1942–1945. The joint Filipino-American struggle to free the Philippines was interpreted as a common sacrifice or a common passion, death and resurrection of Filipino and American soldiers who had fought side by side against the Japanese. What was the "Death March," asked Quirino, if not their common *pasyon* or Christ-like suffering and death? What was Capas, Tarlac, if not, he added, the "Calvary" of the Filipino-American forces?[19] In this way, the post-war leaders could argue that the granting of independence in 1946 was a fulfillment of the dreams of the Revolution *and* tutelage by the Americans.

This official narrative, however, did not extinguish other interpretations of the American return. The Hukbalahap and the Communist Party discovered soon enough that they were excluded from this "Filipino-American" passion story; for them, 1946 did not bring fulfillment. The Huk Supremo, Luis Taruc, understood Occupation Day in a vastly different manner from what we saw in President Osmeña's 1945 speech. He asserted that when the Americans came in 1898, they "crushed a people's movement that had come into being in the struggle against Spain." And when they returned in 1945, they tried to "crush another people's movement that had come into being in the struggle against Japan." The historic US role as liberator and tutor, so emotionally articulated in the speeches of Roxas and Quirino, is belittled by Taruc as a sham so that the US could "make huge profits in our country." He termed the independence ceremony of July 4, 1946 a "performance" that unfortunately deluded many (Taruc 1953: 274–5).[20]

The politics of Philippine history after 1946 involves a complex struggle and negotiation between at least two ways of narrating/remembering the wars against the United States and

Japan. As this struggle for memory got caught up in the Cold War, the pro-US narrative quickly attained a position of dominance. Friend's 1965 book captures quite vividly the picture of the Philippines "caught between two empires," one of which signifies a golden age in memory, and the other, a fall into darkness. But soon after the appearance of Friend's book, Filipino historian and writer Nick Joaquin alluded to the continued presence, if not intensification, of an alternative view of the past. Noting the rise in anti-US student protests and calls for "revolution" from 1965, he observed that "in a sense when we speak of the 'Unfinished Revolution,' we are not referring to 1896–1898 but to 1942–1945."[21] Joaquin was giving credit to Laurel and other nationalists during the supposed "Dark Age" of the Japanese Occupation for having prefigured the radicalizing events of the mid-1960s. From then on, the wars against the US and Japan would have the character of sameness more than difference.

Notes

1. See Philippine Constabulary, *Confidential Reports*, Ms., Bandholtz Collection, Bentley Library.
2. "Remarks by H.E. Ambassador Ryuichiro Yamazaki on the Occasion of the 61st Anniversary of the Battle for the Liberation of Manila," Intramuros, Manila, February 18, 2006: for local media coverage, see "Japan Apologizes over Battle of Manila," *Manila Bulletin*, February 19, 2006.
3. "Address of Sergio S. Osmeña on the Occasion of the Restoration of Commonwealth Government," February 27, 1945 in *At the Helm of the Nation: Inaugural Addresses of the Presidents of the Philippine Repubic and the Commonwealth*, comp. Consuelo V. Fonacier (1973), pp. 33–9.
4. For a detailed discussion, see Ileto (2005a).
5. For an illuminating account of how early American scholar-officials successfully incorporated the history of the late Spanish Philippines into a Latin American narrative, which facilitated the imposition of terms like *cacique*, see Cano (2006).
6. For details, see Ileto (1998), Chapter 6.
7. *Sa Mga Kabataang Filipino* (in Tagalog and Spanish), Manila, 1942. Copy in the Garcia Collection, Sophia University.
8. Dalmacio Martin, "Education and Propaganda in the Philippines during the Japanese Occupation," Manila, June 1952 (Typescript in the Garcia Collection, Sophia University), p. 166.

9. *Sunday Tribune Magazine*, November 29, 1942, in Martin (1952), p. 184.
10. For visual representations of this event, see *Souvenir Pictorial of the Birth of the Philippine Republic*, October 14, 1943.
11. *Forces that Make a Nation Great* (1943). The significance of this work is reflected in its translation into Filipino/Tagalog as *Mga Lakas na Nagpapadakila sa Ating Bansa*, and its publication by the Committee on the National Language Textbook Preparation in 1949.
12. Other details about Laurel's biography and ideas can be found in Agpalo (1992).
13. The "Protected zone" was the predecessor of the "fortified hamlet" during the Vietnam War some 60 years later. While "protected zone" faded from Filipino memory in the course of the American Occupation, ironically it was revived in the term "zona," associated with a similar practice by the Japanese army during their occupation.
14. This information on Recto is from the notable biography by Arcellana (1990).
15. The data for this section, including extensive quotes from *The Tribune*, comes from the unpublished 1952 work by Dalmacio Martin, cited earlier. Martin, an educator, was a participant and keen observer in those events.
16. Editorial, "Beneath American's Velvet Gloves," *Tribune*, August 15, 1944, in Martin (1952), p. 194.
17. E.M. Alip and A.K. Abad, "Gen. Del Pilar, the First to Resent 'Occupation Day' Deception," *Sunday Tribune Magazine*, August 15, 1943, in Martin (1952), pp. 177–8.
18. This notice appears in the inside front cover of the May 1944 issue of *Pillars*, a monthly magazine that had numerous articles on Jose Rizal and other heroes in the issues that came out in 1943–1944; see also Martin (1952), p. 188. Laurel's discourse of heroes was evidently propagated throughout the media and in civic rituals.
19. "Capas: Saga of Heroism," in *The Quirino Way* (speeches compiled by Juan Collas), Manila, 1955, pp. 70–1.
20. It is widely known that this book was ghost-written by William Pomeroy, and that its general arguments reflect the official line of the Communist Party. This does not mean, however, that Pomeroy merely put these ideas into Taruc's head. Even after the latter left the Party, he never distanced himself from the work. The sentiments about US betrayal are also found in the songs of the Huk movement; see Maceda (1996).
21. For the full text of the speech, see Nick Joaquin (Quijano de Manila), "The Law and the Prophet: A Look into the Current Status of the Image of Jose P. Laurel," 1967, reprinted in *The Laurel Legacy*, Memorial Series vol. 2, Manila (1986).

chapter 3

American Impact on Elite Continuity in Post-War Japan and the Philippines

Temario C. Rivera

The Philippines and Japan share a common historical past in having experienced American rule: the former as an American colony for more than four decades and the latter as a defeated power under the American Occupation for about six and a half years in the aftermath of the Second World War. This common historical experience serves as a point of reference in this study for understanding the process of elite reconstitution and restoration in the immediate post-war political development of these two countries.

After the Second World War, both Japan and the Philippines largely succeeded in restoring and reconstituting the "old guard and traditional levers of elite rule" but Japan's post-war electoral system flourished under a stable and dominant conservative hegemonic rule while the Philippines languished under an unstable system of oligarchic electoral rule.

In explaining this major contrast in political and economic outcomes in these two countries, I will focus my analysis on the nature of the reconstitution and reconsolidation of elite rule after the immediate post-war period (roughly 1946–1950) by examining the reforms and policies pursued by the American Occupation as well as the responses of the local elites to this process. In particular, I am interested in examining the opportunities and the constraints created during the occupation period in terms of the capacity of popular movements and non-traditional elite formations and parties to challenge traditional elite rule in both countries.

American Occupation Policy and Reforms in Post-War Japan

The American Occupation in Japan sought a radical restructuring of Japanese society and politics aimed at demilitarization and democratization, and Japan was governed indirectly through the existing governmental machinery and agencies, including the emperor. As John Dower puts it: "… the defeated Japanese were made the subjects of an unprecedented experiment — audacious in its ethnocentrism but also in its ambition and, until devoured by the Cold War, its idealism. This was an undertaking plagued from the start by contradictions, among them the very notion of 'revolution from above'" (Dower 1999: 80).

Three major post-war policy documents provided Gen. Douglas MacArthur vast powers and exceptional latitude in pursuing his mandate as Supreme Commander of the Allied Powers (SCAP) in occupied Japan.[1] The first major decree issued by GHQ/SCAP was the "Civil Liberties Directive" on October 4, 1945, titled the "Removal of Restrictions on Political, Civil, and Religious Liberties." This order abolished the Peace Preservation Law[2] and other ordinances and regulations restricting "freedom of thought, religion, assembly and speech"; ordered the release of all political prisoners; the abolition of secret police organs, including the Home Ministry's notorious *Tokko Keisatsu* (Special Higher Police); the dismissal of the Minister of Home Affairs and various police chiefs; and the removal of all barriers to the "unrestricted discussion of the Emperor, the Imperial Institution, and the Imperial Japanese government."

As a result of the Civil Liberties Decree, "nearly 5000 officials in the Home Ministry and law enforcement agencies were dismissed and the Japan Communist Party (JCP), driven underground and persecuted under the Peace Preservation Law, resurfaced as a legitimate political organization" (Takemae 2003: 238). In the aftermath of the same decree, "439 Communists, Korean nationalists, liberal intellectuals and religious pacifists were freed on October 10, 1945 and the police were forced to suspend immediately the surveillance of another 2,060 "subversives" (ibid.: 240).

The next set of political reforms focused on the revival of political parties, electoral reform, and the purge of undesirable personnel from public office (ibid.: 261–70). The revival of parties not only saw the reemergence of the Conservative parties, but also of the reorganization of the Japan Communist Party (JCP) in October 1945 and the creation of the Japan Socialist Party (JSP) on November 2, 1945. As the first political party to re-emerge, the JCP reconfirmed its policy of overturning the imperial institution through a "peaceful democratic revolution" and sought to establish a broad popular front uniting workers, farmers and the urban poor. The JSP was organized by non-Communist proletarian and peasant groups of various persuasions and succeeded in leading a coalition government from June 1947 to February 1948 under its chair, Tetsu Katayama, a Christian Socialist and former adviser to the labor movement.

Electoral reform aimed at revising voting requirements and broadening the electorate through the following changes mandated by the Lower House Election Law passed on December 17 1945: 1) lowering the voting age from 25 to 20 years, vastly expanding the range of representation; 2) reducing the age requirement for candidates from 30 to 25 years; 3) giving women the right to vote; and 4) enhancing the electoral chances for newcomers through a limited plural system of voting in multimember constituencies.[3] The new election law changed the composition of the Diet and enhanced the participation of smaller political groupings, independents, and women candidates, with this combined sector accounting for about 35 percent of total Lower House seats in the April 1946 elections.

Implemented between 1946 and 1947, the directives on the purging of organizations and individuals listed seven "removal and exclusion categories" as the basis for disqualification from public life. These categories included "active exponents of militant nationalism and aggression," professional military officers, leaders of ultra-nationalist and terrorist societies, officials of overseas financial and economic organizations involved in Japanese expansion, and governors of former Japanese colonies and occupied territories. About 77 percent of those affected were career military men and the purge also disqualified more than 600 conservative party cadres and lawmakers from the April 1946 balloting. The political purges were complemented by the "education" purge of May 1946 and a year later by the "economic" purge which weeded out 1,535 heads of industry, finance and commerce. Ultimately, SCAP screened a total of 717,415 individuals, forcing 201,815 from key positions in public life (ibid.: 267–9).

What were the effects of these purges? A leading expert on the allied occupation of Japan asserts that:

> Despite its inequities, however, the exclusion campaign effected a change of leadership in key areas of social, political and economic life. Many of the middle-echelon officials who had loyally served the Imperial state managed to retain their positions or find comparable work, but the purge decisively ended the political ascendancy of the officer corps and other reactionary elements in society, clearing the way for younger political and business leaders relatively untainted by ultra-rightist ideology. These latter would become the driving force behind postwar Japan's rapid economic recovery and its emergence as a democratic nation (ibid.: 270).

A centerpiece of early occupation reforms was the passage of a new constitution prepared and finalized by SCAP after scrutinizing several proposals from various private study groups (such as the Constitutional Research Association [Kenpo Kenkyu-kai], the Constitutional Discussion Group [Kenpo Kondankai], and the Japan Bar Association, various political parties including the Socialist Party and Communist Party, and influential individuals, notably Iwasaburo Takano, labor leader, scholar and founder of the Ohara Institute for Social Research (ibid.: 273) and other liberal or socialist academics, journalists and lawyers such as Yasuzo Suzuki, Tatsuo Morito, and Hyoe Ouchi (Sims 2001: 244).

Promulgated on November 3, 1946 and taking effect on May 3, 1947, the new constitution "renounced the Meiji charter's authoritarian Prussian legacy, replacing it with liberal Anglo-American legal concepts" (Takemae 2003: 271) and incorporated the following new and radical features: 1) reducing the emperor to a "symbol of the state and the unity of the people" with no powers "related to government" and deriving the emperor's position "from the will of the people with whom resides sovereign power" (Chapter 1); 2) renunciation of war as a sovereign right of the nation and outlawing the maintenance of "land, sea, and air forces, as well as other war potential" (Chapter 2, Article 9); 3) a bill of rights and duties guaranteeing the exercise of basic human and civil liberties, including equality under the law, freedom of thought and expression, freedom of religion, abolition of the peerage system, universal adult suffrage, and the banning of discrimination based on race, creed, sex, social status or family origin in all kinds of relations, and gender equality in marriage and family relations (Chapter 3); and 4) making the national Diet the "highest organ of state power and the sole lawmaking organ of the State" and constituted of two houses (House of Representatives and House of Councillors) whose members are all duly elected (Chapter 4).[4]

While the new constitution was no doubt imposed on the Japanese government, it "was not out of keeping with the popular mood in Japan in 1946 and continued to meet with wide acceptance thereafter" (Sims 2001: 244). The conservative Japanese sectors opposed the change in the status of the emperor, but Article 9 of the Constitution which renounced war and disallowed the maintenance of armed forces provoked more resentment from conservatives and nationalists. However, this provision did not prevent the establishment of substantial Self Defense Forces starting with the creation of a 75,000-strong Police Reserve Force in 1950 in response to the "reverse-course" and reshaping of American policy in the context of the global Cold War and the Korean War in Asia (ibid.: 245).

The next round of reforms targeted by the SCAP focused on a set of institutional and economic changes including police and local government, the bureaucracy, labor controls, the *zaibatsu*, and landlordism. Together with police and local government reforms, bureaucratic deconcentration was seen as a major Occupation goal. Many of the members of the Government Section of GHQ/SCAP considered the bureaucracy as a "bastion of the Old Order comparable in importance to the Tojo war cabal, the great financial combines, reactionary political parties and large landlords." Under strong pressure from SCAP, the Diet passed on October 21, 1947, the National Public Service Law which sought to streamline and modernize the bureaucracy and eliminate favoritism and self-perpetuating distinctions based on social status. However, bureaucratic reform proved to be difficult. As pointed out by one scholar: "Despite its modernizing influence on the civil service, which is undeniable, SCAP ultimately was more concerned with improving bureaucratic efficiency than with reshaping the bureaucracy itself. As a result, the apparatus of state remained prey to the vested interests of its diverse constituencies, with each ministry and agency determined to defend against all comers its prerogatives and particularistic agenda" (Takemae 2003: 307).

Another eminent scholar of the Occupation period asserts thus:

> The American reformers did change the political economy of Japan in significant ways most notably through land reform, the dissolution of family-controlled zaibatsu holding companies, and the promotion of legislation that gave unprecedented rights to organized labor. They also imposed certain specific bureaucratic reforms of lasting importance, eliminating the military establishment and breaking up the powerful Home Ministry that had exercised control over the police and local governments. But they

> did preserve the rest of the bureaucracy, and the '1940 system' more generally, as a matter of convenience. To work through existing channels made implementing occupation policies easier; to fundamentally change the system would have created turmoil in an already confusing situation (Dower 1999: 560).

In addressing Japan's economic reconstruction, SCAP proceeded from the assumption that the country's militarism and imperial aggression were founded on economic and institutional causes that needed to be rooted out. In brief, these factors included a controlled labor force that was underpaid and overworked; the *zaibatsu* system of a few large industrial and financial conglomerates which monopolized the capital-intensive export sector of the economy using semi-feudalistic labor and management practices; and a landholding system dominated by a relatively small number of landlords that perpetuated poverty in the rural areas.

The land reform program was arguably SCAP's most successful reform project. By 1949, it had reallocated two million hectares of arable land or about 80 percent of all tenanted holdings. By the end of the reform, 90 percent of all land under crops was being cultivated by independent growers, and the number of landless tenants had declined to a mere seven percent of farm producers (Takemae 2003: 344). Not only did these reforms boost agricultural production and increase rural incomes, it also effectively undercut the political constituency of support for both the Socialist and Communist movements in the countryside.

In contrast to the overall success of the land reform program, SCAP's campaign to dissolve the *zaibatsu* system faced strong opposition from both Washington policymakers and big businesses in the US who by mid-1947 had become wary of undermining Japanese capitalism and started to emphasize economic recovery, containing Communism, and strengthening conservative rule in Japan. Those who sought to restrain the campaign against the *zaibatsu* included the US Chamber of Commerce, the National Association of Manufacturers, and influential officials such as Secretary of Defense James F.

Forrestal, Undersecretary of the Army William H. Draper, and Secretary of the Army Kenneth Royall. This powerful bloc succeeded in eviscerating MacArthur's deconcentration campaign against the *zaibatsu* system. Thus, by the end of the Yoshida era, a combination of internal American policy disputes and the strong resistance offered by the bureaucracy and big businesses resulted in the "creation of a powerful 'new *zaibatsu*' structure in which, however, the old *zaibatsu* continued to play a leading role" (ibid.: 336–9).[5]

The labor movement was another key target for SCAP's democratization reforms on the economy.[6] Under SCAP's guidance between 1945 and 1947, the labor movement experienced unprecedented freedoms allowing it to grow rapidly. SCAP abolished the reactionary labor fronts established by the militarists in the late 1930s and the Diet passed on December 22, 1945, the Labor Union Law which guaranteed the right to organize, bargain collectively and strike, and established labor relations boards at the central and prefectural levels to mediate disputes. This new environment of freedom unleashed an extraordinary level of popular participation, mass militancy, and union organizing particularly in the face of severe food shortages during the early Occupation years. Workers waged "production-control struggles" in various companies and mounted huge public demonstrations (500,000 on May Day 1946 in Tokyo) calling for the liberation of grain stores in the Imperial Palace, the popular control of hoarded goods, the resignation of the inept Shidehara government, the purge of war criminals, and worker control over production.

This mass mobilization and worker militancy would have climaxed in a general strike planned for February 1, 1947 but Gen. MacArthur directly intervened with a formal decree outlawing the strike, threatening to call the troops if the organizers pushed through with the planned action. This proved to be a turning point in the Occupation policy of liberalization, and henceforth, SCAP clamped down hard on labor organizing and militancy by banning strikes and the right to collective bargaining in almost all public enterprises starting from 1948. This was followed by the "Red Purges" which sought to break radical unions at the company and industry level and involved close collaboration among occupation officials, conservative politicians, government bureaucrats and corporate managers. About 11,000 activist union members in the public sector were purged and about the same number suffered the same fate in the private sector including the media by the end of 1950.

Moreover, this decided drift toward conservatism was further dramatized by the "depurging" or return to public activity of individuals earlier purged "for all time" for their active involvement in militarist and ultranationalist activities. However, as stressed by Dower: "Although the 'reverse course' helped establish a domestic conservative hegemony of politicians, bureaucrats and businessmen that remained dominant to the end of the century, Communists and Socialists continued to be elected to the Diet and to command serious attention in debates over public policy"(1999: 273).

Thus, in the crucible of the war and the American Occupation, a reconstituted conservative elite emerged in Japan that was strong enough to provide the foundations of the subsequent conservative political hegemony under the Liberal Democratic Party (LDP). But the political legacy is more complex than this. As aptly summed up by Dower once again, "the occupation legacy was a new conservatism but within a restructured state in which progressive and reformist ideals, and laws, retained a substantial constituency among the Japanese people themselves" (ibid.: 313).

Elite Restoration in Post-War Philippines

In the context of the overall disruption of the established order in Southeast Asia during the Second World War, the Philippines arguably had the most impressive record of elite resilience. The colonial, pre-war oligarchic families that controlled Philippine politics not only survived the war, but continued to dominate post-war electoral contests. Unlike in

Indonesia, Burma or Vietnam, the local revolutionary movement and radical nationalist popular movements in the Philippines did not emerge triumphant from the cataclysm of war.

In the Philippine context, my main interest lies in examining why the new opportunities and socio-political forces unleashed by the war failed to effectively challenge traditional elite rule. At the international level, one obvious explanatory factor had to do with the further entrenchment and enhancement of American power at the end of the war. The other colonial powers in the region saw their military and political resources severely undercut in the aftermath of the war and found themselves unable to effectively determine the march of events in their former colonies. In contrast, the United States emerged as the most powerful post-war player and sought to dictate the flow of both global and local events. Moreover, the radical nationalist movements in the Philippines were either communist-led, such as the *Hukbalahap*, or pro-Japanese, such as the followers of Gen. Artemio Ricarte and Benigno Ramos. These features of the radical mass movements in the Philippines led to violent American opposition and repression particularly in the immediate post-war years when the American forces under Gen. MacArthur committed themselves to restoring the power of the pre-war oligarchy.

This new post-war arrangement of power gains extreme saliency in the Philippine context in light of another enduring political legacy of American colonial rule in the country. This is the further entrenchment of an oligarchy through an electoral political system formally started in 1901. This meant that elite rule has been perpetuated by a formal electoral system which provided immense advantages to powerful political clans of landlords and big businesses. Under American colonial rule, this oligarchic hegemony was exemplified by the dominance of the Nacionalista Party under the leadership of Manuel L. Quezon, the elite's most consummate practitioner of clientelist-patronage politics. Quezon's role in this system of clientelist politics rooted in and sustained by the local oligarchy is aptly described by one author as follows:

> As Commonwealth president, Quezon perfected a patronage system he had used for 18 years as Senate president to establish his dominion over Filipino politics. No longer restrained by his distance from executive prerogatives, Pres. Quezon soon erected an interrelated, finely tuned clientelist system that reached from the *municipio* to Malacañang, to the White House (McCoy 1988: 120).

However, American colonial rule and the local oligarchy's control of electoral politics could not wipe out the country's long revolutionary tradition of peasant radicalism and trade union militancy that formed the base of both the legal and the extra-parliamentary opposition. The social base of this militant opposition was united by a comprehensive program of land redistribution and agrarian reform, the exercise of full democratic rights and a firm demand for immediate national independence in contrast to the oligarchy's crass manipulation and opportunism on these issues. Shortly before the outbreak of the Second World War, the most organized and militant sections of the peasantry and working class decided to form a single party with the official merger in 1938 of the Socialist Party of the Philippines representing the organized peasants of Central Luzon and the Communist Party of the Philippines representing the radical trade union members.[7] With the outbreak of war, the newly merged party succeeded in organizing the most effective anti-Japanese guerrilla resistance movement, the *Hukbalahap* (Hukbong Bayan Laban sa Hapon [Peoples' Army Against the Japanese]) specifically in Central and Southern Luzon.

In the aftermath of the war, two significant developments emerged as direct threats and challenges to traditional oligarchic rule. First, the guerrilla resistance against the Japanese invaders created an armed revolutionary force rooted in the peasantry, the militant working class, and radical intellectuals whose social roots and political program posed a challenge to the restoration of traditional elite rule. Second, the issue of collaboration with the Japanese Occupation by leading elements of the political oligarchy served to drive a wedge within the elite class and opened up some opportunities for challenging traditional elite dominance. In the unfolding of both of these developments, American policy and intervention proved decisive.

The Hukbalahap waged its anti-Japanese guerrilla struggle in the overall context of an anti-fascist united front strategy in the Second World War. In this strategy, the United States was treated as an ally in the war against fascism and the usual attacks against American imperialism largely ceased during this period. It was also in the context of this worldwide anti-fascist strategy in the gathering storm before the outbreak of war that Commonwealth President Quezon agreed to allow the outlawed Communist Party to resume its public life and to free its imprisoned leaders such as Crisanto Evangelista, the founding chair. However, in pursuing the worldwide communist anti-fascist strategy, the local communist movement may also have lost the flexibility to reach out and respond to anti-American but pro-Japanese mass nationalist movements such as the followers of Gen. Ricarte and Benigno Ramos. For instance, efforts by the pro-Japanese, anti-American *Makapili* (League of Patriotic Filipinos) to form a joint front with the anti-Japanese Hukbalahap against the returning American forces proved unsuccessful (Terami-Wada 1999: 83).

The Huk leadership and rank and file were caught completely unprepared by the ferocity and hostility against them shown by the American returning forces under the command of Gen. MacArthur. Sometime in 1944, the Hukbalahap leadership in fact organized a failed mission to get directly in touch with Gen. MacArthur in Australia to coordinate with the expected arrival of the returning American forces (Lava 2002: 47–60). Tragically, even in face of the systematic persecution perpetuated by the returning American military forces against them, the HUKs initially sought to continue its policy of a working united front with the American military. The historians, Renato and Letizia Constantino, describe the Huk's response thus:

> The Huk fighters and their supporters reacted to American hostility at first with surprise and bewilderment and later with deep resentment. They had sacrificed everything for the anti-Japanese struggle and they never expected their American

> allies in the anti-fascist war to use fascist methods against them. There had been ominous signs of antipathy prior to the reoccupation, but the Huk leadership held fast to the policy of the united front. Even after the local governments they had set up were discarded and their guerrilla organization refused recognition, and even after the first few squadrons were forcibly disarmed, the Huks continued to implement their united front policy. They continued to help in the mopping up campaigns; they helped to organize labor battalions for the construction of army installations; and they even offered to mobilize a strong Huk force to assist in the invasion of Japan (Constantino and Constantino 1978: 168–9).

Suffering enormously from the arrest and killing of its leaders and brutal attacks against its followers by rival guerrilla forces coddled by the American military and private armies of local landlords, the Huks nevertheless decided to participate in the post-war parliamentary process. In the 1946 presidential and congressional elections, the Huks joined the Democratic Alliance (DA), a broad coalition of reformist urban middle and upper class liberals, peasant organizations, militant trade unions, and anti-collaborationist guerrilla groups which allied itself with the Osmeña wing of the divided Nacionalista Party.[8] With its organized peasant and working class base, the Huks and the Partido Komunista ng Pilipinas (PKP) provided the mass constituency of the DA. The Democratic Alliance ran on a five-point program which included immediate and unconditional independence, anti-collaboration, democracy against fascism, social security and agrarian reforms, and industrialization.

With its strong mass base in Central Luzon, the DA succeeded in electing seven members to the House of Representatives, including well-known Huk-PKP leaders Luis Taruc and Jesus Lava. However, the elected DA congresspersons, together with three Nacionalista Party (NP) senators and another NP congressman, were denied their legitimate seats in Congress when the Roxas administration charged them with alleged fraud and terrorism in their election. Behind this disqualification scheme was the Roxas administration's need for a three-fourths' vote of Congress to be able to amend the constitution to accommodate the Parity Amendment of the Bell Trade Act.[9] While the Roxas administration succeeded in amending the constitution and passing the Bell Trade Act, it also foreclosed a golden opportunity of integrating into the legal process the core constituency of the radical opposition by forcing its duly elected representatives out of the parliamentary arena.

The Collaboration Issue

The second major issue at the end of the war that presented an opportunity to challenge the traditional oligarchic power structure in the country was the collaboration issue.[10] Almost all of the leading national elite politicians served in both the Executive Commission under Japanese auspices and the later Japanese sponsored wartime government headed by Jose P. Laurel. Many of the provincial elites were also appointed as local government executives. A key issue that made possible the electoral alliance between the DA and Pres. Osmeña's Nacionalista Party against Roxas' Liberal Party in the 1946 elections was in fact the collaboration issue. However, as successor to Pres. Quezon who died in Washington during the war and as a senior leader of the same pre-war political oligarchy, Osmeña found himself in an extremely ambivalent position to lead the attack on the collaboration issue.

The US collaboration policy vis-a-vis the Philippines was originally set by Pres. Roosevelt in June 1944 when he stated, "Filipinos who collaborated with the enemy must be removed from authority and influence in the political and economic life of the country." In response to this policy, Quezon asserted that although the United States had the "technical legal right" to determine the guilt of and punish collaborators, she "will be wise if she forgoes this right and allow[s] such persons to be dealt with by the Philippine government" because Filipinos "would feel that having failed to defend them ... America was in no position to punish them" (Hayden 1944: 440). Indeed, there was a subtle but important difference between Roosevelt's and Quezon's line on collaboration as explained by one author:

> Roosevelt emphasized the removal of collaborators from positions of authority and influence without concern for their guilt. Behind Quezon's emphasis on the determination of the guilt of collaborators, which would require the sifting of evidence in a deliberate judicial process, was the conviction that his Nacionalista colleagues who had collaborated had been motivated to ease the lot of Filipinos under the Japanese. The Commonwealth president was also determined to stay in power in the islands, and he recognized no need to dismantle the government of Quezonista loyalists he had assembled during the years of Commonwealth rule (Golay 1997: 440–1).

Pres. Osmeña initially organized a cabinet that included hard-line anti-collaborationists, notably two leading guerrilla leaders, Tomas Confesor and Tomas Cabili, who served as secretaries of interior and defense, respectively. Early on, however, Gen. MacArthur, who was the de facto ruler in the first 10 months after the Allied landing in Leyte, asserted his authority on key issues including the collaboration problem. MacArthur's GHQ announced the "liberation" of Manuel Roxas while other officials who served with the Japanese sponsored government such as Jose Yulo, Antonio de las Alas, Quintin Paredes, Teofilo Sison and others were declared as "captured" and consequently detained (Steinberg 1967: 115). During the war, Roxas succeeded in evading formal membership in the Laurel government until he was prevailed upon by Laurel to serve as the "food czar" (minister without portfolio) in a futile attempt to solve the food crisis some five months before MacArthur's landing in Leyte (ibid.: 107).

As a member of the Nacionalista ruling triumvirate (together with Quezon and Osmeña), Roxas was considered Quezon's presumptive heir and was also a close friend and military aide of Gen. MacArthur. By personally absolving Roxas of any collaborationist taint, MacArthur also clearly signaled his choice of Roxas as the post-war Philippine leader. Consequently, Roxas began to build an alternative center of power to Osmeña's and rallied all those suffering from the collaborationist tag. Roxas' base of power was also greatly enhanced with the convening of the Congress elected in 1941 which was dominated by supporters of Quezon and with Roxas himself assuming the Senate presidency and as chair of the powerful Committee on Appointments. Moreover, a Roxas ally, Rep. Jose Zulueta, served as the speaker of the Lower House. With the approaching 1946 presidential elections, Roxas established a new party, the Liberal Party, and brought with him many of the old guards and Quezon supporters from the Nacionalista Party.

Meanwhile, the collaboration issue persisted. Pres. Truman announced in March 1946 that "there is no necessity for any change in our established policy of leaving the disposition of collaborationists in the Philippines to the civil authorities there" (Golay 1997: 453). Osmeña and Roxas compromised to pass a bill creating a People's Court and an Office of Special Prosecutors on September 25, 1945 to try those charged of collaboration. However, these two agencies worked under severe time, personnel and material constraints. For instance, the law required that indictments of those charged with crimes must be filed within six months, a near impossible task for the 25 special prosecutors considering that the Counter Intelligence Corps (CIC) of the American Army turned up more than 5,600 cases in which "presumptive evidence warranted detention."

The final outcome of the trials was absolutely dismal. As summarized by a major author on this subject:

> Of the 5603 cases originally filed before the People's Court, only 156 had been convicted (0.27 percent), and of those, only one, Teofilo Sison, was prominent politically. In percentage terms … 0.6 percent of the wartime leadership was convicted, and 74 percent was never in court. There was no blood bath in which the mob ruled at the end of the war, and there was no purge either internal or external. The elite remained intact, with a remarkable survival rate, considering the risks of war and the average age of the group. The war diminished neither the size nor the authority of the establishment (Steinberg 1967: 162–3).

Conclusion

Thus, in a deeper sense, the restoration of the old order in the Philippines was far more predictable than anything that approximated continuity with the old order in Japan. In defeated Japan, MacArthur's clear mandate included the destruction of the ruling wartime elite (the military bureaucracy but sparing the emperor). In reoccupied Philippines, MacArthur's immediate political objective was the restoration of the old order albeit under the leadership of a more energetic member of the political oligarchy (Roxas as against Osmeña) who was deemed more capable of reconstructing and restoring the old order consistent with overall American interests.

The grouping of progressive forces centered in the Democratic Alliance (DA) that emerged in the aftermath of the war proved to be threatening to both American interests and the local elite. With its main constituency rooted among peasants and workers steeled by the exigencies of the anti-Japanese guerrilla war and animated by a radical program of political and social transformation, the DA mounted a potent electoral struggle. To crush this mass-based political challenge, the administration and its landlord allies launched armed attacks against the leaders and supporters of the Hukbalahap and disqualified the winning DA candidates in the lower House on trumped up charges of electoral fraud to ensure passage of the Bell Trade Act and its Parity Amendment. Thus, under these conditions, the emergence of a legitimate left-wing legal political party in the Philippines was thoroughly undermined.

It would take more than 50 years before political parties representing the interests of the marginalized and disadvantaged sectors could win seats in the lower house of the Philippine Congress with the implementation of the Party List Law in the 1998 elections. The failure of the post-war conservative political leadership to institute fundamental social and economic reforms and effectively incorporate the radical mass nationalist movement in the parliamentary process has resulted in the continuation of a communist-led armed challenge that persists to this day.[11] Contrast that with the Japanese situation where the Socialists and Communists have had a continuing political presence both in the Diet and the daily discourses of political life. Moreover, the most reactionary segment of the old political hierarchy in Japan, the military bureaucracy, was also effectively wiped out by the occupation reforms. But more significantly, it was the structural reforms that vastly improved the lives of ordinary Japanese peasants and workers in Japan particularly through the successful land reform and democratic rights gained by these sectors under the American Occupation. In stark contrast, the American-restored political oligarchy in the Philippines effectively opposed the advance of popular struggles aimed at equally wide-ranging structural reforms in the aftermath of the war. No wonder these absent structural changes continue to be at the forefront of the agenda of change in the Philippines today.

Notes

1. These documents were the Potsdam Declaration (July 26, 1945), US State-War-Navy Coordinating Committee's (SWNCC) "US Initial Post-Surrender Policy for Japan" (September 22, 1945), and the Pentagon's "Basic Directive for Post-Surrender Military Government in Japan Proper" (November 3, 1945).
2. Passed in 1925, the Peace Preservation Law imposed harsh penalties of up to ten years' imprisonment for those found guilty of involvement in organizations aimed at the overthrow of the emperor system or the system of private property and targeted communists, anarchists, and other radicals.
3. The New Election Law, which favored women and smaller political parties, was revised in March 1947 by the Yoshida-led government, which restored the pre-surrender electoral precincts and replaced limited plural balloting with a single vote.
4. See The Constitution of Japan at <http://www.solon.org/Constitutions/Japan/English>.
5. See also Theodore Cohen, *Remaking Japan: The American Occupation as New Deal* (1987), pp. 353–77.
6. This section on the labor movement draws heavily from the works of Eiji Takemae (2003), pp. 310–24 and Theodore Cohen (1987), pp. 187–239.

7. The merged parties officially became known as the Communist Party of the Philippines (Merger of the Socialist and Communist Parties). For an account of the convention merger of these two parties, see James S. Allen, *The Radical Left on the Eve of War: A Political Memoir* (1985), pp. 56–9. Today, this merger party is referred to as the Partido Komunista ng Pilipinas (PKP) to distinguish it from the new Communist Party of the Philippines (CPP) established in 1968.
8. The Democratic Alliance (DA) was composed of three guerrilla groups — the Hukbalahap, the Free Philippines and the Blue Eagle; a peasant union, the PKM (Pambansang Kaisahan ng mga Magbubukid [National Union of Peasants]); a labor group, the CLO (Committee on Labor Organization); and four other progressive organizations — the League for National Liberation, the Anti-Traitors League, the Anti-Japanese League, and the Civil Liberties Union. See Renato Constantino and Letizia R. Constantino, *The Philippines: The Continuing Past* (1978), pp. 182–3.
9. The Philippine Trade Act, better known as the Bell Trade Act was passed by the US Congress in 1945 and provided for eight more years of duty-free trade until 1954 and gradually ascending tariffs for 20 years until 1974. It also fixed the rate of exchange at two pesos to one dollar, thus depriving the Philippines of its currency sovereignty. Its most notorious provision was the so-called Parity Amendment which granted Americans the same rights as Filipinos in the exploitation of natural resources, acquisition of lands of the public domain, grazing, fishing and mineral rights, and the ownership and operation of public utilities.
10. On the collaboration issue, see David Joel Steinberg, *Philippine Collaboration in World War II* (1967); Hernando J. Abaya, *Betrayal in the Philippines* (1970); and Teodoro A. Agoncillo, *The Burden of Proof: The Vargas-Laurel Collaboration Case* (1984).
11. For an extended discussion of these problems, see Temario C. Rivera, "Transition Pathways and Democratic Consolidation in Post-Marcos Philippines," *Contemporary Southeast Asia* 24, 3 (December 2002): 466–83.

Part II:
Images of Nations and Nationalism

chapter 4

The Japanese Analogy as Liminal Crisis-Effect in Initial Filipino-American Encounters, 1898–1899

Oscar V. Campomanes

> "The political representative is the political image."
>
> Raymond Williams

Reporting to General Emilio Aguinaldo about his first diplomatic mission to the United States on behalf of the Filipino revolutionary government, Felipe Agoncillo recalls the strange reception that awaited him upon arriving in San Francisco on September 22, 1898:[1]

> Sapagkat bantog [sic] sa Estados Unidos at sa Europa ang pagka-alis ko sa Hongkong, dahil sa mga cablegramas ng mga corresponsales ng mga periodicos, ay ang unang panukala ng bayang amerikano ay akoy darating doon ng hálos *hubad* at *may bahag*. Kayà pag pasok namin ng puerto ng California ay ilang corresponsales ng periodicos ay nag presenta sa akin sa vapor at humihingi ng conferencia; tinanggap ko po silang lahat ng mahusay, bagaman guinao-an ko ng paraan na u[a]la silang masimot sa aking pananalita tungkol sa aking lakad. Noong

> ding arao na iyon, na publicar sa mga periodicos, na itinalâ nila na ang ating Bayan ay di salvage at may katampatang civilizacion kaparis ng iba.
>
> (Because the newspaper correspondents cabled the news of my departure from Hong Kong extensively throughout the United States and Europe, it was the first expectation of the American people that I would arrive *half-naked*, and *with nothing on but a loincloth.* So it was that after our entry into the port of California, several reporters introduced themselves to me upon coming aboard, and asked for a press conference; I received all of them ably, sir, although I endeavored with some reticence not to disclose the object of my mission to them. On that very day, the newspapers reported that we are not a savage people, and possess a civilization comparable to any other.)

Advance cable dispatches from newspaper correspondents had not only screened his identity and his trip to the United States before he could verify them for interested and curious North Americans. Felipe Agoncillo avers that after catching a glimpse of him and seeing something different, the expectant throng on the scene (which included newspaper reporters) corrected their preconceptions about Filipinos as "uncivilized savages."

Teodoro Agoncillo's seminal account of Filipino republican formation at the turn of the 20th century notes this singular event and keeps to the spirit of Felipe Agoncillo's anecdotal report, with some elaboration (1960: 322):

> Since it had been known in the United States and Europe that Agoncillo left Hong Kong on his way to America, the Americans, in their staggering ignorance of geography expected that he would arrive on civilized American soil naked, except for the G-strings. They were, however, dumbfounded to see a highly educated man, complete with hat and well-pressed European suit, go down the gangplank with superior airs.

This historical account provides no more analysis of the event/ encounter beyond emphasizing the transformative effect of Felipe Agoncillo's arrival "on civilized American soil." But it suggests a curious reversal of roles for both the observed and observer, adding inferential details of its own. Felipe Agoncillo is pictured as "superior" in air and attire, his clueless and credulous North American reception committee, "ignorant in geography," and "dumbfounded" by the portrait before them.[2]

What, exactly, did these curious American onlookers see with the first ever Filipino they had laid their eyes on? How could have it been possible for initial American colonial stereotypes of Filipinos to be transformed this radically, and with such instantaneousness, at such a particular moment? In what specific forms did such transformations express themselves as a force field? With what catalyzing significance, thereby, was Felipe Agoncillo's political image charged? To what proximate objects or ends, if discernible at all, was it oriented? Within what specific historical and political contexts, and given what contingencies, did Felipe Agoncillo's representational act and its political effects take place? What politics and semiosis of representation in historiography can be limned in the coverage of events of this sort?

In this essay, we consider closely the diplomatic politics of Felipe Agoncillo and the Filipino revolutionary leadership, through the Comité Central Filipino (hereafter the Comité or CCF), as it brought American imperial politics of authority and knowledge to heretofore unexamined thresholds of breakdown and crises. Between 1898 and 1901, Filipino revolutionists challenged American sovereignty claims upon the Philippines in the wake of the Spanish-American War, but specifically and closely during the short but crucial period before the outbreak of the US-Philippine War in February 1899. What the Filipino intellectual and diplomat S.P. Lopez calls "the initial encounter" between Filipino and American authorities takes place within these temporal bounds and in the thick pall of these political — and as we shall indicatively illustrate, historiographic — disputes (1966: 10).

We focus on the antebellum phase of the war on the argument that it has been easily glossed over when, in fact, it can tell us much about the fateful turns that Filipino-American neocolonial relations of representation would shortly, and thereafter, take. Particularly in the crucial months from late

1898 to early 1899, the crises in US imperialist representations of Filipinos and the Philippines expressed themselves in the momentary emergence and disappearance of a shadowy Japanese Analogy (and of Japan as a cultural icon or as a third term), mediating, and indeed, eventuating as concrete crisis-effects of such Filipino revolutionary-diplomatic cultural politics and campaigns. For to the extent that what can be alternatively called here "the Japanese bogey" seemed to have functioned as a telling symptom of a politics in process and progress, it is nonetheless striking that it arose at all. The political process that ensued, or in which it emerged as a telling critical effect, is thus understood here as more open-ended, highly-contingent, closely contested, and vexed by serious problems of political will or initiative than most standard accounts of the American conquest of the Philippines and anti-colonial Filipino resistance would typically permit.

As a crisis-effect, the Japanese Analogy, while emerging and fading away as a liminal margin of *fin-de-siècle* Filipino-American representational scuffles, clearly bore portents for a much later contestation between Japan and the US over the Philippines. It is a Japanese-American discord over the archipelago in which revolutionary strategy and diplomacy itself would play a precipitating part or might be seen as having exhibited such astute foresight.[3] Although this essay will not be the space to explore the many critical implications of this particular phenomenon, it suggests some beginning or tentative interpretations. The focus here, in other words, remains the contested dyad of Filipino-American neocolonial relations and the initial engagements that first provided the templates that would shape its future expressions.

To appreciate the Japanese Analogy as a liminal crisis-effect, and as engendered by Filipino revolutionary diplomacy within the self-confident politics and rhetoric of American imperial and representational discourses, one must set this Analogy's shadowy onset and egress within the larger frame of the antebellum anti-imperialist campaigns of Felipe Agoncillo and the Aguinaldo government. After a brief introductory segment on Agoncillo and the Comité as historical actors, the section that follows performs this necessary contextualization, highlighting important events in the two Filipino diplomatic missions before and after the conclusion of the Treaty of Paris negotiations. The final section details the critical effects of the Japanese Analogy that quite curiously resulted from such an immediate context and which showed up the veridical uncertainties and anxieties in the initial (arguably, even subsequent) US political and cultural representations of Filipinos. But we do so in the form of, and by concluding with, historiographic critique — particularly of certain strains of American history-writing that remained blind to (if not actively suppressing) the critical valences of such Filipino revolutionary and historiographic acts/texts of political agency and "self-representation."

Felipe Agoncillo and the Comité's Propaganda Work

Felipe Agoncillo and the Comité consistently advocated for an exacting public and international interrogation of the various claims made by American imperialist/orientalist discoursing over the Filipinos as colonial subjects, and over the Philippines as a prospective dominion. A strenuous advocate of international diplomacy among the revolutionaries, Agoncillo, with the able and punctual assistance of the then-newly constituted Comité Central Filipino under Galicano Apacible, presided over the propaganda campaigns that kept the issue of international and North American recognition of Filipino independence burning, even as all indications pointed to eventual US imperial hegemony in the Philippines (Alzona 1971: 65–142). As a sign for and an agent of the many-sided struggles that preceded and paralleled the actual US-Philippine War, Agoncillo deserves more than the hagiographic or biographical, episodic or fleeting, treatments of his story thus far.[4] Apart from Gen. Aguinaldo, Agoncillo was probably the only Filipino leader (with Sixto Lopez who accompanied him as his secretary on his diplomatic missions to the West/United States) who performed a sustained metonymic function and acquired a centrally symbolic value as the Filipino Other for the North American imagination in the official and public realms.

A lawyer by training and vocation, Agoncillo drew from international law, diplomatic protocols, and precedents in the US Declaration of Independence, Constitution, and revolution against Great Britain, to delimit and argue against maturing US imperial claims over the islands. Performing as a *political representative* for the Filipino republican government, Agoncillo engaged US imperial ambitions in a close contest for legitimation through diplomatic politics, rational or legal discourses, and a creative or pleasurable play of signs and images (semiosis).[5] From these positions, he self-consciously spoke to the contingent convergence of epochal developments in US empire-building and Filipino nationalism as the 19th century sped toward its momentous close. His Hong Kong exile, after he narrowly escaped deportation to a Southern Philippine island for his political agitation against the Spanish colonial dispensation in the late 1880s and early 1890s, was what provided him a more than ample opportunity to monitor global developments that would bear heavily on the Philippine revolution (May 1993). Such a transitive nature of his political engagements and displacements enabled him to tackle unratified US claims of imperial sovereignty, with indisputable competence and political efficacy, on their own ground. His political and symbolic self-representations formed part of the inescapable or irrepressible references to which subsequent North American political acts would allude during the US-Philippine War (and after this war was declared over in 1902 by McKinley's presidential successor, Theodore Roosevelt).

After closely tracking various developments in the international sphere which could shift the opportunities for Filipino revolutionary success or spell the defeat of revolutionary aspirations, Agoncillo advised the Aguinaldo government to adopt a "balanced policy."[6] One prong of this policy called for a formal and systematic diplomatic campaign to establish the legitimacy of the inchoate republic by appealing to other (imperial) nations and the US itself for diplomatic recognition and material/moral support. Its other prong involved equipping the revolutionary army without cease for armed defense against possible aggression by the US and other imperial powers in case diplomacy failed. Such policy guidelines must be considered from an extended historical perspective. Within the many scenarios that Agoncillo envisioned with his colleagues as early as December 1897 and before the Spanish-American War, the United States emerged as an inevitable factor in the Filipino project of emancipation from Spanish colonialism because of its then heightening involvement (and escalating intervention) in the contemporaneous Cuban revolution.

Agoncillo and his CCF colleagues had to plan their diplomacy and propaganda work from an acute awareness of ethnographic constructions of the "Filipino" percolating in instant forms, which paralleled now-beginning and hotly contested constitutionalist and generally political debates over "the Philippine Question." This emergent and instant colonial ethnography pervaded the popular/public discourse in the United States in ways that could cause despair for them who were, of course, concerned to launch a reactive and effective counter-discourse of self and on the legitimacy of their revolution. Writing later for the *North American Review* in 1899 under the *nom de guerre* "Semper Vigilans" (Latin for "Always Vigilant"), Agoncillo faults the cultural information that the American empire's army and emissaries produced for US public consumption, while dealing with their prospective subjects in the critical antebellum phase, for the then seemingly interminable state of war between both peoples. He recalls these problematic US cultural descriptions of the Filipino as a racial phenotype, or even as a peculiar kind of political genotype, and their lusty preponderance in the "popular press" before and in the immediate aftermath of the war's outbreak (1899a: 426–7):

> The Filipinos have been described in serious American journals as akin to the hordes of the Khalifa; and the idea has prevailed that it required only some unknown American Kitchener to march triumphantly from North to South to make the military occupation complete. We have been represented by your popular press as if we were Africans or Mohawk Indians. We smile, and deplore the want of ethnological knowledge on the part of our literary friends. We are none of these. We are simply Filipinos.

Agoncillo and the CCF, in other words, were obviously cognizant of, and strategically based their diplomatic campaigns on, the political portents and consequences of this concordance between instant American ethnologies of the Filipino and US public discoursing of "the Philippine Question." Agoncillo's own act of self-representation during his missions, and the Filipino desire for *representative* government on whose behalf he presumptively stood, clearly and directly spoke to this politically unfavorable state of affairs for Filipino revolutionary aspirations.

The Filipino Diplomatic Campaign and its Political Semiosis

Agoncillo's story as recounted here covers the specific period between September 1898 and February 1899 when he shuttled between the US and France in pursuit of US/international recognition of Filipino belligerency and independence. Three events of extreme importance in relation to the "Philippine Question" occurred during this period: the Treaty of Paris negotiations between the US and Spain from October to December 1898; the ratification battle around the Treaty in the US Senate in January 1899; and the outbreak of the US-Philippine War in early February 1899. Armed with "a power of attorney" signed by Gen. Aguinaldo and designating him as "minister plenipotentiary of the Philippine Revolutionary Government," Agoncillo's immediate mission was to call on President McKinley to inform him firsthand of the Philippine situation and to press, specifically, for Filipino representation in the Spanish-American peace and treaty negotiations. To understand the exigencies which informed Agoncillo's missions, we must note the breathless pace at which these moments for struggle actually shifted, endowing Agoncillo's missions with almost the same sense of contingency and unpredictability as the very questions then being framed, in vibrant public discourse and international press speculations, about the US rise to world power.

The problem for the Filipino revolutionists, in fact, was how to read US intentions toward the Philippines at this juncture when they seemed unclear to the Americans themselves. In the overarching question through which this general prevarication among the American public and its politicians was framed: "Republic or Empire?" The signs and signals emanating from Washington seemed rather mixed, as to be judged from either dissimulating or vacillating pronouncements and actions of the McKinley government alone. Did Americans want part or all of the Philippines, if they wanted it at all? (Clearly, the outright annexation of the Philippines or any of its parts would ratify the reality of American imperialism and signify the now-anticipated and anxiety-ridden departure of the country from its vaunted republican traditions.) Any careful reading of the political scenario in the US would note the unsettled — even troubled — character of US thinking concerning the islands, whether among cabinet members, the commissioners eventually chosen for the peace negotiations, the senators and opinion leaders, or indeed, the public at large. The much-discussed debate(s) on the Philippine Question, already swirling at this time in its initial torrents, then presented the revolutionists with manifold possibilities for speaking to the claims being made about the Philippines by various US sectors while simultaneously making the Filipinos' own readings of the signs (for an effective politico-diplomatic campaign) vexed and difficult.

To return to the primal scene commencing this essay, we might imagine the massive wave of disorientation that swept through the large turnout of Americans (ordinary citizens and newspaper correspondents alike) at the San Francisco port where Agoncillo disembarked on September 22, 1898, when he walked down the plank, not half-naked — as newspapers and magazines would have them believe — but in a well-pressed "European" suit. But what this San Francisco welcome certainly foreboded for Agoncillo and what he learned in due time was that President William McKinley was not going to receive him *officially*, credentials from the revolutionary government and all, but only as a "private individual." Given the curious reception at San Francisco, Agoncillo was ostensibly aware that for McKinley to do otherwise was in effect to recognize the Filipino cause or legal personality, and to violate the US agreements with Spain to settle the matter of the disposition of the Philippines between them as the concerned powers.

The non-recognition of Agoncillo and concomitantly, of the Filipino republic, began in McKinley's requirement that Agoncillo *strip* himself of his credentials from Gen. Aguinaldo before he could be admitted to the president's office on October 1, 1898. Although he was allowed to review the Philippine revolution against Spain, according to some skimpy accounts, his request for the rights of Filipino belligerency and representation in the Paris conference for the Aguinaldo republic elicited no significant comment or expression of commitment from the US President (see undated note of Agoncillo to Aguinaldo, in Taylor, vol. 5; Gould 1982: 103). What Agoncillo merely gained from this exercise was the privilege of filing a memorandum on the Filipino case although again, as a historian's interpretation emphasized, "with a chilly injunction that this did not imply recognition" ("Memorandum [of] Felipe Agoncillo, of Manila, Philippines," in Taylor, vol. 5; the "interpretation" is from Morgan 1963: 406). This document, which US Paris Treaty chief negotiator Whitelaw Reid called and did concede as "an extraordinary paper," became the basis for Agoncillo's subsequent press statements and polemical publications, including his *Memorial to the US Senate* and his contribution to the US Presidential election debate on imperialism, *To The American People*.[7] Reid summarized it in a diary entry as a point of interest: "In [this] paper he claimed an independent government for the islands, asserted an alliance with the United States invited by us and accorded [by the Filipino insurgents], and quoted the language of the Declaration of Independence, which he requested Spain and the United States to make effective as to the Philippines" (October 17, 1898 entry, Reid 1965: 82).

In a very important sense, Agoncillo's revolutionary strategy, even with such a seemingly innocuous request for an audience with the US President at the White House — and under whatever terms it might be granted — was working to serve on US state authority a *fait accompli* that had the effect of initiating the crises now poised to haunt, without cease, McKinley's (and the USA's) maturing claims of sovereignty over the "Philippine Islands." The instances of non-recognition of Agoncillo himself, and there are plenty of them, are not the issue here. That he actively *figured* himself — and did so, in extensive American and international newspaper coverage — as *the representative of a right to representation* is what is semiosically significant. Indeed, in his polemic against the final deal of December 1898 in which Spain ceded the Philippines to the US for $20 million, Agoncillo limited his own importance to protesting "resolutions agreed upon at the Peace conference in Paris, as long as the juridical, political, independent personality of the Filipino people is entirely unrecognized and attempts are made to impose on these inhabitants resolutions which have not been sanctioned by their public powers" ("Official Protests Against the Paris Treaty," in Taylor, vol. 5).

After the imperialist power dealing in Paris was concluded, the arena for decision-making shifted back to the US where the treaty had to be ratified by a two-thirds majority vote in the Senate for US authority over the Philippines to be formalized. Naturally, the larger public debates about the now-controversial US sovereignty claims over the Philippines ascended to new heights with such highly contingent developments as the ratification battles in the US Senate and the possibility of war with the Filipino revolutionary forces in case the treaty were ratified. The Senate ratification battle promised the same contentiousness as that of the larger public culture debates (which were far from settled), and it was this political equation that apparently drove Agoncillo to suggest to the CCF in Hong Kong to establish a Washington legation as their "last recourse." In a prescient earlier reading of a snag in the Paris negotiations over the Philippines, Agoncillo suggested that the revolutionists should speed up their arms purchases, and predicted that if the US took the Philippines, "Independence will not be granted us. Their ambition is great ..." (Cablegram from Kitapalad [Agoncillo] to Kant [G. Apacible], received November 18 [1898], in Taylor, vol. 5).

Agoncillo quickly returned to and arrived in Washington (from Paris) in late December 1898 and was later joined by three emissaries sent by the Comité from Hong Kong.[8] With more help, Agoncillo lobbied against the treaty and flooded the State Department with requests for another meeting with McKinley, and absent that, with Secretary of State John Hay, to re-present his credentials and to press his case that a war could be averted if the US recognized that "the U.S. has no jurisdiction, natural or acquired, through any of its agencies to adjudicate in any manner upon the rights of [the Philippines and Filipinos]."[9] All such entreaties were, of course, studiously ignored by the McKinley government. But with the treaty winning approval by a one-vote margin in early February — charged by American historians to last-minute backroom dealings among some tipping-point senators and the nearly simultaneous outbreak of the US-Philippine War — Agoncillo's continued stay on US soil became untenable. Agoncillo, however, would milk this moment for whatever critical effects it could yield for the republican cause, even as his legation members now received instructions from the CCF for redeployment elsewhere, and he himself faced possible arrest and deportation by US authorities.

In his public and press statements up to his precipitated flight to Montreal, Canada, on the eve of the outbreak of the US-Philippine War on February 4, 1899, Agoncillo rhetorically emphasized the dubiousness of the claim of US authority over the Philippines by invoking international law to question the Treaty's binding powers. He copiously quoted from the US Declaration of Independence and the Constitution to reiterate as well as resound the parallel but now raucous anti-imperialist critique. The Anti-Imperialist League critique, as we know, expressed interminable anxieties — later to be shared by tons of exceptionalist American ideologues and by post-colonial scholars — over the unconsidered consequences of imperialism (and the Philippine conquest which was its touchstone) for the future, and future forms, of American republicanism. Earlier, the *Washington Evening Star* had inadvertently ratified Agoncillo's running arguments against US authority when it reported that the State Department, in considering what to do to rid Washington DC of "the unwelcome visitor," was hogtied by the pending Senate action on the treaty: "To regard Agoncillo in the light of a spy might be tantamount to an admission that we are still in an active state of war, while to hold him guilty of treason would involve the assumption that he is an American citizen and indirectly that our jurisdiction over the whole of the Philippines is complete" (January 27, 1899: 1; see also *Washington Post*, January 28, 1899: 1). What a triple bind, indeed, if one added that to do either was also for the USA to, in effect, recognize the Filipinos as rightful belligerents and itself, finally, as an imperialist state.

The State Department certainly (and quite understandably) did not bother to acknowledge Agoncillo's various attempts to be received as an envoy, even as a US Secret Service detail was deployed to keep tabs on his and the Filipino legation's movements under these politically intensifying conditions.[10] Anywise, the Secretary of State John Hay could not grant Agoncillo both the audience and recognition which the latter continued to seek, obviously fearful that to do so meant, yet again, the grant of nominal status to him and the government he represented. Still, the radical effect of Agoncillo's semiosic standing in the whole economy of claims and counter-claims may be gleaned from a *Washington Post* editorial: "It seems an absurd condition of affairs in which the government of the United States cannot protect itself against the nuisance represented by Agoncillo, who pretends to be the diplomatic representative of Aguinaldo's opera-bouffe establishment in the Philippines ... [S]urely we can devise some plan by which we may administer the great American bounce to this pestiferous Malay, and the sooner we do so, the better for our moral and political sanitation" (January 26, 1899: 3; see also front-page cartoon from the *Washington Post*, February 1, 1899). But as the war broke out on February 4, 1899, at a time when the crucial voting on the treaty remained highly contingent, the Washington press reported Agoncillo's flight to Canada and pronounced that this "act of cowardice" on his part had relieved the State Department of the *fait accompli* (now successfully established as far as Agoncillo was concerned), or worse, the inexplicable embarrassment itself of having him arrested or deported.

The Japanese Analogy as Semiosis in Diplomacy and Historiography

Teodoro Agoncillo, otherwise noted for the rigor of his groundbreaking research into the Philippine revolutionary papers, did not "document" his account of the diplomat's arrival scene with Felipe Agoncillo's letter.[11] Recently, Teodoro Agoncillo has been under sustained attack or subjected to withering critique for his interpretive contributions as a "nationalist" historian as well as for his scholarship. Among the Filipino scholars of his generation, Teodoro Agoncillo had offered the most closely researched "Filipino point of view" against the claims of US imperial intervention in the Filipino revolution against Spain. He discerned, and passionately argued for, anti-imperialist Filipino nationalism to be as much a phenomenon among the population-at-large as it was among the elite Filipino revolutionists. North American scholars had implied or explicitly claimed otherwise by active omission of Filipino agency or by echoing contemporary US imperialist pronouncements that limited the "insurrection" to certain sections of the Filipino elite or the "Tagalos." Polemical North American claims of Filipino incapacity for self-government and the necessity for US intervention had rested on this vision of the Filipino revolution as internally divided and "tribal," verging on anarchy and atrocious anti-colonial and punitive violence if unassisted by external police power.

Something of this interpretive contention drives the recent and highly-engaged critique of Teodoro Agoncillo's work. But in most particular instances, the question raised about his interpretive claims also concerns his competence as a scholar and his research practices. Frederick Hoyt, for example, shouldered what he calls "the onerous task of researching old [US] newspaper files for this period" after finding Teodoro Agoncillo's account of the above event "fascinating" but "undocumented."[12] After examining US newspaper coverage of Felipe Agoncillo's first diplomatic trip to the United States (from September 22 to October 8, 1898), Hoyt asserts that no "evidence" exists for the historian Agoncillo's contentions. On the contrary, for the event in question, Hoyt finds Felipe Agoncillo to have been accorded respectful reception, extensive coverage and detailed description, and "rather consistently discussed in flattering terms" by US periodicals ("AMA": 48). He then quotes various newspapers copiously to demonstrate how Felipe Agoncillo was not received with malevolence as he expected, but with benign tolerance.

Ample evidence from the extensive newspaper coverage that Hoyt patiently scoured through does seem to bear him out. Among the reportorial proofs he marshaled but to whose fascinating implications he seemed rather (and conspicuously) oblivious is what we have been calling here the Japanese Analogy. In specifying quite a few instances when the Filipino diplomats, throughout their first sojourn in the United States were likened by credulous American writers or reporters to the Japanese, Hoyt inadvertently and unwittingly called attention to two important aspects of our historiographic critique here. First, given that Agoncillo "quite naturally attracted" such widespread press and popular attention as he did, being "the first Filipino [continental Americans] had ever seen" at that important juncture of initial Filipino-American contacts, Hoyt observes in passing that this might have had something to do with the absence of an adequate language of (racialist or ethnological) representation through which Americans could report their new alien others to themselves. And second, the Japanese Analogy is here read by Hoyt to signify benign popular and journalistic American treatment of the first and apparitional Filipinos (although Agoncillo was accompanied by Sixto Lopez who acted as his secretary, and with Lopez's rudimentary knowledge of English, as his interpreter, Lopez merely functioned as the shadowy foil to Agoncillo's symbolic centrality) — the basis, therefore, for his claim of "the flattering terms" by which they were represented in US public culture during the period concerned. Hoyt writes: "Seeking to find a racial parallel with which Americans would be familiar, these accounts often compared Agoncillo to a Japanese. His manners and conduct were routinely praised as those of a civilized, polished, well-educated gentleman" ("AMA": 32, 35).

In short, the Japanese Analogy, as it seems to have worked, meant that the "Filipino" struck most American reporters and observers as almost like the "Japanese." The "Japanese," in this context, works less as a racial and racializing marker than as a sign for being "civilized, polished, well-educated" — very positive and flattering terms indeed. Strikingly, the very Japanese Analogy that American writers had applied to the "Filipino" — ill-equipped as they were (as Hoyt notes) to appreciate or understand the novel difference that Agoncillo represented to Americans at this radical juncture — also operates, by itself, in another way worth remarking. It also analogizes the Japanese in respect of a determinate set of characteristics presumably and preferably applicable only to American or Western equivalents (civilization, education, and the term which couches both: "polish"). The work of signification/representation that the "Japanese" here is made to bear as a term of positivity, both as *vehicle* in regard to the Filipino as *tenor*, and as simultaneously *tenorial* and *vehicular* in respect of the implicitly ultimate term "American/Westerner," is sociologically understandable.[13] The typical American diplomatic historian will tell us that after Japan's conquest of the Northern China territories in 1894, its own attendant colonization of Taiwan, and the emergence of a modern Japan from the Meiji Restoration, Japan and the Japanese finally earned the begrudging admiration and collegial embrace of the United States as a civilizationally kindred nation.

For the Filipino to be likened to the Japanese (and by unwanted implication, the fledgling republic that Agoncillo as "Filipino" represented, to the modern Japanese nation that the sign "Japanese" symbolized in the contemporary [and post-contemporary] period) is therefore nothing less than remarkable. It testifies, first of all, to the onset of a crisis in American representational authority (which was to become endemic and from which it was never to recover) in regard to Filipinos and the Philippine Revolution at this *critical* juncture of early encounters. This is a crisis-effect, in the form of the Japanese Analogy, which is instantiated by the problematic specter that Agoncillo as Filipino represented to his American observers: it gave "lie" to the early and denigrating American racializations of Filipinos and the Philippines as alien subjects, revolutionary antagonists, and territorial objects. The semiosic crisis can be seen in the symptomatic juxtapositions of racializing tropes with apparently positive ones in the newspaper coverage that Hoyt examined.

The *Oakland Enquirer*'s unequivocal assertion, right after the sighting of Agoncillo at the port of San Francisco, that Agoncillo could impress any American as "a distinguished native Philippine islander" was, in fact, rather rare ("AMA": 34). The *San Francisco Bulletin* on September 23 felt compelled to point out that "Agoncello [sp.] is a quick-witted dark-skinned man of rather small stature" and Lopez "is a sharp-looking half-caste"; to which a *San Francisco Call* reporter, confounded by a discovery of the latter as an unlikely English-speaking Filipino (surely a rarity), had to chime in, on that same day's issue, that Lopez's "command of English is that of a stuttering schoolboy with a year's experience in the vagaries of Anglo-Saxon grammar" ("AMA": 33–4).

Later elaborations came with more and more racializing specificity. Although the *Chicago Tribune* would early on tag Agoncillo as "a small brown man, with a Malay face and polite manners" (September 23), its correspondent who had opportunity for closer inspection by being on the same Overland Limited train that took Agoncillo and Lopez from San Francisco to Washington (with a stopover in Chicago), testified in a front-page story for September 26 that Agoncillo looked as "dark as the darkest American Indians," a telling phrase and another racial analogy echoed word for word by the *New York Sun*. The *Chicago Times-Herald* agreed the next day with a near satirical characterization of Agoncillo as "a swarthy diplomat." Newspaper reports and reporters throughout this time quite generally fixated on Agoncillo's diminutive size, a characteristic phenotypical criterion in American racialism. The *Chicago Evening Post* called Agoncillo "a swarthy little man" (September 26), with the *Chicago Journal* swearing that the "pleasant little man" stood "not more than 5 feet, 2 inches in height" in a story on the same day, and the *Chicago Inter-Ocean* fudging and demurring in its issue the next day (September 27) that this "little man" actually stood "not much over five feet." Apparently, a two-inch difference mattered much. In all, the *San Francisco Call* seems to have set the summarative terms for these *racializations*, with its observation that Agoncillo possessed "all the racial characteristics of the Malay product" and that Lopez, "His secretary is the typical Filipino" ("AMA": 33, 35–7).

The Japanese Analogy characterizations seemed to have been yoked to this emphasis on Agoncillo's "littleness" and in relation to rather odd analogues and qualifiers (at a loss for an adequate characterization, in face of Agoncillo's multiplicity as a "sign" and representational figure, one newspaper even compared him to a Frenchman). This is where the Japanese Analogy *as a liminal crisis-effect* — i.e., as both a shadowy juncture of crisis and as an actively induced effect — in the veridical uncertainties and claims of American representational authority/practices most conspicuously appears hydra-headed. Such US representations might be authoritative in their overtones but are already self-deconstructing in their telling lacunae and contradictions. It is not very difficult to imagine that this crisis-effect was directly engendered by Agoncillo's self-representations, as evidenced, for example, in the self-conflicted terms of the extended or simple similes that proliferated given the visage he offered to his American observers. Although the *Chicago Tribune* expressed confidence that Agoncillo "looked more like any Japanese than any other nationality with which Chicago is familiar" (September 27) or that, in the unhesitating words of the *Chicago Evening Post* report the day before, "His appearance has that of an educated and polished Japanese," an earlier *San Francisco Examiner* report on September 23 had maintained that "the dapper-looking little fellow" might seem "somewhat like a Japanese, but his features are of the Spanish cast." The *Washington Post*, five days later, would strongly disagree with this West Coast newspaper, while ratifying the *Midwestern Evening Post*'s claim of a Japanese analogy to paint Agoncillo, patently maintaining that he "[has] the appearance of a polished and well-educated Japanese rather than a Spaniard." Little wonder that the *San Francisco Chronicle* seemed to have anticipated the problem quite early by portraying the racially intractable Filipino in its front-page September 23 story as "a little young man of *Spanish-Japanese* appearance" (see also "AMA": 33–6; emphasis supplied).

Its reporters having personally tailed Agoncillo who had checked in with Lopez by early October at the Waldorf-Astoria hotel, preparatory to their trans-Atlantic voyage to Paris after the meeting with McKinley, New York papers *Herald* and *World* might have had the last word on the culturally (and a bit racially) contradictory quandary of whether, in fact, Agoncillo as Filipino was, by analogical reasoning, Japanese or Spanish (as incongruous in the ways cultural comparisons/differences could go). In the form of a qualifying refinement, the *Herald*'s characterization would strike a present-day reader as peerless, even if a tad too sophistical: "Although he [Agoncillo] speaks the language of Spain, he is of the Japanese type of appearance"; and as if to settle the matter once and for all, the newspaper published a large picture of Agoncillo, quite interestingly given a verbal supplement by Hoyt the historian as looking "alert, intelligent, well-groomed, and properly dressed" (see "AMA": 44). Nothing in this exuberant coverage, however, better summarizes *and* embodies the critical semiotic puzzle/ patchwork that Agoncillo represented to American readers than the *World* report (October 8):

> The revolutionary envoy is for all the world, except for his language, which is that of Spain, a typical Japanese ... He is small and slight, with little hands and feet and a tiny black moustache to match. His cheekbones are high, his hair is short, coarse, and jet black, and his complexion is that of any dozen Japanese one would meet … [He spoke] in low modulated tones ... [and he was] most courteous and considerate …

Recall that on the strength of a singular lapse of documentary procedure by Teodoro Agoncillo, Hoyt speculates about why a Filipino historian of his stature should make such a reading of one historical event (the San Francisco arrival of Felipe Agoncillo) and not provide the requisite "evidence." Unaware of Teodoro Agoncillo's use of Felipe Agoncillo's letter, Hoyt argues that the Filipino historian might have simply repeated a claim made by US historians and by Felipe Agoncillo himself (publicly, upon arrival) on the subject of "American ignorance." It should be clear from our discussion that the crisis-effect of the Japanese Analogy, fading away as quickly as it emerged (being specific only to the political effects of Felipe Agoncillo's semiosic and culturally productive diplomacy), does show up the matter of American "ignorance" in respect of its Filipino Other(s) in rather demotic ways. "American ignorance" is not only a Filipino revolutionary-diplomatic counter-claim in response to their prospective and actual neocolonizer's own insistent claims about Filipino incapacity for representative government, but as this conclusion hopes to demonstrate, is a politically charged and obsessively historiographic question.

As Hoyt himself recognizes, a "tenacious myth, created and nurtured by two generations of historians" posits that North Americans knew next to nothing about the Philippines before Admiral George Dewey's feat at Manila Bay on May 1, 1898.[14] On this view, Dewey's victory over the Spanish armada came as a "stunning surprise" to Americans that then, presumably, spurred their interest in the Philippines to grow in leaps and bounds. Hoyt critiques this proposition as he finds it rearticulated by the Filipinos, faulting historians like Samuel Flagg Bemis, Thomas Bailey, and John Hicks, for reverberating contemporary claims to this effect (by William McKinley and Theodore Roosevelt, for instance). For Hoyt, the "myth" of ignorance apparently held Teodoro Agoncillo in its thrall, who had "simply accepted [it] from his distinguished American colleagues." Just as North American historians were held captive by their privileged historical actors, so was the historian Agoncillo swayed by the myths affirmed by his professional betters in the United States. Hoyt then reproves Teodoro Agoncillo "for rather casually extending the period of American ignorance of all things Philippine from May 1, 1898, until Felipe Agoncillo's arrival in the United States on September 22, 1898" ("AMA": 48–9).

Hoyt quotes Felipe Agoncillo's press statement upon his subsequent arrival in Washington DC on September 28, 1898 as another possible source for the Filipino historian's claims:[15]

> I am afraid that many Americans have formed an erroneous idea of the Philippine Islands and their people[.] Prior to the outbreak of the Spanish-American War, the American people knew little or nothing of us or our islands[.] You were led to believe that we were a savage or a barbarous race, half civilized[.] You have heard little of us, and the American people know nothing of our struggles and trials which we have endured under the rule of Spain, and our many efforts, futile and unsuccessful, to throw off the galling yoke of that country, whose colonial government has been the worst, the most heartless, cruel, and unsympathetic of any in the history of the world.

After this reference to a public utterance by Felipe Agoncillo, however, Hoyt shifts the register of critique from the Filipino historian to the Filipino historical character himself. Like historian Stuart C. Miller, Hoyt "discovers" that the Filipino "insurrection" against Spain had indeed hogged part of the limelight of US public interest from the open Filipino rebellion of August 1896 to the Filipino standoff with Spanish forces in 1898 (see Miller 1982: 13, 279n1). Accordingly, he wagers that "[i]f Agoncillo had come to the United States two years earlier and had been able to read major American daily newspapers, he would never have made such statements." Hoyt finds Felipe Agoncillo's "ignorance" to be doubly unconscionable given what he sees as an exponential increase in US newspaper coverage of the Philippines after the day of Dewey's feat. Yet again, "if Agoncillo had picked up any of the four dailies published in San Francisco on the day of his arrival ... he would have discovered them filled with extensive news reports, feature stories, articles, letters, editorials, and illustrations related to the Philippines" ("AMA": 49). To be *imaged* as shorn of clothing thus becomes, by extension, to know little or nothing, to suffer an epistemological lack or nudity demanding some redress.

Even under better circumstances, knowledge of Felipe Agoncillo's report to General Aguinaldo would not clearly alter Hoyt's arguments, given the now-widened compass of his historiographic critique to embrace both diplomat and chronicler. In fact, in thrust and substance, Felipe Agoncillo's Washington arrival statement differs little from his post-departure report to Gen. Aguinaldo, supplying the very elaboration that Teodoro Agoncillo's paraphrase enables. What clearly emerges is Hoyt's presumption that both Agoncillos (Felipe and Teodoro) had not done their homework and both of whose authority, therefore, could only but invite the gentle disdain of the assiduous and obsessive researcher. Claiming to know "American ignorance" about Filipinos, they now stand revealed as guilty of the very crime they impute to the Other. If Teodoro Agoncillo had cited Felipe Agoncillo's letter, in Tagalog and with its immediate contexts, Hoyt (who knew no Tagalog) would still have recourse to Felipe Agoncillo's arrival statement in translated English. Paradoxically, being shunted from vernacular knowledge by the other historian's procedural lapse is the lack upon which Hoyt unwittingly predicates his will to positivist and empirical research.

The point would thus remain. It would not matter who between the Agoncillos (historian or historical character) could positively know the state of North American affairs and knowledge during the period with respect to Filipinos and their cultures. Seeking to represent the Other's representations of their people, they could only but, perforce, be subjected to the accustomed measures of veracity by the historian and found wanting. Both of their attempts to "read" the Other seemed, after all, to be more ambitious than the contemporary ambition of the Filipinos to practice the art of representative government. Filipinos would earn much animus in the United States for not realizing that "racial" fitness came hand in hand with such aspirations (and American "Filipinologists," from Dean Worcester in the days of empire to Glenn May and Brian Linn in the post-colonial epoch, would not lack in reminding us about the intimate link between one's *race* and one's capacity, either for representative government or historical narration/ research). But precisely after Felipe Agoncillo's departure for Europe from his "unsuccessful" US trip to represent Filipino desires for independence in the Spanish-American negotiations, their so-called racial incapacity for self-government became the object of spirited public debates in the United States, in which many writers and opinion leaders began to express lingering doubts about such pertinent racialist and political claims of US imperial ideologues.

Strikingly, Hoyt concentrates on and finds positive images of Filipinos during, and not before or after, Felipe Agoncillo's US sojourn(s). All he asserts in contrast to the kind of US knowledge questioned by the Filipinos for the pre-arrival phase is its positive bounty (which Felipe Agoncillo precisely critiques for its paradoxical poverty), and nothing about its particular forms. Hoyt does not tell us if Felipe Agoncillo and the people he represented (or of which he was the veritable portrait and proxy) were indeed imagined in the US as half-naked savages. He merely responds to one aspect of the latter's claim which has to do with the deficiency of such available information. He does not find what he is looking for (and what he finds gets generalized as counter-evidence) because he looks in the wrong place, the period during which precisely the sudden transformation reported by Felipe Agoncillo occurs. The diplomat is discussed "in flattering terms" (such as those of the Japanese Analogy) and in contradictory detail after his arrival, because the fiction of Filipino savagery could not be unproblematically sustained with the alternative self-portrait or opposite visage that he offered to American observers.

While able to dispute the claim of ignorance by a generalized notion of extant foreknowledge, Hoyt fails to synchronize it with the diplomat's chronological frame of transformative effects. Indeed, by finding a flattering picture of Filipinos upon and immediately after Felipe Agoncillo's arrival, Hoyt ratifies the sequence of transformation that the envoy sketches (*Noong ding arao na iyon ... itinalâ nila na ang ating Bayan ay di salvage at may katampatang civilizacion* [On that same day, the newspapers reported that we are not a savage people, and possess a civilization comparable to any other]). Felipe Agoncillo specifies the "ignorance" of North Americans as, in fact, a form of egregious foreknowledge that was not irredeemable ("I am afraid that the Americans have formed an erroneous idea of the Philippine Islands and their people ... You were led to believe that we were a savage and barbarous race, half civilized.") It is not the case that North Americans did not know or had no occasion to know about the Filipinos and their historical conditions as well as aspirations. Rather, what they knew, especially what the media of representation purveyed or charted (at least before and immediately after the shadowy Japanese Analogy), was deficient and in dire need of political and semiotic texture.

"You have heard little of us," Agoncillo says, and it is little to the extent that North Americans had not understood "our struggles and [the] trials which we have endured under Spain." In raising the specter of the other imperial Other (Spain) and the revolution against it for their intending liberators, Felipe Agoncilo begins to hint at the forms of knowledge and disputes that his mission would bring to the brink of precipitant anxiety and crisis. In this light, the ensuing disputes between Filipino nationalists and US imperialists over sovereignty after Spain's defeat begin to coincide with a more bracing dispute over knowledge or ignorance, and the authority for policing it. It is not so much the kinds of representations that arise (partial and racial, on the part of Americans; oppositional and polemical, on the part of Filipinos), as their effects. And these effects, including those of the politically significant Japanese Analogy, persist and spill over from a now remote historical moment in which they have remained sealed off, for the longest time, in the absence of the kind of semiotic readings and historiographic critique as we have here attempted.

Notes

1. Felipe Agoncillo, Paris, to Emilio Aguinaldo, October 22, 1898, Philippine Insurgent Records (PIR) 451.6, R.G. 94, US National Archives, Micrcopy 254, Reel 28.
2. We return to Teodoro Agoncillo's narrative interventions toward the latter part of the essay, in our critique of certain acts of history-writing as consequential *discursive* events in the historiography of United States imperialism.
3. For a well-documented and extremely compelling analysis of the considerable general impact of Philippine revolutionary propaganda/ foreign policy politics on the other triadic relationship of the Philippines, Japan, and China, see Rebecca Karl's *Staging the World*, especially the chapter on Comité member Mariano Ponce's activities in the East Asian region to which he was assigned, pp. 83–115.
4. Agoncillo first chaired the Filipino Revolutionary Committee that was established in the British Colony in December 1896 to support the revolution against Spain after it broke out in August that year. This loose organ became the Hong Kong Junta upon the voluntary exile to Hong Kong of Aguinaldo and some of his advisers and line generals in December 1897, as a consequence of a conditional truce with the Spanish colonial regime (Pact of Biak-na-Bato).

When Aguinaldo returned to the Philippines to reorganize the revolutionary forces in May 1898 and after Agoncillo headed for the West for his diplomatic missions, the Junta was recast as the Comité Central Filipino, with broadened powers to coordinate "insurgent" foreign policy and propaganda campaigns. In sum, Agoncillo dispensed influential advice and legal expertise for Gen. Aguinaldo as a member of the Filipino government-in-exile and its various antecedent organs (through April 1898), and as its effective coordinator from May to August 1898; as the emissary sent to the United States and abroad to consolidate international support networks and to argue for the Filipino cause (September 1898–July 1903); and as the moderating presence in various revolutionary committees that considered the policy, publicity, documentary, and logistical needs of the fledgling government.

5. On semiosis or sign-production, see Pierce (1931), Eco (1979), and Kristeva (1989).
6. See Respe (Agoncillo) to Mr. Rost (Aguinaldo), August 1, 1898; Agoncillo to Mabini, August 2, 1898; Respe to Mr. Rost, August 15, 1898, all in Taylor, *The Philippine Insurrection against the United States*, vol. 3 (1971 [1901–1905]), hereafter cited in the text by volume number.
7. *Memorial* was republished by the Anti-Imperialist League in a slightly different version in 1899 and Agoncillo privately printed *To The American People* in Paris in 1900.
8. The Washington *Evening Star* identified them as "Dr. Jose Lozada, Sr. Juan Luna and Capt. Marti Burgos" (January 23, 1899, p. 1).
9. *Memorials from Senor Felipe Agoncillo and Constitution of the Provisional Philippine Government* (Boston: Anti-Imperialist League, 1899), n.p.; Agoncillo to Aguinaldo, April 6, 1899, John R. Thomas Jr. Papers, Library of Congress, Manuscript Division.
10. Sixto Lopez (Secretary to Agoncillo) to John Hay (US Secretary of State), January 5, 1899; Memorandum, Lopez to Hay, January 5, 1899; Lopez to Hay, January 7, 1899; Agoncillo to Hay, January 11, 1899; Agoncillo to Hay, January 24, 1899, all in Taylor, vol. 5.
11. Shortly in the chapter in which such an account occurs of Felipe's arrival scene, Teodoro Agoncillo cites the same letter/report by Felipe Agoncillo to Gen. Aguinaldo but as a source for his own recounting of Felipe Agoncillo's subsequent conference with President William McKinley at the White House on October 1, 1898, on which the letter dwelt at length (ibid.: 323, 707n28).
12. Hoyt, "Agoncillo's Mission to America: Reality Confronts Mythology," (1979), pp. 32, 49; hereafter cited in the text as "AMA.".
13. Analogy, in literary study, is not only a distinct form of establishing resemblance(s) between two ideas, things, or actions, but as with

its kindred figure of metaphor, involves the elucidation of the one term (called "tenor" in metaphor, that which is being talked about) by means of the other (called "vehicle" in metaphor, the way it is being talked about, that which carries the charge of comparison). But unlike metaphor, which might allow for the yoking together of terms that are either verisimilar or otherwise differential in the qualities they possess (provided in either case that there exists some conceptual/linguistic basis for comparability) and which requires a kind of interpenetration or transference of qualities between such verisimilar or differential terms (the Latin root word *metaphora* derives from the Greek *metapherein*, "to transfer" or "carry across"), analogy is predicated upon the separability of the terms under comparison; and involves, in short, the construction between these terms of an imaginary identity that is otherwise countervailed by their constitutive difference. Analogy shares with simile this kind of predication which the *literal* and metamorphic comparison of metaphor (given its repression of simile's explicit conjunctions of "like" or "as") naturally disallows. Not surprisingly, therefore, analogies tend to express themselves in the form of simple or extended similes rather than in metaphorical accents.

14. For a historiographic critique of this notion of American ignorance, see Miller (1982) p. 13.
15. Published in *Boston Evening Transcript*, *New York Sun*, *Washington Evening Star*, *Washington Post*, September 28, 1898 ("AMA," p. 49).

chapter 5

Japan and America in the Filipino Nationalist Imagination: From Rizal to Ricarte

Floro C. Quibuyen

Imagining the Nation: The Colonial Self and the Imperial Other

A productive way to explore how we Filipinos have imagined ourselves as a nation is by exploring how we have imagined the two countries that have, for better or for worse, intervened in our modern history — Japan and America. National consciousness is not simply a matter of imagining oneself, but of imagining oneself in relation to others. This may be a truism. But in a colonial or neo-colonial context, the imperial Other is primary and the colonial self is derivative. Indeed, Filipinos can learn more about themselves by studying how Japan and America have figured in their colonial imagination — before, during, and after the Second World War.

The national consciousness that emerges out of the colonial experience is constituted not only by what the colonized remember, but also, and perhaps more importantly, by what they have forgotten. As one character in Milan Kundera's

(1983: 5) novel laments: "The struggle of people against power is the struggle of memory against forgetting."

My task in this paper is to trace the development of the Filipino national consciousness — the genealogy of our imagined affinity with the United States, and at least before the Second World War, with Japan. This earlier affinity with Japan is important as it has been overlooked by historians trying to understand the Filipinos' so-called "bi-nationalism" or "binational and bicultural bonding" with the United States. In his recent attempt to understand Philippine nationalism, the pre-eminent Southeast Asianist Benedict Anderson seems to have overlooked the place of Japan in the Filipino national consciousness, as if the only relevant external factor was American imperialism (Anderson 1994).[1] Among Philippine Studies scholars, Theodore Friend comes closest to addressing the issue of Japan's place in the Filipino psyche. In his interesting work, *The Blue-Eyed Enemy: Japan Against the West In Java and Luzon, 1942–1945* (1988), Friend discusses the contrasting responses of, on the one hand, the Indonesians to the Dutch and the Filipinos to the Americans, and on the other, the Filipinos' hatred of the Japanese and their love for the Americans. "Whereas the Malagasies and the Indonesians accepted and then revolted against a 'blue-eyed stranger' and the Japanese fought a 'blue-eyed enemy,'" notes Friend, "the Filipinos in some manner adopted a 'blue-eyed friend'" (Friend 1988: 280). Then Friend (285) asks, "How to explain the contrasting behavior of the Filipinos vis-a-vis Americans?" This is the fundamental question that Friend asks repeatedly (at least three times) in his concluding chapter. The exceptional loyalty of the Filipinos to America during the three and a half years of the Japanese Occupation, notes Friend (285), cannot be simply explained in terms of political factors, such as the overwhelming presence of American forces in the Philippines or the imminent realization of American promises of Philippine independence. Culling from received wisdom, Friend (280) offers his thesis:

> The causes of binational and bicultural bonding reached deep into Philippine history. They include the lack of a native god-king, the Western bias of Catholicism, the concord of priests and principales, the normality and even prominence of mestizo ethnicity, and the size and power of the United States, not to mention the unconscious, sloppy, acceptable prevalence of American cultural influence. The result was that long after sovereignty, Filipinos continued, on balance, to appear to prefer the constraining security of psychological dependence to the creative insecurity of psychic and cultural independence.

But Friend's account begs the question of why Filipinos prefer "psychological dependence" to "psychic and cultural independence." Friend's attempt to frame the Philippine experience in terms of his conservative reading of Hegel (i.e., Friend's borrowing of Hegel's concept of "lordship" and "bondage") leads him ultimately to fall back on the pop psychology of his two favorite Filipino commentators, whose one-liners he loves to quote.[2] "We fell in love with your culture," says the journalist Carmen Guerrero-Nakpil; the Filipinos were "colonized with love" by the Americans, declares historian Alfonso Felix (Friend 1988: 275, 285). Of particular import to Friend are these words of Nakpil: "Those who survived Japanese hate did not survive American love. Both were equally deadly; the latter more so because sought and longed for." "The sting and meaning of that remark," Friend (1988: 286) enthuses, "would require another book to analyze."

There is one fundamental flaw in Friend's otherwise impressive 287-page comparative study: he glosses over the fact that prior to the Second World War, the Filipinos looked up to Japan as an ally, if not as a source of inspiration. Indeed, Nakpil's love hypothesis loses its sting once we take into consideration the Filipinos' earlier bonding with Japan. Our understanding of Filipino national consciousness will remain hazy if we fail to explore this crucial fact. To fully explore the genealogy of our national consciousness, we need to depart from the historiographic practice, exemplified by Theodore Friend's work, of focusing on the Second World War as the only significant moment in the Filipinos' imagining of Japan.

First of all, we need to rethink the prevalent assumptions. It is now taken for granted that the arrival of the Japanese armed forces in the Philippines in 1941 polarized the Filipinos: "roughly speaking it was the elite who collaborated and the peasantry who resisted" (Preston 1987: 200). This has been construed by American scholars and Filipino nationalist historians, from Alfred McCoy to Renato Constantino, as a manifestation of the "true nationalism" of the masses and the calculating and self-serving "collaborationist mentality" of the bourgeoisie. McCoy (1981: 55–6) explains it as a unique combination of the "rational calculation and bi-national patriotism" typical of the elite. Implied here is the proposition that collaboration with the Japanese was antithetical to a genuinely nationalist stance. Thus, the elite, motivated primarily by calculations of what they could gain, collaborated; whereas the masses, driven by a primordial desire for independence, resisted.

This orthodoxy in Philippine history becomes problematic when viewed in the context of what happened during the Second World War in the rest of Southeast Asia, where locals collaborated with the Japanese in pursuit of nationalist goals. As Anthony Reid (1981: 134) observes, "alienation from the colonial regime (the Dutch and the British) was universal by 1942, and the Japanese were welcomed as liberators." The Indonesian nationalists collaborated with the Japanese to drive away the Dutch, the Malays and the Indians in Malaya (now Malaysia) — except the Malayan Chinese who hated the Japanese because of the latter's military atrocities in China[3] — and the Burmese nationalists did the same to drive away the British. And they succeeded without compromising their nationalism. When the Japanese were defeated in the war, the Indonesian and Burmese nationalist movements were already well-organized, with a strong mass base and a solid army — thanks to Japanese sponsorship — to resist and drive away their former colonial masters. Thus, in regard to the rest of Southeast Asia, it was the experience of the Japanese

Occupation that "both destroyed the old order and fostered the new": it destroyed for good the European colonial empires and fostered the independent nation-states (Preston 1987: 202–6).

Historians like Theodore Friend are of course well aware that the exact opposite happened in the Philippines, where the experience of the Japanese Occupation in fact reinforced existing ties with the American colonial masters. By 1941, the attachment to the US was so strong that the resistance to the Japanese was motivated not only by a racist hostility to the Japanese, but also by an abiding devotion to the Americans. However, students of Philippine history have failed to address a crucial double puzzle. First, how did this devotion to the Americans come about when not that long ago, the Filipinos fought them to the bitter end and continued resisting them for some more years after their military debacle? Second, how could the Filipinos develop such a racial hatred for the Japanese when, after the failure of the so-called Propaganda Movement and during the revolutionary period, and some years after that, the Filipinos believed that their redemption laid on the Japanese?

The conventional wisdom after the war, inscribed in textbooks and the popular media, explains this antipathy in terms of the unusual brutality of the Japanese. To this day, whenever the opportunity arises, Japanese war crimes are invoked — from the infamous April 1942 Death March to the February 1945 "sack of Manila," which has been described as "The Most Vicious Crime in Philippine History." In a paper read at the Oral History Conference marking the 60th anniversary of the Battle of Manila (February 4–5, 2005), Benito Legarda Jr. asserts, "No other single event in our history even remotely approximates it in the extent of the material destruction, the number of casualties, the manner of dealing with death, and the loss of cultural heritage" (2007: 11). Legarda estimates that 100,000 civilians died. However, he obscures the fact that the material destruction, in particular, the virtual obliteration of Intramuros — which must have significantly added to the number of civilian casualties — was caused by massive bombing and artillery fire from American forces. Admittedly, the infamous Bataan Death March in April 1942 led to the death of 17,200 prisoners-of-war (Prichard and Zaide 1981, cited in Rummel 1997), but the total number of Filipinos who died as a result of the Philippine-American War at the turn of the century, when measured proportionate to the population, far exceeds the total casualty of Filipinos in the Second World War.[4] Indeed, the record of American atrocities in the earlier war matches, if not exceeds, that of the Japanese in the second war.

In the early stage of the Japanese Occupation, the Japanese tried hard to win the Filipinos to their side, as they had done in Indonesia, Burma and Malaya.[5] A year after their conquest of the American forces in the Philippines, the Japanese "granted" the independence of the Philippines and sponsored an independent Philippine Republic, which was inaugurated on October 14, 1943. The ceremony, witnessed by half a million Filipinos, took place before the Legislative Building in Manila, where the revolutionary national anthem was played and the national flag was hoisted by none other than the aging General Emilio Aguinaldo, once President of the First Philippine Republic, and his former comrade-in-arms, General Artemio Ricarte, who to his dying day, never recognized the sovereignty of the United States over the Philippines. But the Japanese, finding their gesture of friendship rebuffed, and realizing that they could not win the loyalty of most Filipinos, let alone wean them from their attachment to the Americans, launched a series of bloody "punitive expeditions" which led to countless atrocities and the massacre of thousands of civilians across the archipelago (McCoy 1981: 56).

For their part, Aguinaldo and Ricarte could do nothing to rally the Filipinos to the old nationalist tune. But then, the two aging *veteranos* were already in their late 70s, and the young Filipinos who were fighting the Japanese had not been born during the two revolutionaries' heyday. The real significance of that event may have dawned on these two pathetic veterans at the twilight of their once glorious lives. Their hoisting of the national flag may have signaled the end of the nationalist era that they, together with Jose Rizal and Andres Bonifacio, represented. That ritualistic act of collaboration in fact totally discredited Aguinaldo and Ricarte in the eyes of the new generation of Japanese-hating and American-adulating Filipinos.

The tragedy of Aguinaldo and Ricarte lies in the fact that they had survived the revolution and lived long enough to witness the passing away of their own era and the coming of the "immense subterranean shift," to borrow Benedict Anderson's (1994) phrase, in Filipino consciousness. If the two former *Katipuneros* recalled their youth in the 1890s and at the turn of the century, a different scenario must have flickered in their minds. During their time, the Filipinos did not hate the Japanese; in fact, they sought the aid of the Japanese in their life-and-death struggle against the Spaniards, and subsequently, the Americans.[6] To explore this intriguing story, we need to excavate forgotten memories and sift their significance, placing them alongside remembered ones.

Romancing Japan: Jose Rizal

A definitive study of the place of Japan in the nationalist imagination prior to the Second World War has yet to be written.[7] While we await such a study, we shall begin by highlighting some instances of how Japan figured in the life and times of Filipino nationalists from Jose Rizal, the moral and intellectual leader of the nationalist struggle against Spain, to the revolutionary leadership in the *Katipunan* and the revolutionary government of Aguinaldo. Indeed, given the high regard that Filipinos had for Japan in the late 19th century, the fact that Japan was viewed with fear and trepidation at the outbreak of the Second World War tells a lot about how profoundly Filipinos have changed since the American conquest.

Rizal might have set a trend among his countrymen when he visited Japan in 1888, on his way to America, after his first return to the Philippines in 1887. From his diary, we know that he stayed in Japan for about one and a half months (February 28 to April 15), during which he visited several places, notably Yokahama (where many Japanese spoke English, he wrote Blumentritt) and Tokyo (it is bigger than Paris with a million inhabitants, an imposing city with its somber edifices, wide streets, Cyclopean walls, he wrote his parents), met a Filipino fugitive from Pangasinan, Feliciano Espino (Japan was then a haven for Filipino patriots escaping the wrath of the authorities in the Philippines), learned enough Japanese to get by, and had a fleeting love affair with a Japanese beauty by the name of O-Sei-San.

On 13 April 1888, shortly before his departure for America, Rizal (*Reminiscences*: 145) wrote of his feelings for Japan, and the woman he had loved, in his diary:

> I like Japan. Most beautiful scenery, the flowers, the trees, the peaceful inhabitants, so courteous, so willing to please. O.S.S. [O-Sei-San]. *Sayonara, sayonara*! I spent a golden month. I don't know if I shall have another one like it in my life. Love, money, friendship, esteem, distinctions, I did not lack.[8] ... I am going to dedicate to you the last chapter of these reminiscences of my early youth. No woman better than you has loved me, no woman like you has sacrificed herself. As the flower of the *chodji* falls from the stem fresh and perfect without either being stripped of its petals or withered, tender and poetic even after its fall, thus you fell. Neither did you lose your purity nor did the delicate petals of your innocence wither — *Sayonara, sayonara*!

What is remarkable about this diary entry, which was after all confidential, is that at that time, Rizal was already engaged to his childhood sweetheart, Leonor Rivera. Perhaps his love affair with O-Sei-San is the poetic epitome of his falling in love with Japan, its culture and people whose courtesy and quiet ways, and honesty, cleanliness and industry impressed him deeply. "They make no noise; loud voices are not heard; they sit quietly in their stores," Rizal relates to his parents in his March 1, 1888 letter from Tokyo. In his March 4, 1888 letter to his Austrian confidant and mentor, Professor Ferdinand Blumentritt, he observes,

> The Japanese are considered a people without God. I don't know if this is justified. It would be interesting to study this point. There are very few thieves among the Japanese. It is said that houses are left open; their walls are made of paper, and in the hotels one can leave money on the table without fear of losing it. The Japanese are very merry and they are courteous; in the streets fighting is not seen. Their houses are clean. Rarely are beggars seen. They are very industrious. What a difference there is between them and the religious and superstitious Chinese! If I could stay here a couple of years, I would study this and I could do it with greater ease than a European, because I have the look of a Japanese, and here, *like in the Philippines, the European is not much trusted* (*Rizal-Blumentritt:* 163–4; italics mine).

On his last week in Tokyo, he writes his parents (April 7, 1888):

> I have stayed here longer than I intended, for the country seems to me very interesting and because *in the future we shall have much to do and to deal with Japan* (*Reminiscences*: 291; italics mine).

The contrast in Rizal's impressions between Japan and the United States is quite telling. From Japan, Rizal proceeded to the United States where he stayed for nearly three weeks, from April 28 to May 16, traveling by train across the country from San Francisco to New York, his point of departure for London (where he would work on his project of reconstructing Philippine history).

Rizal's first experience of America was a bad one — a six-day quarantine upon the ship's arrival in San Francisco. Being a medical doctor, it was obvious to Rizal that something anomalous was going on. As he related in his July 27, 1888 letter to Mariano Ponce, they were quarantined despite having met the following requirements: the American consul had given the clearance, they had been at sea for about one month with no single case of illness aboard, the governor of Hong Kong had sent a telegram certifying that the port of Hong Kong was free from epidemic; but what gave the whole thing away was that, on the very day of the ship's arrival, 700 bales of silk were unloaded without being fumigated, the ship's doctor was allowed to go ashore, many customs inspectors had lunch onboard, including an American doctor from the hospital for cholera victims. The real reason for the quarantine was quite jarring for Rizal (*Rizal-Fellow Reformists*: 186):

> We were quarantined because there were on board 800 Chinese and, as the elections in San Francisco were approaching, the government wanted to boast that it was taking strict measures against the Chinese to win votes and the people's sympathy[9] … Afterwards only the passengers of the first class were allowed to land; those of the 2nd and 3rd classes — Japanese and Chinese — remained for an indefinite period. It is said that in that way they got rid of 300 Chinese, letting them gradually die on board. I don't know if it's true.[10]

Except for a passing comment in his letter about Washington as "the great man whom I believe has no second in this century," and some jottings in his diary, written while onboard the train, on the beauty or the vastness of the American landscape, Rizal's impression of America was not exactly favorable, largely on account of the racism that he saw. But he did not seem curious about the plight of the native Indians; at this time, Rizal, it seems, had not yet read Bartolome de las Casas, the Spanish friar who launched a campaign for justice and human rights for the indigenous peoples of the Americas in the 16th century.[11] To his compatriot Mariano Ponce, Rizal (*Rizal-Fellow Reformists*: 186) writes:

> I visited the largest cities of America with their big buildings, electric lights, and magnificent conceptions. Undoubtedly America is a great country, but it still has many defects. There is no real civil liberty. In some states the negro cannot marry a white woman, nor a negress a white man. Because of the hatred of the Chinese, other Asiatics, like the Japanese, being confused with them, are likewise disliked by the ignorant Americans … However, as they say rightly, America offers a home to the poor who like to work.

Strangely, Rizal never wrote a more serious study of America and Japan, the rising empires whose destinies would eventually clash in the Pacific region and would exert, as Rizal had foreseen in his *Filipinas dentro de cien años* (1890) (Rizal 1961d), a far-reaching impact on the destiny of the Philippines.

Be that as it may, Japan again would intrude on Rizal's life during his political hibernation in Dapitan. In June 1896, Dr. Pio Valenzuela, on instructions from the revolutionary party *Katipunan*, surreptitiously visited Rizal on a twofold mission: 1) to seek his advice on the question of starting an uprising; and 2) to get his approval for a *Katipunan* scheme to whisk him off Dapitan and take him to Japan, where he could presumably plan for and direct the revolution. Rizal's receptive response regarding the Japan scheme is recorded in Valenzuela's 1914 memoir:

> Rizal: Tell our countrymen that, at the same time that we are preparing for a war against Spain, I desire to see a college established in Japan which will be converted later into a university for Filipino youths. I shall be greatly pleased to be the director of said college.
>
> Valenzuela: I shall bear in mind all what you say and counsel, but I believe you would rather direct the revolution than manage a college.
>
> Rizal: I am ready for both.

In the *Katipunan*'s eyes, Japan appeared brightly as the likely champion of Asian liberation from European oppression. And so, a month before Valenzuela's conference with Rizal, a *Katipunan* delegation, led by Andres Bonifacio and Emilio Jacinto, met with the Japanese consul and a visiting Japanese naval officer at a Japanese bazaar in Manila to establish an alliance with Japan against Spain. The Japanese agreed to sell arms to the *Katipunan*, but the deal did not push through due to a lack of funds (Valenzuela 1978a: 102–3).

To Filipinos reared under American tutelage, this penchant for soliciting Japan's aid, which continued under Aguinaldo's revolutionary government and up to the early years of American colonial rule, may seem strange. But as the case of Feliciano Espino attests (13 April 1888, Friday, 11:15am, as noted in Rizal's *Reminiscences*), and as Rizal's own experience exemplifies, Japan had been a congenial place and had even served as sanctuary to Filipino fugitives. "Many Filipinos who had fled from Spanish persecution had been welcomed there and given the full protection of the law" (Zaide 1957: 159).

The Revolutionary government of Aguinaldo sent Mariano Ponce, Rizal's collaborator in the *Solidaridad*, to solicit Japan's aid as the Philippine-American War loomed menacingly in the horizon. Upon his arrival in Tokyo in June 29, 1898, Ponce was welcomed by Japan's Premier and concurrently Minister of Foreign Affairs, Shigenobu Okuma (diplomatic representations by the revolutionary government never reached this level in the United States).[12] We now know that although Japan wished to extend her influence on the Philippines, she was careful not to get embroiled in a deadly conflict with the United States, especially because she did not want any power to interfere with her ambitions over Korea, as Rizal had already inferred in *Filipinas dentro de cien años* (1890). Nevertheless, it appears that Ponce's diplomatic mission bore some fruit, although short of securing a formal alliance with Japan.

With the cooperation of prominent Japanese and the tacit approval of the Japanese government, Ponce was able to purchase arms and ammunitions (10,000 Murata rifles, six million rounds of ammunitions, and other war supplies) and charter a Japanese vessel (the *Nonubuki Maru*) under the command of Captain Nagano. Unfortunately, the whole thing went kaput when the ship sank on its way to the Philippines. A second attempt was made by the persistent Ponce and this time with the help of his friend Dr. Sun Yat Sen, then a Chinese exile in Yokohama, to bring desperately needed arms and ammunitions to the Philippines. The arms deal was closed but again, as fate would have it, the military cargo did not reach its intended destination (due to the American blockade) and ended up, in January 1900, in Taiwan, where it was picked up by Sun Yat Sen's revolutionary forces and used in the struggle against the Manchu dynasty in China. After this failed second attempt, the project of getting arms from Japan was given up (Zaide 1957: 210–1).

Nonetheless, unofficial Japanese support continued: newspapers in Japan openly called for the recognition of Philippine independence, and in fact, many Japanese officers (most of whom were veterans in the 1894–1895 Sino-Japanese War) served as military advisers in the General Staff of Aguinaldo's government, an arrangement made possible by Ponce.

Mariano Ponce stayed long enough in Japan to fall in love with a Japanese woman, but unlike the restless Rizal who slipped away after a momentary affair (only to lament it later in his diary), Mariano Ponce married his Japanese girlfriend, whom he brought back to the Philippines to settle down with in his hometown in Bulacan during the American regime. As time went on, however, Mariano Ponce and his Japanese adventure would be forgotten by the Filipinos.

Romancing Japan: Artemio Ricarte

But the most poignant case in this romance with Japan is the story of the one revolutionary general who probably deserves to be the most remembered and honored by the present generation of Filipinos, the never-say-die General Artemio Ricarte. Together with Ponce, Ricarte has faded away in the nation's collective memory. Instead of extolling his revolutionary efforts against American imperialism, today's historians deride him for being a "dissembler" and a *balimbing*, akin to a *trapo* (traditional politician) (May 1996),[13] a "collaborator" and "a scheming opportunist" (De Viana 2003).[14]

Ricarte's life story summarizes the rise and fall of the radical nationalist tradition of the late 19th century. As David Sturtevant (1976: 196) puts it:

> Ricarte remained loyal to the 'spirit of '96.' Rather than compromise his principles, he endured exile, solitary confinement, and expatriation. Predictably, he became a symbol of selfless patriotism to chauvinistic islanders of the post revolutionary generation.

A nationalist and a Rizalist to the core, Ricarte drafted, during his exile, a Constitution for an independent Philippine Republic which he hoped would be established once the Americans had been driven away. The most interesting feature of his proposed constitution, which did not depart substantially from the 1899 Constitution of the first Philippine Republic, was the provision to change the country's name from the "Philippines" to "Rizaline Islands," and the "Filipinos" to "Rizalinos" (Ricarte 1963: 139–41). Ricarte also advocated patriotic names for children. For example, he had his grandson christened *Bislumino* — *Bis* for Bisayas, *lu* for Luzon, and *mino* for Mindanao — the three major islands of the Philippines (Sturtevant 1976: 196n2).

Ricarte's relentless agitation not only for complete and immediate independence, but also for the equalization of wealth, made him anathema to both the Americans and Filipino elite. But his message appealed to the masses, especially those whose lot did not change, or even got worse, under the new order. And the fact that the Americans could not apprehend him caused them considerable embarrassment and frustration, even if they knew that he did not, nor could ever pose a real threat to American rule. For here was one nationalist they were not able to tame, a recalcitrant revolutionary who could neither be frightened nor bought off into acquiescence. Indeed, Ricarte's uncompromising nationalist stance is, as Ileto (1984: 104) puts it, second only to martyrdom.

Ricarte was perhaps the first and only general to plan for an immediate assault on the American troops in Manila as soon as he suspected that, as early as in December 1898, the Americans would not willingly withdraw from the Philippines (Goodman 1966: 48).[15] Nothing apparently came out of this plan for it was the Americans who started attacking the Filipino forces. Not long after, Aguinaldo's Malolos headquarters was overtaken by the Americans, thus forcing Aguinaldo to run away and his field generals to resort to guerrilla warfare. General Ricarte formed his own guerrilla unit called the "Vipers" (from his mother's family name Vibora). But Ricarte soon fell to the Americans in 1900 and was promptly sent to Guam for a three-year exile by then Military Governor Arthur MacArthur (General Douglas MacArthur's father) when he, together with other political prisoners like Apolinario Mabini and Fr. Gregorio Aglipay, refused to take the oath of allegiance to the United States. The last of the exiles to be brought back in 1903 were the intransigent duo, Ricarte and Mabini. Because of his failing health and wish to die in his native land, Mabini relented and took the oath. He died within the year, at the age of 39. The healthier 34-year-old Ricarte remained adamant, despite MacArthur's threat to extend his exile. And so, Ricarte was not allowed to disembark and was shipped to Hong Kong straightaway for an indefinite exile. He was told that until he swore allegiance, he could not come home again. Undaunted, Ricarte slipped through the American cordon the following year to organize an uprising in his native province of Ilocos. He was relentless in "attacking almost every one of his former co-revolutionaries as having sold out to the Americans and giving a low estimate of the value of their political parties" (Salamanca 1968: 181). By then, however, the Americans were already well entrenched and police security was well in place, so that his uprising was subdued before it could do any damage. Thus, in 1904, Ricarte was once again captured. This time, he was put behind bars and subjected to a punishment that could have broken any man: a six-year solitary confinement in Bilibid prison. However, Ricarte's request for pen and paper was granted, which enabled him to keep his sanity by writing his memoir on the Philippine Revolution (published as *Memoirs of General Artemio Ricarte*). At the end of his jail term, his oath of allegiance was again demanded. Again Ricarte refused; consequently, he was again exiled to Hong Kong, where he stayed from 1910–1915.

But being exiled for the third time after a harrowing six-year solitary confinement did not deter Ricarte from agitating for independence and engaging in conspiratorial acts aimed at subverting the American regime. In Hong Kong, Ricarte gathered around him fellow Filipino exiles and formed the *Consejo Revolucionario de Filipinas* (Revolutionary Government of the Philippines). He also published revolutionary propaganda which was distributed in the Philippines. A year after his arrival in Hong Kong, on 11 February 1911, Ricarte wrote a letter to the Secretary of the Japanese Ministry of Foreign Affairs in Tokyo, Count Komura, announcing the formation of the "Revolutionary Government of the Philippine Islands and the coming revolution, which," declared Ricarte, "I am planning in order to overthrow the sovereignty of the United States of America in my country and to restore the Philippine Republic under the old Political Constitution of Malolos" (cited in Goodman 1966: 49). The letter of course surprised the Japanese government, which forthwith requested a complete report from the Japanese consulate in Hong Kong about Ricarte and his Hong Kong organization, as well as his Japanese connections. After a month of surveillance and investigation by Japanese agents, Acting Consul General Funazu forwarded, on March 14, 1911, his report to Tokyo, detailing Ricarte's activities and sources of funding.

Most interestingly, the report revealed that on several occasions, the Americans attempted to buy off Ricarte through former Filipino revolutionary leaders who had joined the American regime with "several tens of thousands" of dollars to entice him to cooperate with the United States, or to at least stop his subversive political activities. The report added that Ricarte had refused all offers and continued his agitation in Hong Kong. "I would [rather] die poor, a martyr to the Filipino cause, than to abandon my convictions," Ricarte said.[16]

The last straw for the American regime was the abortive Christmas Eve Rebellion on December 24, 1914, an urban uprising in Manila, planned by Ricarte in Hong Kong. Ricarte had hoped that such an uprising would trigger a chain reaction throughout the archipelago, but the regime, which knew of the plot from the very beginning, was able to round up the would-be rebels before they could even get started. After this, the regime decided that it had had enough of Ricarte's conspiracies and demanded the extradition of Ricarte from Hong Kong to the Philippines. A combined team of the Philippine Constabulary and the Manila police, headed by Detective Lieutenant Edwin

C. Bopp, arrived in Hong Kong to arrest Ricarte. This triggered a chase up the China coast worthy of a James Bond thriller. Ricarte evaded his hunters up to Shanghai, where he boarded, amidst the cheers of delighted Filipino journalists (so the report goes), a Japanese freighter, the *Kasuga Maru*, which took him safely to Yokohama, where he was warmly welcomed by his Japanese admirers. This incident created a sensation in Manila, and according to David Sturtevant (1976: 202), should have been a fitting conclusion to Ricarte's colorful career as a revolutionary.

From 1915 to 1941, Ricarte settled down to the life of a retired revolutionary in Yokohama, where he raised a family (with his Filipina wife from Cavite) and supported them by teaching Spanish in a mission school in Tokyo and running a small restaurant in Yokohama with his wife called *Cafe Karihan*. It became a Mecca for travelling Filipinos, students, tourists, and politicians who paid courtesy calls to the retired rebel. During this period, Ricarte mellowed and gave up his advocacy of violence. He began to counsel moderation and welcome the use of legal methods in the fight for independence. His anti-imperialist and nationalist perspective however remained intact, and he began calling for a pan-Asian solidarity. He said, "In order to protect our motherland and to make firm its foundation and in order to counteract the predatory whites, we must joyfully participate in the formation of an Oriental Union so as to secure our mutual defense and to guarantee peace and security."[17]

Through Ricarte's initiative, Rizal Day was always celebrated by the Filipinos and their sympathizers in Japan.[18] For example, a Japanese police report tells of a December 30, 1924 commemoration held in Yokohama Public Hall to honor Filipino revolutionary leaders. About 50 people attended, which aside from the Filipinos, included Japanese, Spanish and American sympathizers and their families. The confidential report noted that Ricarte delivered a speech eulogizing Rizal and urging the Filipino expatriates in Japan to take the lead in creating a "Philippines for Filipinos" (Goodman 1966: 56).

There are two conflicting views regarding Ricarte's influence on Filipinos during this period. Goodman (1966: 53) thinks that even as early as 1914, Ricarte was already "becoming a somewhat remote figure already relegated to the historical past." This view is disputed by Ileto (1984) and Sturtevant (1976), who observe that, if anything, time and distance added imposing new dimensions to Ricarte's image. "During the 1920's and early 1930's," observes Sturtevant (1976: 203–4), "legends concerning Ricarte's feats accorded him all the attributes of a popular champion." Ileto (1984: 101–5), following Brian Fegan's (1979) unpublished research on the radical tradition in the Tagalog province of Nueva Ecija, notes that Ricarte's exile in Japan, in fact, enhanced his image among the folk: for one thing, his actions embodied the myth of the returning hero. More importantly, Japan at that time was looked up to by both the nationalist *ilustrados* and the masses as the Asian power that could challenge the United States, as well as a potential redeemer for the colonized peoples of Asia.

In the popular imagination, Fegan points out, the Japanese emblem of the rising sun eventually got linked to notions derived from the Easter vigil of the Holy Week — the "light in the east," the source of light (*liwanag*) and the coming of a redeemer. Thus, from 1905 (following Japan's victory over Russia) to 1914 (shortly before the outbreak of the First World War), rumors of an approaching cataclysm abounded, such as an impending "great war" between the US and Japan, in which, it was prophesied, Japan would emerge the victor. In 1910, the influential *espiritistas* (spirit mediums and faith healers) in Malabon and Caloocan (neighboring districts of Manila) were spreading the "advice" of the spirits of Rizal and Bonifacio that in the coming war between the US and Japan, the Philippines would gain independence if it sided with Japan. Such forecasts gained more force in the popular imagination when Haley's Comet appeared in mid-1910, a phenomenon that was interpreted as an apocalyptic sign. According to confidential intelligence reports of the Philippine Constabulary headed by Colonel Bandholtz, the king-maker in Philippine colonial politics and patron of the rising Filipino politicians, Manuel L. Quezon and Sergio Osmeña, public commemorations, in particular the death anniversaries of Rizal and Bonifacio, became occasions not only for spreading these rumors but also for spontaneous mass rallies and demonstrations agitating for independence, in which the name of Ricarte was oftentimes invoked (Ileto 1984: 102–3).[19]

Sturtevant (1976: 204) notes that although Ricarte disengaged himself from any conspiratorial activities during his exile in Japan, his reputation continued to cause headaches for the Philippine Constabulary. Ricarte's attempts at urban insurrection, his idea of an equal sharing of the nation's wealth, and his rumored links with Japan's national leadership appealed to the new generation of aspiring, albeit marginal, rebels. A variety of insurrectionary secret societies that proliferated in North-Central Luzon between 1915 and 1930 used Ricarte's regional fame, and promised Japanese naval and military assistance when the day of reckoning arrived, to rally peasant support. One such group, the *Tanggulan* of Pangasinan, exploded into a bloody rebellion, which as always, ended in the massacre of its members.[20]

Thus, the neo-colonial state could not ignore Ricarte, or for that matter, write off the popular aspiration for complete and immediate independence. When the November 1935 inauguration of the Philippine Commonwealth was being planned, notes Sturtevant (1976: 303), colonial administrators vied with prominent leaders of the dominant Nacionalista Party in extending cordial invitations to Ricarte to attend the inaugural ceremonies — an honor he declined. But to avoid appearing impolite, Ricarte sent his wife to represent him. In an interview with the *Tribune* newspaper shortly before her return to Japan, Mrs. Ricarte revealed that Commonwealth President Manuel L. Quezon had made a standing offer of a cabinet post to her husband if he would return home, which Ricarte had also refused (Goodman 1966: 58–9). Ileto (1984: 110) states, albeit without documentation, that Ricarte "pointedly refused a stipend and the rank of 'Superior General-in-Chief of the Filipino Army' offered by Quezon" because he was concerned that if he acquiesced, he would have to return the favor.

Since then, Ricarte's star started to dim. Sturtevant's view (1976: 203) that Ricarte's rebuff of the Commonwealth Inaugural was a political error seems to have been borne out by subsequent events. Goodman (1966: 59) writes that during the Commonwealth administration, events passed General Ricarte by at an even faster rate than had earlier been the case during his prolonged self-exile in Japan. Goodman does not explain, however, why events overtook Ricarte during the Commonwealth administration.

What seems to have happened during this period was the complete weaning away of the Filipinos from their nationalist past and their absorption into an "official nationalism" that looked up to America as the model to emulate. One aspect of this new consciousness was the erasure of the revolutionary heroes from collective memory, augured by the resounding landslide victory of the ebullient Quezon over the aging General Aguinaldo in the presidential elections for the Philippine Commonwealth.

So why was Ricarte forgotten? Sturtevant's answer expresses the orthodox view: Ricarte's association with the invaders during the Occupation shattered his heroic image. Thus, he fell from "nationalistic grace," equally despised by the collaborating oligarchs and the resisting masses. Writes Sturtevant (1976: 196):

> By the time W.W. II ended and the seventy-nine-year-old Ricarte expired, both in 1945, insular opinion had consigned him temporarily to the status of a Filipino Marshall Petain. Of all the irreconcilables at the century's turn, only Artemio Ricarte y Vibora suffered a fate akin to that meted in Greek tragedy.

The Eurocentric cast of Sturtevant's explanation, comparing Ricarte with Marshall Petain of France, begs the question. In the case of Southeast Asia, as we have mentioned, the general rule among the nationalist leaders was collaboration with the

Japanese. While in exile (as a result of his nationalist activities against the Dutch), Sukarno, like Ricarte, had pinned his hope of returning to Indonesia (to resume the struggle for national independence) through the sponsorship of an emergent Japan (Dahm 1969: 406). Aside from Sukarno and Hatta of Indonesia, we must mention Aung San of Burma, who after fleeing Burma and getting some military training in Japan, returned to his country in 1941 under Japanese sponsorship.[21] On top of this, Aung San had formed the Japanese-trained-and-armed Burmese Independence Army (BIA), which became part of the invading anti-British Japanese force in Burma. And like Sukarno and Hatta, Aung San's one-time association with the Japanese did not diminish his towering stature among the Burmese masses, who did not mind collaborating with the Japanese to drive away the British (Silverstein 1972).

The case of Ricarte does not befit, as Sturtevant would have it, a Greek tragedy but an American farce: he came home at the twilight of his years hoping to rally his people, with the aid of the Japanese to be sure, against the American regime (which after all had destroyed his own generation) only to discover that his own people had committed themselves body and soul to his generation's arch enemy. Moreover, when the 77-year-old Ricarte finally decided to come home, under the sponsorship of the Japanese and at the beginning of the Japanese Occupation, he could not have chosen a worse time: the Filipinos were still reeling from the shock of the debacle of the combined American-Filipino forces in Bataan and Corregidor and the national trauma and rage over Japanese atrocities in the so-called Death March. Thus, when Ricarte arrived, after 27 years of exile in Japan, there was no hero's welcome for him. The unrepentant *Katipunero* had come home uncelebrated. He died a broken man — and in obscurity — three years later. With Ricarte's death, the nationalist romance with Japan that had started with Rizal finally ended.

According to Goodman (1966: 60), Ricarte died retreating with the Japanese army in Northern Luzon in July 1945, as the American forces were re-establishing their control over the Philippines. Agoncillo (1965: 919) however writes that the reports are conflicting: some say Ricarte died retreating to the mountains of Rizal province; others say he went with the fleeing Japanese General Yamashita; still others claim that he died of illness in Northern Luzon, possibly in Nueva Viscaya. The point is that nobody knows for sure how or where he died; the forgotten hero had passed away with not even a marker placed on his grave.

Teodoro Agoncillo is the first, if not the only one, among Filipino historians to view Ricarte's collaboration with kindness. According to Agoncillo (1965: 917–8), Ricarte urged his countrymen to support Japan's scheme of a Greater East Asia Co-prosperity Sphere because, first, he "sincerely believed, wrongly to be sure, that Japan could give his country better independence than the one promised by the United States," and second, "he could not have done otherwise, for he owed the Japanese a debt of gratitude, in the same manner that the Filipinos could not have been expected to turn against the United States because of their debt of gratitude to the Americans."

Postscript: Imagining Japan and America Today

The implication of Agoncillo's kind words is, of course, that Filipinos who grew up during the American period owed so much to America, and therefore had every reason to be loyal, even at the cost of their own lives. Filipinos then, as now, believed that the Americans fought the Japanese for their sake, that they offered their lives to defend the Filipinos against Japanese aggression.

And so, as the maverick nationalist senator Claro M. Recto (1951: 172) remarked, when independence was finally "granted" to the Philippines by the United States in 1946, "it was not so much an act of separation, as one of more perfect union."

The far-reaching effects of that union in the political and economic spheres are still being debated. But as far as the national psyche is concerned, the signs are unmistakable. In a

1982 Philippine survey, when 207 grade-schoolers were asked what nationality they preferred, only ten replied, "Filipino" (cited in Fallows 1987).[22] Today, the situation is even worse. In early January of 1998, the Catholic Bishops Conference of the Philippines sounded the alarm over the Filipinos' precarious sense of identity. They called attention to Maria Luisa Doronila's latest study of Filipino schoolchildren which showed the latter's order of preferences with respect to country and nationality. For role models, first preference went to the American cowboy, followed by the Japanese *samurai*, and then the Chinese *kungfu* master, with, alas, the Filipino heroes coming in fourth. As to the countries they admired and wanted to live in: the first choice went to the United States, followed by Japan, and third, the Philippines. The study also found that as the schoolchildren got older, their preference for other countries and for things foreign, far from being diminished, even intensified.

Rizal and Artemio Ricarte must be turning in their graves.

Notes

1. See Anderson (1994). I critique Anderson's perspective and misreading of Rizal's novels in Chapter 3 of my book, *A Nation Aborted: Rizal, American Hegemony, and Philippine Nationalism* (1999; revised 2nd ed. 2009).
2. Friend (1988) is an expansion of an earlier essay, "Lordship and Bondage: The Philippines, Indonesia and Japanese Impact, 1942–1945" (1984).
3. Fenby (2003), cited in Petras (2006), estimates that around 10 million Chinese were killed by the Japanese between 1937–1942. Rummel (1997) provides a Chinese death toll range from 1.578 million (low estimate) to 6.325 million (high) from 1937 to 1945.
4. R.J. Rummel (1997) estimates a low 90,000 to a high 180,000 Philippine death toll, directly attributable to Japanese military forces, from 1941 to 1945. Regarding the Philippine-American War, the two most cited estimates are those of John Gates (1984: 367–78), from a low 127,593 to a high 362,659 war-related deaths, and General James M. Bell of the US Army, 600,000 for Luzon alone. Gates dismisses Bell's 600,000 estimate on the basis of James LeRoy's observation that it was "based on an unverified newspaper interview." Gate's estimates cover the 1899–1903 period, based on the 1903 census. His method was to subtract the estimated Christian population in the 1903 census — that is,

6,987,686 — from a projected population growth had war not occurred (based on the 1898 Spanish census), which ranges from 7,115,279 (estimated from an annual growth rate [a.g.r] of 1.2%) to 7,350,345 (1.86% a.g.r). The difference — 127,593 to 362,659 — "represents the potential range of war-related deaths among the Filipino population." See Gates (1984), p. 374. Even granting the validity of Gate's method, the problem is that his figures cover only the period from 1899 to 1903. The pacification campaign of the US continued way beyond 1903. See Francisco (1973), p. 11.

5. Commenting on the Japanese propaganda effort in Southeast Asia, Masuo Kato, a Japanese journalist who visited Manila during the occupation, wrote: "My personal estimate was that Japanese propaganda failed most in the Philippines and was most successful among the Burmese." See Kato (1946), p. 146, cited in Zaide (1957), p. 35n31.
6. By 1895, when it became clear that the Solidaridad reform campaign was doomed, members of the *Comite de Propaganda* started, as Mabini put it, "looking in another direction," that is to say, toward Japan. Thus, Jose Ramos went there in 1895. He was later joined by Doroteo Jose and some others in 1896. Their mission was to solicit Japanese intervention. See Josefa M. Saniel (1965), pp. 171–5, cited in Schumacher (1973), p. 264.
7. The pioneering study of Josefa Saniel, *Japan and the Philippines, 1868–1898* (1962) breaks some ground on the official and unofficial relations between the Filipino revolutionaries and the government of Japan and the Japanese *shishi* (nationalist military as well as civilian activists). However, it does not delve deeply into how the Filipinos imagined Japan during the Revolution and the Philippine-American War. For example, it never explores Rizal's reactions on his visit to Japan or Ricarte's attachment to Japan in the aftermath of the Philippine-American War.
8. Rizal received several offers of employment in Japan but declined them all.
9. The government that inhumanely quarantined the Chinese to win more votes in the coming elections was that of President Cleveland, who as it turned out, lost to Harrison.
10. Rizal was among first-class passengers. There is a discrepancy between Rizal's letter to Mariano Ponce, in which Rizal states that their quarantine lasted 13 days, and Rizal's diary, in which he notes that it lasted six days. It could not have been 13 days as Rizal's length of stay in America was only 19 days. The anomaly in Rizal's letter to Ponce could be a typographical error in the translation or even in the transcription of the original letter, which was handwritten (I have yet to check the Spanish original).

11. See Benjamin Keen (1977) and Bartolome de las Casas (1974). Many of the military officers who led the American conquest of the Philippines were veterans of the pacification campaigns against the Indians. Rizal, in his "The Philippines A Century Hence," envisioned a bloody war with the Americans in which "the Filipinos will defend with indescribable ardor the freedom [from Spain] that they had won with so much blood and sacrifice." Unfamiliar with American history, General Aguinaldo failed to anticipate the horrific atrocities that the invading Americans would wreak on the Filipino civilian population.
12. See Josefa M. Saniel's pioneering study, 1962 and 1965.
13. In their critical review of May's *Inventing a Hero* (1996), Guerrero and Villegas (1997) argue: "But since we have been discussing speculative allegations, we may as well posit another: Could May have been skeptical of Ricarte's memoirs because, of all the revolutionary generals, Ricarte went into self-exile in Japan rather than live under the American flag? Is it because Ricarte's sense of nation was able to resist the personal comfort and accommodation which the American colonial masters provided to all the revolutionaries who surrendered? It is this same notion of nation which runs through the works of Filipino historians that so offends May's idea of historiography."
14. Relying solely on Aguinaldo's self-serving memoirs, De Viana (2003), p. 76 insinuates that the 77-year-old Ricarte was a vengeful and scheming opportunist: "Was Ricarte a scheming opportunist? This may be partly true judging from Ricarte's conversation with Aguinaldo that he intended to "square things up" and "settle accounts" in the [Japanese installed] dictatorial government he was to lead. Ricarte was referring to the Americans who took away more than 40 years of his life by exiling and publicly humiliating him with six years of solitary confinement. The coming of the Japanese forces to the Philippines was a heaven-sent opportunity to get back at the hated Americans. He also talked about using threats and blackmail to all those who would oppose him."
15. My main sources regarding Ricarte's activities during the American regime are: Grant K. Goodman (1966); Teodoro A. Agoncillo (1965); and David R. Sturtevant (1976).
16. Quoted by J.K. Eyre, Jr., "General Artemio Ricarte y Vibora," *The Military Engineer* (November 1944): 369 (cited in G.K. Goodman [1966], pp. 55–6).
17. As quoted by Ricarte's wife in an interview in Manila after she attended the inauguration of the Philippine Commonwealth in November 1935 (cited in Goodman [1966], pp. 55–6).

18. The practice of commemorating Rizal's December 30, 1896 martyrdom was started by Aguinaldo's revolutionary forces in 1898. The American regime appropriated this practice in 1902 by declaring December 30 as a national holiday in the Philippines.
19. Indonesian historians, in particular, Professor Ruslan Abdulgani of Padjadjaran University, have claimed that the first Southeast Asian leaders to predict the Great Pacific War between Japan and the Western Powers were the Communist Tan Malaka (in 1925) and the nationalist leader Sukarno (in 1928). See Bernhard Dahm (1969), pp. 404–6. As we have seen, rumors about an impending war between the US and Japan have been floating among Filipinos as early as 1905!
20. The full name is *Kapatiran Tanggulang Malayang Mamamayan* or Brotherhood for the Defense of the Free People. For details of the Tangulan insurrection, see Sturtevant (1976).
21. In 1940, Aung San fled Burma when a warrant for his arrest was issued due to his attempts to organize a revolt against the British. He went first to China, seeking assistance from the communist Chinese, but he was intercepted by the Japanese military occupiers in Amoy, and was convinced by them to go to Japan instead. In February 1941, Aung San returned to Burma, with an offer of arms and financial support from the Fumimaro Konoe government. He returned briefly to Japan to receive more military training, along with the first batch of young revolutionaries who came to be known as the "Thirty Comrades." On December 26, 1941, with the help of the *Minami Kikan*, a secret intelligence unit (headed by Colonel Suzuki) formed to close the Burma Road and to support a national uprising in Burma. Aung San founded the Burmese Independence Army (BIA) in Bangkok, Thailand (then under Japanese occupation). Source: http://en.wikipedia.org/wiki/Aung_San.
22. This may have been the survey done by Maria Luisa C. Doronila, "The Nature, Organization and Sources of Students' National Identity Orientations" (1986).

chapter 6

On the Same Terrain of Colonial Modernity: The Mystification of Jose Rizal and the Symbolization of the Japanese Emperor

Yoshiko Nagano

Introduction

This essay attempts to compare the mystification of Jose Rizal under the American Rule of the early 20th century with the symbolization of the Japanese Emperor after the Second World War, with the assumption that the "Benevolent Assimilation" policy toward the Philippines during the American colonial period could be understood as the forerunner of the US occupation policy toward Japan in 1945–1952.

The Philippines and Japan seemingly did follow divergent historical paths in the modern period from the late 19th century to the present. The Philippines was colonized in the mid-16th century by Spain, and after the outbreak of the Philippine Revolution of 1896–1898, briefly emerged as an independent nation, but through the Philippine-American War of 1899–1902, was annexed by the United States as its first and only formal colony in Asia till the Second World War. The Philippines was even subsequently placed under Japan's control during the

Second World War through a fiercely militaristic regime. The Philippines gained its independence after the Second World War, but got quickly counted among the "developing countries" due to its economic disadvantage. Japan, by contrast, experienced the Meiji Restoration in 1868 as the point of departure for its formation in short order as a modern independent state, and later colonized Taiwan and Korea, a political emergence as a modern power highlighted by its victories in the war with China and the Russo-Japanese War earlier, and which greatly impressed the West. In the early 1930s, Japan invaded Manchuria in a move that served as the major stepping-stone for Japan's entry into the Asia-Pacific War of 1941–1945. Due to the defeat in the Second World War, Japan once lost its independence under the US Occupation but regained it in 1952, and then with US military procurement for both the Korean War and Vietnam War, it gained economic strength, serving as the successful model of economic development for other Asian countries until the end of the 1980s.

However, Japan's fatal economic crash in the early 1990s has triggered its almost endless economic recession for over a decade, making the 1990s Japan's fabled "lost decade," similar to the 1980s for Latin America and the Philippines. Since then, Japan has willingly absorbed much more direct US political and economic influences, particularly with the post-Cold War "globalization" that the United States led. All these phenomena seem to provide us with occasions to rethink the historical experiences of their countries and for exploring the similarities and common threads between them under the framework of "Americanization of the Philippines and Japan" beyond the differences of time frame and historical matrix.

In terms of the US entry into both societies in various ways, the Philippines is obviously well ahead of Japan, with its experience of US colonization since the early 20th century, while in the case of Japan, it was only after the Second World War that the United States became an inseparable factor for understanding the nature of its 20th-century social reconstruction and modern development. Arguably, pervasive social and cultural effects of Americanization have been particularly felt in Japan since the early 1980s, even as Japan's political and economic ties with the United States have been notably strengthened right after the Second World War. This American influence has been further strengthened under the US-led "globalization" since the early 1990s.

If we understand the US project of remaking the Philippines and Japan in its image as a result of their defeat in the two wars, that is, for the former in the Philippine-American War of 1899–1902,[1] and for the latter in Asia-Pacific War of 1941–1945, we might begin to discover and uncover the otherwise intertwined and common natures of these two countries in Asia in the larger context of colonial modernity. The colonial modernity is one of the most attractive new concepts to emerge in recent years for grasping the distinctive features of Asian historical, social, and cultural formation. This concept offers critical possibilities for breaking the impasse in our conceptualization of Asia's "modern period," particularly since the latter formulary still carries with it the long dominant notion of "modernization." It opens up spaces to think and rethink the more profound meanings of modernization and colonization as processes that have had decisive impact on Asian societies, beyond the binaries of West/Asia, imperialism/nationalism, colonizer/colony, rulers/ruled, and developed countries/developing countries (Shin and Robinson 1999; Barlow 1997).

In this essay, first, I will discuss the historical meanings of the US Occupation of Japan from a critical consideration of John Dower's influential Pulitzer Prize-winning book, *Embracing Defeat: Japan in the Wake of World War II* (1999). Second, I will go on to the discussion on the similarity between the US occupation policy of Japan and its "Benevolent Assimilation" policy toward the Philippines. Third, I will see the meaning of the mystification of Jose Rizal during the early American colonial period in the Philippines, and fourth, the symbolization of the Japanese Emperor after the Second World War will be assessed in the light of the historical origin of emperor system.

John Dower's *Embracing Defeat*

One obvious reason why Japan and the Philippines have not been considered as comparable nations is that while for Filipinos, US colonial rule in the first half of the 20th century has been a staple of their official collective memories, the US Occupation of Japan technically lasted only for seven years (1945–1952) except for Okinawa (until 1972), so that such historical experiences as covered by this period have been mostly forgotten or effaced from public memory among the Japanese. Although only for a relatively short period, the US Occupation decisively reshaped Japan in the post-war era, a fact widely acknowledged today but which has been gradually forgotten in Japan by the early 1970s, given the decade-long economic miracle of the 1960s. Japan's phenomenal economic recovery and success lasting till the end of the Cold War very much relied upon the political or economic structure primarily established under the US GHQ's (General Headquarters) occupation policy implemented by General Douglas MacArthur in the late 1940s. At the same time, it is important to note that, as John Dower excellently discusses in *Embracing Defeat* (1999), the nature of the US Occupation policy in Japan could be understood as the "SCAPanese model" or "a hybrid Japanese-American model." The "SCAPanese model" means the collaboration between the Supreme Command for the Allied Powers (SCAP), namely the US GHQ and the Japanese political elite. As Dower's clearly describes and explains the SCAPanese model:

> ... To understand the Japan that stands at the cusp of the twenty-first century, however, it is more useful to look not for the *longue durée* of an inexorably unfolding national experience, but rather at a cycle of recent history that began in the late 1920s and essentially ended in 1989. When this short, violent, innovative epoch is scrutinized, much of what has been characterized as a postwar 'Japanese model' proves to a hybrid Japanese-American model ... This bureaucratic capitalism is incomprehensible without understanding how victor and vanquished embraced Japan's defeat together ... [T]he so-called Japanese model could have been more aptly described as a 'SCAPanese model.'

> The short cycle of Japan's modern experience coincides almost perfectly with Emperor Hirohito's reign. He was the ever-present ideological touchstone of these decades — the symbol of a seamless transition from unbridled militarism to imperial democracy, the most obvious rallying point, in peace as in war, for those who would emphasize the racial and signaled 'unity of the people.' For his subjects, Hirohito's death in 1989 signaled the literal end of an era ... (1999: 558)

Dower's book's title itself, *Embracing Defeat*, carries the connotation of "mercy," and to see such a miserable situation from every corner of defeated Japan suggests that Dower, although an excellent American scholar of Japanese history, has not completely freed himself from the blind spots that inhere in regarding post-war Japanese history from "outside of Japan." I assume that the national sentiment varied from the elite to the populace right after the war; however, as far as I have been able to collect the stories from the contemporary Japanese as well as various writings during and after the Second World War, it appears that generally speaking, Japanese citizens did not so much "embrace defeat" as they simply welcomed "the end of war" because "the end of war" meant for them the end of the massive US air raids (conducted by American bombers over 60 times) in various cities throughout Japan, starting from November 1944 until August 1945. The culmination of this type of US bombings, known as the Tokyo Raids, on March 10, 1945, wiped out approximately 100,000 citizens, including children, the aged, and the sick and infirm within one day alone, not to mention the H-bombs in Hiroshima and Nagasaki (Toshi Kushu [City Raids] 2006).

As widely known, the Asia-Pacific War had double meanings for Japan; for one, it was the imperial war against the United States, while it was the war of invasion against Asia. In the dual war structure, the Japanese military brought immense atrocities and destruction in Asia, while so many Japanese civilians were killed in their homeland by US bombings. Some Japanese official statistics estimate that 20 million lives were killed in Asia, while 3.1 million Japanese and over 60,000

Western Allied lives were lost during the Asia-Pacific War (Bix 2000: 4, 690–1). However, in the eyes of Japanese populace, the dual structure of the war was generally invisible; what they were concerned with was the lives of the husbands or sons who were sent out to the battlefields in Asia, while protecting their own lives from US bombings in their homeland. The most striking evidence that Japanese citizens had accepted "defeat" as "the end of war" is that "August 15" has been recognized as the Day for the End of War when the Japanese Emperor announced to accept the Potsdam Declaration in 1945. For them, it generally and strategically meant "the end of war," as retrievable public memories of the immediate post-war phenomena in Japan can eloquently attest.

In spite of my strong feeling of ambiguity about the book's inordinately telling title, however, what I have found useful from Dower's otherwise exhaustive and compelling account is that post-war Japan was not the mere creature of the GHQ, but the product of the collaboration between the GHQ and Japanese political elite. I retain my opinion that Dower's frame of analysis is substantially correct and Part 4 of the book (on "Democracies") gives us a chance to rethink the embryonic nature of Japanese democratic development. Dower sees post-war democracy in Japan to consist of three natures or features: "imperial democracy," "constitutional democracy," and "censored democracy." Of these three, "imperial democracy" is what Dower seems to consider most important for understanding the nature of post-war Japanese society or the hybrid nature of the Japan-American model thereby formed.

In the post-war constitution, the emperor was newly placed as the "national symbol" (instead of the "sovereign" in the pre-war constitution), crucially placing the emperor at the center of Japanese citizens' efforts to rebuild the country after its devastation by its rather ill-considered dalliance with fierce militarism with its Second World War aggressions. Paradoxically, however, to makeover the emperor into the national symbol, the post-war constitution does not state explicitly who should occupy the position of sovereign in Japan. We might read this particular ambiguity of the post-war Japanese constitution as a reflection of the ambiguous motives underpinning the "SCAPanese model" itself, swinging as it does between measures of keeping the old political and administrative system intact and schemes for creating a new system of Japanese democracy, no matter how hybrid. It also mirrors the ambiguous attitude of the post-war Japanese government when relating to the question of its responsibility for the Asia-Pacific War and to the Asian countries affected by its destructive consequences up to the present.

Benevolent Assimilation in the Philippines: The Origins for Post-War Japan?

In the context of colonial modernity, what is conspicuously lacking from the work of Dower and other Japanese studies scholars is the perspective that the "SCAPanese model" or "hybrid Japanese-American model" is a kind of replica of United States pacification policy in the Philippines and the establishment of its colonial rule there under the mantle of "Benevolent Assimilation" during the first half of the 20th century. One can say that the "SCAPanese model" or the "hybrid Japanese-American model" is not the mere creature or product of United States Cold War policy and politics; arguably, it is rather the product of an American colonial policy that had already embedded itself and germinated in the American Philippine experiment half a century earlier. Considering the later Japanese variant in terms of its earlier precedent, I propose that it allows us to conceptualize the distinctive features of US empire-building historically and in a critically comparatist fashion heretofore missing from existing studies.

It is widely known that American colonial policy for the Philippines was first and best expressed by President McKinley's "Benevolent Assimilation" proclamation issued on December 21, 1898, to wit:

> ... [I]t should be the earnest and paramount aim of the military administration to win the confidence, respect, and affection of the inhabitants of the Philippines by assuring them in every possible way that full measure of individual rights and liberties which is the heritage of a free people, and by proving to them that the mission of the United States is one of benevolent assimilation, substituting the mild sway of justice and right for arbitrary rule ... (Agoncillo and Guerrero 1973: 263).

To pursue the principles of colonial rule as enunciated here by McKinley, one important agenda that the United States needed to tackle was the establishment of an autonomous political and legislative system in the Philippines. The United States' own experience as a British colony until its independence of 1776, and given its historical formation, found itself, from the onset of Philippine pacification and reconstruction policy, actively seeking to avoid a situation where the Philippines should be fatally bound to it under the strict bondage or relationship between the ruler and ruled. Thus, the United States pragmatically chose to promote or enhance the institution of autonomous government by Filipinos under US tutelage. Such a policy, often acclaimed as exceptional in the annals of colonial rule, meant the introduction of an American-type political and legislative system in the Philippines but one largely ran by the Filipinos themselves. This master narrative of benign and enlightened US colonial state-building thus undertaken, and generally, "exceptional" US imperial rule in the Philippines, is a story well-told and much-rehearsed by previous and current American Filipinists. To remake the Philippine political and legislative system in the American image, it was imperative for US government officials — as it was to prove equally so, in the case of post-war Japan and the Japanese leadership — to forge close ties with an emergent Filipino political elite from whose ranks could be drawn the manpower for autonomous and surrogate government under American guidelines.

At this point, it is noteworthy that when the first general election for the Philippine Assembly was held in 1907, it was the Nacionalista Party headed by Sergio Osmeña and Manuel

Quezon that won the majority of the seats. Since then, with several stages of conflicts and despite its division into various fractions as well as the plague of turncoatism that was to characterize colonial Filipino party politics, the Nacionalista Party went on and continued to dominate the Philippine political process throughout the American colonial period. What is also important to point out here is that these two prominent national political leaders, Osmeña and Quezon were not the direct "descendants" of the inchoate elite political groupings that led the Philippine Revolution, but rather belonged to the new political elite formation that was now being incubated by the American colonial context. They stepped into power in the national political arena by fostering, at times intrepidly risking, close personal and official ties with American proconsuls or military officers in the Philippines in the crucial first decade of US colonial rule. Thus, the new Filipino political elite became the prime mover for establishing so-called "colonial democracy" in the Philippines under American encouragement and pragmatic considerations for the sustenance of the administrative regime that was instituted. It was after the First World War or in the early 1920s that the "hybrid Filipino-American model" in Philippine politics was firmly established under the leadership of Manuel Quezon, which in a series of master strokes, managed to displace and supersede Osmeña's overwhelming power in the Nacionalista Party that had lasted nearly 15 years (Paredes 1988) from the establishment of the American colonial state.

By discussing the historical experiences of the two US Occupation regimes in the Philippines and Japan in the context of colonial modernity, we have shown what was previously ignored or neglected as historical facts; that is, the salient similarities between these two countries, which have been otherwise considered as completely different nations in their historical, cultural, or social features and aspects. One of the most striking discoveries here is that the hybrid Philippine experience and experiment of the US can actually be understood, and must be further explored, as the forerunner of its history of decisive interventions in modern (and in the "colonial" modernization of) Japan. In this highly important sense, we might and should begin to construe the historical experience of "Benevolent Assimilation" in the Philippines as the "shadowy" origins for post-war Japan's "SCAPanese model" or the "hybrid Japanese-American model" discussed and explained in Dower's *Embracing Defeat*.

The Mystification of Jose Rizal

Floro Quibuyen's provocative book, *A Nation Aborted: Rizal, American Hegemony, and Philippine Nationalism* (1999), offers a detailed examination of Rizal's role as a national symbol for American colonial rule in the Philippines. It is a critical effort in rethinking the instrumentality of the United States in transforming the image and role of Jose Rizal in the Philippine Revolution, at the initial stages of US colonial conquest. The book's tenth chapter, "Remaking Philippine History," amply hints at the process initiated by the US colonial administration to appropriate, selectively, the image of Jose Rizal as a major ideological sanction for their colonial policy in the Philippines, with the willing collaboration of Filipino counterparts. Quibuyen declares:

> The hegemonic aspect of colonial rule, aimed principally at the co-option of the nationalist movement ... involved two related dimensions; the cultural and political. The political aspect involved co-opting the local elite into effective partners in the colonial enterprise, through the creation of a civil government. The marvelous products of this co-option, a success story for the American regime, were the so-called nationalist leaders and stalwarts of the alleged "pro-Independence" Nacionalist Party, Manuel Quezon, Sergio Osmeña, and Manuel Roxas.
>
> The cultural aspect involved the co-optation of the independence-oriented nationalist movement and its transformation into an "official nationalism" in which the revolutionary tradition of 1896 was cut off. For this purpose, the symbol of Rizal was appropriated and deployed (1999: 276–7).

Quibuyen cites three major readings of Rizal during the American colonial period by quoting Reynaldo C. Ileto's highly acclaimed piece, "Orator and the Crowd." Ileto has argued that one of these readings consisted in a "nationwide hero worship of Rizal ... to transfer Filipino adoration away from the revolutionary heroes towards an advocate of pacifist and constitutional nationalism" (1984: 92). This influential reading was first noted in Katherine Mayo's *The Isles of Fear: The Truth about the Philippines* (1925), as cited by Usha Mahajani's *Philippine Nationalism: External Challenge and Filipino Response, 1565–1945* (1971). Mahajani has analyzed the ways that President Theodore Roosevelt enlisted Rizal's legacy in the "negation of independence" given that Rizal's controversial repudiation of the Katipunan uprising applied "with tenfold greater force to those who foolishly or wickedly opposed the mild and beneficent government we were instituting in the islands." The second reading Rizal pointed out by Ileto concerns "that of the conservative *ilustrado*'s view of Rizal as a symbol both of the opposition to friar supremacy and of "evolutionary ... change." Quibuyen contends that this version complemented the American view (1999: 282–3).

The third reading totally competed with the American view and Ileto calls it the "subversive reading of Rizal." As Quibuyen succinctly summarizes Ileto's arguments, this is "a popular image of Rizal that was shared by the Malolos Republic under Aguinaldo and by peasant millennial groups such as the Corolum, and that persisted through the American colonial regime" (ibid.: 283). Earlier in this same chapter, Quibuyen noted precisely that Rizal Day was not proclaimed by the American administrators but by the Filipinos. The first commemoration was held on December 30, 1898 by the Aguinaldo revolutionary government to mark the second anniversary of Rizal's execution at Bagumbayan. According to Quibuyen, Katherine Mayo's account in *The Isles of Fear* successfully captures and reproduces the scenes whereby all the towns in Tayabas province under the control of the revolutionary government commemorated the death anniversary of Rizal on that day (ibid.: 277, 283).

Backed by the abovementioned narratives, Quibuyen contends that "It was a stroke of genius, therefore, on the part of the American regime to have seized the symbol of Rizal to further their own colonial agenda. However, during the early years of the new regime, the American appropriation of Rizal was resisted" (ibid.: 277–8). But how exactly did the American administration maneuver to remake or mystify the symbol of Jose Rizal to ensure the success of its colonial project? This should be for Filipinos' "welfare" but not for independence. In order to pursue this purpose, Americans had to write Philippine history and reinvent Rizal with their orientalist views. Quibuyen details this process by dividing it into two stages as set by the two Philippine Commissions, namely Schurman's and Taft's.

According to Quibuyen, one of the most important matters that the Schurman Commission busied itself with was the matter of Rizal, although this was not explicitly mentioned in its policy recommendations. The Commission learned about Rizal through its interviews with some prominent Filipino *ilustrados* like Trinidad H. Pardo de Tavera or the Spanish bibliographer Wenceslao E. Retana. Above all, it is revealed that Pardo de Tavera provided the Commission its first image of Rizal, as exemplified in his interview with the Commission that was included in the *Philippine Commission Report* in 1900. Later, W. Cameron Forbes, who served as one-time Governor-General, expressed this view in *The Philippine Islands* (1928), which was to be among the more representative castings of the American Rizal: "Rizal never advocated independence, nor did he advocate armed resistance to the government. He urged reform from within, by publicity, by public education, and appeal to the public conscience." From authoritative American statements of this kind, Quibuyen deduces American intentions of seeking to delink Rizal from Bonifacio and the Revolution of 1896 (ibid.: 285, 287, 290).

The Taft Commission began on July 1901 the practical implementation of the colonial policy whose grand design was basically drawn up by the previous Schurman Commission. Quibuyen argues that the propagation of an Americanized

Rizal was achieved by "aggressive American sponsorship and the enthusiastic cooperation of the Filipino elite." Thus were provinces and streets, here and there, named for Rizal and his signature statues erected in every town plaza or park. Among others, two legislative acts were most instrumental in disseminating and implanting the American image of Rizal. Act No. 243 on September 28, 1901 led to the erection of the Rizal monument at the Luneta. Act No. 345 on February 1, 1902 made December 30 an official public holiday. The designation of Rizal Day was important for two reasons: first, in religious and civil elements being merged in his person, Rizal became both the national symbol and the Tagalog Christ; second, in so setting the solid grounds for the yearly commemoration of Rizal as has been achieved by US colonial authorities, with the help of their native partners, the active participation of the entire Filipino from the elite to the masses was quite effectively elicited (ibid.: 292–5).

How did Jose Rizal relate to the populace as a mystical figure in the Philippines or influence them through his writings by or right after his death in 1896? Reynaldo Ileto's "Rizal and the Underside of Philippine History," first published in 1982, gives us an answer to this question (1998, Chapter 2). Together with his seminal work, *Pasyon and Revolution: Popular Movements in the Philippines, 1840–1910* (1979), Ileto's provocative and critical projections, in these works of the politically contested portrayals of Jose Rizal in post-revolutionary Philippine history, provide us with equally helpful clues for understanding Rizaline mystification and the role it played in the evolution of Filipino political modernity.

Here, it is clear that what the United States essentially attempted was to cut off the intimate ties of Jose Rizal, as a martyr of a Filipino nation that was in emergence, with popular sentiment, by projecting an image of Jose Rizal as a mere reformist. This attempt by American colonizers seems to have succeeded, indeed, through various means like the workings of public education and systematic institutional pedagogy during the American colonial period and afterward. However, since the 1980s, a more balanced and critical portrayal of Jose Rizal, including a trenchant critique of his American mystification, has been disclosed in a whole host of revisionist efforts by Filipino scholars.

The Symbolization of the Japanese Emperor

The question of the emperor has always been somewhat of a "taboo" nature in Japanese history and it is particularly so in the case of the previous Showa Tenno or Emperor Hirohito who lived a long and dramatic life before and after the Second World War. Along with some others, these four books may be taken as the standard readings on this topic: Masanori Nakamura, *Shocho Tenno-sei eno Michi* (*A Path to the Emperor as National Symbol*) (1989); Masanori Nakamura, *Sengoshi to Shocho Tenno* (*The Postwar History and Emperor as National Symbol*) (1992); Yutaka Yoshida, *Showa Tenno no Shusen-shi* (*Showa Tenno and His End-of-War History*) (1992); and Herbert Bix, *Hirohito and the Making of Modern Japan* (2000).

For depicting the historical process of making Emperor Hirohito a national symbol in relation to post-war Japanese politics, Yutaka Yoshida's *Showa Tenno no Shusen-shi* is certainly the most successful work. It scrutinizes the original documents not only in Japan but also in the National Archives in Washington DC, particularly in the files of the International Prosecution Section (IPS) (RG: 331).

The most striking achievement of Yoshida's book is its compelling attempt to locate a document newly disclosed to the public in 1990, that is, "Showa Tenno no Dokuhaku-roku" (Memoirs of the Monologue of Showa Tenno), within the framework of Japanese post-war politics. By doing so, Yoshida was able to read clearly from the memoirs the political intentions of both American officers and some Japanese elite leaders in their contentions for hegemony on the terrain of post-war Japanese political processes. Yoshida has determined that the US GHQ's treatment of the emperor system was already clear by late August 1945: while introducing the indirect rule system, the GHQ held the view that the emperor system ought to be maintained. This did not necessarily mean, of course, that the United States had already decided how to keep the emperor system and how to treat Showa Tenno himself. Indeed, some American administrators even considered the possibility of the abdication or prosecution of Showa Tenno, were it not for the antagonism from the Japanese populace that might result from such an act and likely prove to be detrimental to the purposes of American rule in Japan (1992: 41–2).

Under this fluid situation involving the American treatment of Showa Tenno, some fractions of the Japanese conservative elite started to maneuver in various ways for seizing the hegemonic position in post-war politics. The first group that approached the US GHQ was the so-called "Emperor's court." This group was composed by the emperor's close aides and their followers who made active representations to protect Showa Tenno from the prospect of abdication. Their major achievement was the meeting between General Douglas MacArthur and Showa Tenno on September 27, 1945. During the meeting, MacArthur did not question the emperor's responsibility for the war, treating him as sovereign. Thus was how the GHQ itself firmly established its policy for governing post-war Japan: by utilizing the authority and power of the emperor. This decision led to the declaration of a "human emperor" by Showa Tenno on January 1, 1946 (ibid.: 67–9, 81–3).

The second move among conservative Japanese elites came from some members of the first group headed by the members of the royal families directly related to the Showa Tenno, like Naruhiko Higashikuninomiya and Takahito Mikasanomiya. Separating themselves from other members of the "Emperor's court," they supported the idea that Showa Tenno should abdicate after taking responsibility for Japan's role in the Second World War. This kind of opinion was even disclosed during the meeting of the Privy Council of the Emperor in February 1946. Naturally, the GHQ was very sensitive to this move among some Royal family members because by that time, GHQ had firmly established its policy to utilize the Emperor system for the stabilization of its occupation policy. Thus, the GHQ quickly responded to this move. On March 6, 1946, Brigadier General Bonner F. Fellers, MacArthur's military secretary, candidly told Mitsumasa Yoneuchi, an important member of the Privy Council of the Emperor thusly: Hideki Tojo, former Prime Minister, was to take full responsibility for the war (against the United States); and that then Showa Tenno was to be completely freed from any imputation of war crimes (ibid.: 92–4).

Hence, there was a dilemma. Yoshida explains that the Emperor system is better understood as a political system that could only function in spreading among the Japanese populace the image of the Emperor as a non-political or trans-political figure. For instance, were the Emperor himself to denounce some particular persons in public on any account, the image of the Emperor as this "politically neutral" figure is certain to be jeopardized. Here lies the reason why the GHQ, the International Prosecution Section (IPS), and the Japanese political elites had to maneuver or consider some means secretly to relieve Showa Tenno from the pressure of taking responsibility for the war (ibid.: 97–8).

According to Yoshida, "Showa Tenno no Dokuhaku-roku" was the one that was prepared exactly for such a crucial political motive and intention. In this document, the point is stressed why Showa Tenno did not use his veto power when Japan declared war against the United States. The Emperor emphasized the traditional custom of following and standing by any decisions of the cabinet and he feared that to exercise his veto power in contravention of tradition at that point might bring about a military coup d'état. In this light, "Showa Tenno no Dokuhaku-roku" is therefore the document that absolves the Emperor of responsibility for the war. It is also noteworthy that this document merely concerns the Emperor's responsibility for the war against the United States and does not include or address the question of his responsibility for the war against Asia (ibid.: 97–8, 145).

On the other hand, Takashi Fujitani discussed the newly discovered documents of the US War Department in 2000. This is the "Memorandum on Policy towards Japan" written by Edwin P. Reischauer in September 1942. In this memorandum, Reischauer proposed to use the Emperor as "the best possible puppet" or the tool for post-war rule. What Reischauer meant as "the puppet Emperor" is nothing but the Emperor as the national symbol enacted under GHQ after the war. Here, Fujitani emphasizes that Reischauer conceived "the puppet Emperor" based on American racism against Asians and paid keen attention to the fact that Reischauer discussed the issue of the Emperor by linking it to the problem of how to deal with Japanese Americans in US combat units. Reischauer proposed that the inclusion of Japanese Americans into the US military would be "the best possible proof that this is not a racial war to preserve white supremacy in Asia, but a war to establish a better world order for all, regardless of race ..." (Reischauer 2000). For Fujitani, this statement means that Reischauer proposed to use both of the Emperor system and the Japanese Americans as tools in US post-war strategy based on its national consciousness generally shared by white elites (Fujitani 2000: 137–46).

After more than 60 years since the Second World War, it seems that the Emperor system as a national symbol has deeply taken root in Japanese society. However, the success of the post-war Emperor system cannot be only attributable to the US occupation policy. As Yoshida explains, the Emperor is better understood among the Japanese populace as a non-political or trans-political figure. It is also true that, as Takashi Fujitani argues, one of the paradoxes of the modern Japanese Emperor system is that it lies embedded in the vicinity of violence and death despite the fact that the Emperor has otherwise worked as the very symbol for peace and prosperity (Fujitani 2003: 276). The origin of this paradox can be historically traced back to the distinctive nature of the formation or establishment of the Japanese Emperor system that Yoshihiko Amino, one of the most provocative Japanese historians specializing in its medieval history, brilliantly discusses (Amino 1974 [2001]; Amino 1978 [1996]; Amino 1986 [1993]).[2]

Amino poses his major question to Japanese history. Why has the Emperor system lasted for so long in Japan beyond various time periods and despite the various and intermittent criticisms leveled against it as an institution? Looking at Japanese history from the perspective of the present, Amino argues that the 14th century constitutes the most important crossroads throughout the entire span of Japanese history from the ancient and medieval to the modern and contemporary periods. The external crisis of Mongolian invasion precipitated the internal crisis in Japan and had the effect of strengthening the centralized ruling system. It was in the middle of the 14th century that Godaigo Tenno (Emperor) crucially accomplished this purpose. He organized the *hinin* or "outcasts" as his military guard and used the prayers or rituals of Tantric Buddhism to neutralize the independent warriors near Kyoto as well as Kamakura Bakufu (Shogunate) who held political power, and thus consolidated various warriors in the east of Japan within the sphere of his influence (Amino 1986 [1993]: 226–7, 232, 237).

The reign of Godaigo Tenno lasted for only three years. However, in the nature of the Emperor system that Godaigo Tenno established in Kyoto, Amino locates the origin of the modern Emperor system that was subsequently reorganized during the Meiji era (1868) and essentially lasted to the present. More concretely, Amino implies that the present Emperor system has survived up till now with its hidden or dark side of a historical relationship with the *hinin* or "outcasts," and now with the *buraku* or outcast community (ibid.: 246). For Amino, the Emperor system has served as a kind of surrogate religion in Japan to control or give a measure of comfort to the common populace, taking the risk of dragging along with itself its dark side of *hinin* complicity and the deep involvement with Tantric Buddhism as its twin necessary evils. If so, what is most important for Japanese is to question the meaning of the long-lasting Emperor system that has been embedded in the deep structure of Japanese mentality in post-war Japan.

Concluding Remarks

The symbolization of the Japanese Emperor in the post-war period was materialized through the interwoven relationships between the American administrators and the conservative Japanese elite factions. The ambiguous status of the Emperor in the post-war Japanese Constitution brought out the dual ambiguities of the Japanese responsibility for the Second World War, particularly the Asian-Pacific War against the United States and also the war against East Asian and Southeast Asian countries. In multiple historical contexts we have laid out so far, we might regard the symbolization of the Japanese Emperor as something constituted under US occupation policy to serve certain administrative purposes, in much the same way as the mystification of Jose Rizal was accomplished by the US colonial state for Philippines's own earlier pacification and post-war conjuncture. Both of them, the symbolic emperor and the mystic Rizal, would come to occupy politically pivotal positions in the popular mind and memory of the two countries respectively. But it seems equally true that there are some differences in their external implications. While the American image of Jose Rizal as national hero functioned to maintain the Philippines as America's colony, the symbolization of the Japanese Emperor remained as the principle of ambiguity in Japanese attitudes toward the question of their responsibility for the Second World War or the Asia-Pacific War. It would be also important to point out that while the Japanese have accepted the symbolic emperor after the Second World War, Jose Rizal might have served as a national martyr among Filipinos during the Philippine Revolution and the Philippine-American War beyond its American image that should have functioned as the basis for the Filipinos' resistance against American colonial rule.

For the Japanese, the Second World War holds two primary meanings: the first concerns the imperial war against the United States, while the second concerns the colonially aggressive or invasive wars against Asia. The symbolization of the Japanese

Emperor under the GHQ reflects the American policy of saving Showa Tenno from his responsibility of using the institution which he stood for as the bedrock for the stabilization of Japanese society under US administration after the war. Paradoxically, however, this policy had the unfortunate effect of depriving the Japanese government or its citizens of the chance to squarely confront the grim Asian realities of the Asia-Pacific War and their responsibility for them. This post-war situation in the country certainly differs from that of Germany whose Nazism was immediately aborted, thus clearly showing the international crime that the Holocaust represented. Why do the Japanese still face some formidable barriers in our relations with the citizens of our neighboring countries in Asia? Why do other Asian countries still regard the Japanese with suspicious eyes? We might find the roots of this problem beyond a mere focus on the US occupation policy of 1945–1952.

After this comparative discussion of the strategic recasting of national symbols in the Philippines and Japan under the US' Shadow, we have reached the inescapable conclusion that to grasp the effective and political nature of national symbols in particular societies, it is imperative that we look into the interrelationship between such national symbols and the communities they represent, and more importantly, at how these national symbols are indigenously worshipped or regarded by the populace. Only in undertaking this kind of historical research on national symbols are we able to begin to disclose, critically, their genuine natures in particular societies like the Philippines or Japan beyond the US' Shadow.

Notes

1. For an illuminating anthology on this topic, see Shaw and Francia (2002).
2. For an introductory review of Yoshihiko Amino's works in English, see Johnson (1996).

chapter 7

Memory and Mourning: Six Decades after the Two Wars

Satoshi Nakano

Introduction

Reynaldo Ileto's *Pasyon and Revolution* sets off on its soul searching journey of the Philippine history with a vivid account of the Lapiang Malaya's "uprising," which is today referred to more often as a massacre, on Sunday, May 21, 1967 (Ileto 1979: 1–3). The clash between the police forces and the Lapiang Malaya members broke out at dawn on Taft Avenue in Pasay City, killing one constabulary soldier and at least 33 Lapiang Malaya members, who were armed only with *bolos* and *anting-anting*.[1] They were led by the 86-year-old "*supremo*" Valentine de los Santos, a charismatic leader and a perennial presidential candidate in 1957, who was diagnosed as schizophrenic and sent to the National Mental Hospital where he was allegedly mauled and beaten to death, while he was officially pronounced to have died of pneumonia in the middle of June (Sturtevant 1969: 256–9).

It was a few months after this incident that Reynaldo Ileto left for the United States to take a graduate course in the Southeast Asian Studies program at Cornell University. There, by the end of 1973, he completed his PhD thesis, which was to be published as *Pasyon and Revolution* in 1979. In his preface to the long-awaited Japanese version (*Kirisuto Junanshi to Kakumei*) published in 2005, Ileto recalled that this groundbreaking work was a reflection of a number of things he found *new to him* during these turbulent years of anti-war, anti-imperialist and anti-establishment movements he himself was involved in both in the United States and the Philippines. One of the *new* things he learned *then* was the history of the Philippine-American War, "America's first Vietnam" as anti-war Asian studies scholars in the United States then called it. Ileto says, however, that the war is "nearly completely forgotten" among the Filipino people while the memories of Japanese Occupation during the Second World War are still fresh and graphic among them (Ileto 2005b: xviii–xix).

In 2000, two decades after the publication of *Pasyon and Revolution*, Reynaldo Ileto tackled the question of remembering and forgetting the two "colonial wars" in another conference paper he presented in Tokyo, in which he argued that the forgetting of the one event (i.e., the Philippine-American War) and the remembering of the other (i.e., the Japanese Occupation) are facilitated by the following factors: (1) the purging of aging memories (of the Philippine-American War) by fresh and intense experiences (of the Japanese Occupation years); and (2) politicizing the past by the colonial states (i.e., the US and the Philippine government) with meta-narratives emphasizing the difference of the two wars. Ileto concluded his discussion by foreseeing that "more exhaustive micro studies and the deconstruction of historical meta-narratives" will show the two wars really are "the same bananas" (Ileto 2001: 118). The word was borrowed from what Pedro Calosa, leader of the Tayug Colorum Uprising in 1931, uttered in 1966 during the interview conducted by David Sturtevant and F. Sionil Jose, an American scholar and a Filipino writer. Calosa was soon killed by an unknown murderer in 1967, the same year the Lapiang Malaya movement was destroyed by the government (Sturtevant 1976: 269–76). The content of Calosa's interview would later intrigue Reynaldo Ileto and one more scholar, Vicente Rafael, whose arguments will be discussed later in this chapter.

The chronology of these events tempts one to give much thought to the life of war memories or how memories of war would live, die, resurrect and be haunting in the course of time in either collective, individual, or intellectual ways. Particularly interesting is the significance of the "six decades after." *We* (*Japanese, Filipinos and Americans*) all passed through the six decades after the end of the Second World War in 2005, while 1967, the year of Lapiang Malaya massacre, could also be the six decades after the end of the Philippine-American War if 1907, the year of Macario Sakay's execution and the inauguration of the Philippine Assembly, could be chosen as the truly final year of the war instead of 1902, the year Theodore Roosevelt declared the "pacification" on July 4 though the war in fact was far from over. Some might say, of course, the war's end should be 1912, the year Felipe Salvador was executed. This would make 1972 the year of martial law declaration "six decades after." Whatever the case may be, the Philippine-American War did not have a clear-cut end date but was only gradually winding down during the decade between 1902 and 1912, so the "six decades after" may be placed somewhere in the decade between 1962 and 1972.

This chapter, however, will choose 1967 as the year of "the six decades after," since there is another story to tell. From November 22 to December 30 that year, a major "bone-gathering" (*ikotsu syusyu*)[2] mission organized by the Kagoshima prefecture government visited the Philippines to recover remains of what they believed to be the Japanese war dead in the Philippines. The event embarrassed the Japanese national government while marking one of the emotional beginnings of the Japanese pilgrimage tours to the former battle sites in the Philippines, which reached its peak in the middle of the 1970s but continues to this date with a shrinking number. The Kagoshima mission brought more than 4,000 remains back to Japan and the memorial was erected in April 1968 on the Cape Hanase beach in Satsuma Peninsula, which is located at the southwest end of mainland Japan, where they built a spacious beautiful park named Hanase Bo'hi Ko'en (Hanase Philippine

View Park). Since then, they have had the annual memorial services at the park every March 27. I had an occasion to observe their 38th memorial service in 2004, one year before the 60th anniversary of the end of the Second World War, which turned out to be another occasion to think about the life and death of war memories.

Of course, these two instances of "six decades after" the wars cannot be "the same bananas." We, however, may find a number of clues to understand in what manner war memories have been functioning in each society by paralleling and cross-referencing these two cases. Focus will be on the issues of mourning, i.e., the people's reaction to a sense of great loss they suffered in the past. How have the issues of mourning been addressed in the course of 60 years *and beyond* in each society? Asking this question would provide a good venue to discuss and understand the different but interrelated attitudes of the three peoples (Filipinos, Japanese, and Americans) toward the past. Then, it may be useful to apply the psychoanalytical conception called work of mourning, which has been adapted to multiple disciplines in their discussion of the post-war and other post-violence memories.

Object-Loss, Mourning, and Melancholia

Sigmund Freud's monograph titled "Mourning and Melancholia," which was written in 1915 and published in 1917, stands as a classic about the human reaction to the loss of "a love-object," which can be not only a person but "some abstraction" such as "one's country, liberty, and ideal, and so on" (Freud 1953: 243). Freud initially thought he could distinguish between the two types of reactions to object-loss, i.e., "normal mourning" and "ill of melancholia," even though they are very much alike in their appearances with such similar symptoms as obsessive behaviors, inhibition, loss of interest, and so on. In case of "normal mourning," the mourners went through a psychological process Freud named "work of mourning," which is painful and full of inner struggle but is expected to end after a certain period of time, enabling them to move on. It is a normal process because the mourners understand what they lost and they are sooner or later expected to accept the fact that they lost it. On the other hand, Freud argued, those who are "ill of melancholia" continue to be stuck and cannot move on to the process of mourning, because the melancholic are neither aware of nor willing to know what they lost; even if they know, they would not acknowledge the significance the loss holds for them. In denial of loss, they often tend to identify themselves with the lost ones and recreate them within the egos of themselves (ibid.).

Object-loss has since been an important subject of clinical psychology, developmental and social psychology as well as an increasing number of various disciplines of social sciences and humanities (Eng and Kazanjian 2003). One of the most cited works adapting object-loss theory to social and political issues was Alexander and Margarete Mitscherlich's *Inability to Mourn*, published in West Germany in 1967 (Mitscherlich and Mitscherlich 1975), which argues that post-Second World War Germans have avoided confrontation with those years of their Nazi past, using the conception of manic defense to describe their inability of mourning. Their handling of object-loss theory has been criticized as rough and the accuracy of their statement about post-war Germans' manic defense has been questioned. Their argument, however, has since had a tremendous impact on German endeavors for "the overcoming of the past" which was considerably rewarded in gaining the trust of its neighboring countries (Rabinbach 1995: 313–28; Wielenga 2003: 551–72).

Recent scholarship on object-loss has paid attention to such aspects as persistence of mourning as well as indivisibility between mourning and melancholia. Freud himself recognized difficulty to distinguish between the two in his writings in response to the First World War, noticing the possibility of "endless mourning" (Clewell 2004: 43–67). Today's clinical psychology considers work of mourning not a one-way process to move on. Instead, it claims "people do not necessarily 'get over' major loss, but learn to live with it, with struggles to do so persisting far longer than previously thought" (Kasterbaum 2002: 592–7). Then, if the mourning is not to be finished in a certain period of time as initially expected by Freud, are there any differences between mourning and melancholia? In conjunction with this question, Freud already stated that "it is only because we know so well how to explain mourning that it does not seem pathological" (Freud 1953: 244). Then, melancholia will not seem pathological anymore if it is better explained. Eng and Kazanjian in their introduction to *Loss: The Politics of Mourning* (2003) argue that one can even appreciate the potential of melancholia, since it can take much more free-wheeling forms, in which "the past remains steadfastly alive in the present" with "an ongoing and open relationship with the past — bringing its ghost and specters, its flaring and fleeting images, into present," while in mourning, the past is clearly defined and declared resolved and dead (Eng and Kazanjian 2003: 3–4).

Claiming lives and destroying what was once taken for granted, wars would cause massive individual and collective object-loss experiences to people, especially of the defeated and the victimized. One important aspect of wars' object-loss experiences is that the mourners always need the help of "the others" in the broader sense of the term for their work of mourning. If they want recognition for their lost loved ones, they need society to recognize them in such forms as commemorations and memorials; if they want apologies and reparations, they need the victimizer to make atonement to them; and if they want to make reprisals, they need the enemy to attack. Such dependence on "the others" in the work of mourning could be another cause of prolonged mourning. A sense of satisfaction one may gain from the social recognition could easily be harmed by forgetting later; memories of victimization could easily collide or tangle up emotionally between the self and the others especially in case of wars, which after all were massive complicated experiences of killing one another.

Prolonged mourning certainly is the case of the Second World War, whose 50th anniversary in 1995 did not mark the end of remembering and mourning as had previously been expected. On the contrary, 1995 pulled the trigger for the flourishing of memory politics around the world as shown by the Holocaust controversies in Europe and the Middle East as well as *Rekishi Mondai* (History Issues) in North East Asia. In the Philippines, a civic group Memorare Manila 1945 started its quiet campaign against the forgetting of the battle for Manila in 1995 (Nakano 2003: 368–9). Iris Chang's *The Rape of Nanking* was published in 1997 (Chang 1997), bringing about a storm of controversy across the Pacific. Japanese Prime Minister Junichiro Koizumi revived the Yasukuni controversy by his series of visits to the shrine through his tenure (2001–2006). Then, 2005 came and went. *We* found memory politics to be still alive and going on in many parts of the world. In these cases, the people claim they cannot conclude their work of mourning satisfactorily unless their sense of loss is more properly recognized, addressed, and atoned by "the others."

This chapter will discuss how the Lapiang Malaya movement in 1967 can be understood as a melancholic popular reaction to the forgetting of the lost revolution and war, which was then diagnosed as pathological but does not seem pathological anymore with better understanding given by *Pasyon and Revolution* and the following works of the Philippine history. On the other hand, the Kagoshima bone-gathering mission in 1967 and other Japanese endeavors to memorialize *their* war dead in the Philippines certainly had aspects as a melancholic protest against post-war Japan's forgetting of *their* war dead. Their mourning work, however, soon turned out to be a case of successful and smooth mourning as far as Japanese mourners were concerned. This was made possible with the collaboration of Filipinos as *the helpful others*, while completion of mourning work has resulted in amnesia on the part of the Japanese, making another melancholic protest from the Philippines a possibility.

1967 Lapiang Malaya Movement

The significance of "six decades after" stems from the fact that it is difficult for any survivors of any wars to live long after this point in time except the extremely blessed ones. This makes "six decades after" more or less a pronouncement that the living memories are soon to be gone. It may, however, still stay around for several more years or even a decade, which would be the time for the last stand of the living memories. This is what *we* now live in the six decades after the Second World War and what *they* lived in the six decades after the Philippine-American War in 1967. Newspapers of those days carried obituaries of the last living veterans of the war, including Emilio Aguinaldo, President of the First Republic, and Douglas MacArthur, whose life was deeply tied with the Philippines since his first assignment in 1903; both of them died in 1964 at the age of 94 and 84, respectively.[3] The Lapiang Malaya's *supremo* Valentine de los Santos, who was 86 years old in 1967, and a few of the senior members of the Lapiang Malaya, belonged to the very last of the generations who could claim to have living memories of the lost revolution and war, whether or not they actually participated in them.

What little is known about the movement tells that this militant and patriotic sect with 40,000 members emerged during the late 1940s. De los Santos claimed he had the spiritual power to communicate with the deity as well as the living personalities of the dead Filipino heroes, especially with Jose Rizal. In 1957, he ran for the presidential elections but received only 21,674 or 0.4% of the total vote (Commission on Elections 1958: 207). Their patriotism increasingly became anti-foreign in the 1960s while the members were encouraged to practice *bolos*, wear uniforms imagined to be bulletproof, and carry *anting-anting*. In October 1966, the 1,000 *bolo*-equipped members attempted to interrupt the summit of the seven nations allied with the United States in the Vietnam War, which was proudly hosted by Ferdinand Marcos. The police dispersed them without violence. In early May of 1967, however, De los Santos called for the resignation of Marcos and declared the formation of the Lapiang Malaya government. The Philippine Constabulary and the police forces responded by placing a cordon around the Lapiang Malaya's headquarters in Pasay city. On Saturday May 20, *Manila Times* publisher Chino Roces and Pasay City Mayor Pablo Cuneta visited the headquarters to persuade De los Santos to lay down their arms but his "generals" refused, saying they were the "sons of Andres Bonifacio" and they "were not afraid of anything as the followers of Bonifacio were not while fighting against the Spanish oppressors" (Zapanta 1967: 13). On the dawn of Sunday May 21, the tense situation eventually led to the massacre by the heavily armed constabulary and police forces when the members allegedly attempted to break the cordon in order to proceed to Malacañang Palace seeking to meet Marcos to receive his resignation (Sturtevant 1976: 256–60).

One of the few contemporary scholastic accounts was written by David Sturtevant, a pioneer scholar on the Philippine popular movements and a rare sympathetic observer of the Lapiang Malaya,[4] who deplored "the apparent willingness on the part of prominent Filipinos to dismiss the incident as a relatively unimportant and largely inexplicable event" (ibid.: 260). Credit should go to Sturtevant for his argument that the incident had the same magnitude of significance as Pedro Calosa's Tayug Colorum uprising of 1931 and both movements show the persistence with the notions of independence, nationhood, and patriotism. Sturtevant stressed the evil of class division and indifference of the Filipino urban elite toward the peasant society while equally and rightly criticizing Americans' shared indifference as well as collaboration with the Filipino elite (ibid.: 58–60, 265).

In retrospect, however, even Sturtevant's pioneering work seems to share the contemporaries' pathological treatment of the movement in the narrative depicting the villagers rallying to De Los Santos as "messianic" and "millennial" waiting for the "Judgment Day" with a sense of "omnipotence." Within the thesis of dichotomy and see-saw between traditional supernaturalism and modern secularism in the Philippine popular movements, the Lapiang Malaya was categorized as a resurgence of traditional supernaturalism which was brought about by the failure of contemporary modern secularism in the 1950s marked by the defeat of the Huk rebellion and the death of the "commoner" president Ramon Magsaysay in 1957 (ibid.: 260–1). Even though Sturtevant used the term "revitalization movement" for the Lapiang Malaya, the argument seemed not to examine the possibility that the old war Filipinos fought against Americans might have any substantial connection to the character of the Philippine popular movements. Sharing more or less the same view, a US Embassy official casually noted the incident in a dispatch of their weekly summary reports to the State Department, discarding the movement as "traceable more to the ignorance and superstition of the misguided fanatics; and it serves as a sad reminder of the uneven political and cultural development in the Philippines."[5]

What Sturtevant seems to have missed while Reynaldo Ileto would later salvage from the obscurity of the inexplicable, is the popular movement's sustained devotion to the past as the lost-object, evidenced by such usage as the Lapiang Malaya's "triangular symbols, the colorful uniforms, the title of 'supremo' and even the very idea of a radical brotherhood" (Ileto 1979: 3) and *ating-ating*, showing their strong attachment to the tradition and cause of Katipunan of 1896. In this light, spiritual worlds of the popular movements which previously were understood as pathology of millennialism would not seem pathological anymore. The Lapiang Malaya turns out not to be the fanatics but the last revolt of the living memories, a protest against forgetting, and a reminder to the nation of the huge loss they suffered some 60 years before. The other post-Philippine-American War popular movements may be interpreted in this way as well.

In his 2000 paper, Reynaldo Ileto revealed an episode of forgetting in his own family history. His father, General Rafael Ileto, born in 1920, grew up as a typical America's boy without knowing that his father (Ileto's grandfather,

"Lolo Ysco") once got involved in the revolution and was watched by the US Army Intelligence as a "revolutionary spy," a fact Ileto discovered among the archives in the United States (in the Philippine Insurgent Records). Ileto inferred that Lolo Ysco probably had kept his silence since 1904 when he was recruited as a schoolteacher by the Americans. The implication of this episode is that for many post-war Filipinos, if forgetting was a necessary survival strategy to succeed in "the new era," then they had to forget "there ever was a war" (Ileto 2001: 103). Forgetting by choice in one generation was then to be inherited by total ignorance about the past in the next generation, resulting in collective amnesia at the level of a family as well as the whole society. Public education in English might have helped the replacement of revolutionary memories with American colonial discourse.

It is then only natural, Freud would say, that this magnitude of inhibition of mourning would set off a revolt as an angry expression of melancholic frustration over the mainstream society's inability to mourn. Such might have been the case of the Colorum uprisings, including the Tayug uprising led by Pedro Calosa in 1931 when the living memories could be still very fresh among many even 24 years after the war's end. Calosa himself claimed he knew Felipe Salvador personally in his boyhood. This does not necessarily mean that the factual history of the Philippine-American War was well shared among the participants of the movements. On the contrary, most of the younger participants might not have even the slightest idea of the war. They could still be the rebels of the memories because memories of the revolution and war could be built-in into the forms and idioms of the movements as in the case of the Lapiang Malaya movement, making the participants the guardians of memories even without knowing it. In this way, the Lapiang Malaya movement certainly deserves the name of the revolt of the living memories and was the last one. The revolt, carrying the Katipunan tradition with the same kind of melancholic emotion as the Tayug uprising and the Lapiang Malaya movement, would not appear on the Philippine political scene anymore. Though tradition and idioms of the revolution would still be remembered and even revived, the mode of protest would change as the old soldiers fade away from the scene.

1967 Kagoshima Bone-Gathering Mission to the Philippines

Turning our eyes to the Japanese bone-gathering mission from the Kagoshima prefecture in 1967 might certainly seem abrupt and even absurd. The mission and its aftermath, however, could be interestingly paralleled, compared, and contrasted with the revolts of the memories in the Philippines if we could choose the Colorum Tayug uprising in 1931 and the Japanese bone-gathering mission from Kagoshima as early instances of revolts of the memories in each case.

While there was without doubt a small minority of nationalist intellectuals who lamented the loss of such abstractions as pre-war Japanese heroic patriotism and masculine tradition, the prevailing feelings shared among the Japanese public in the mid-1960s was still one of pacifism and anti-militarism. Post-war Japanese heroes were the victims of wars (Orr 2001: 118). It was thus almost exclusively the war dead that the post-war Japanese mourned and that is why the Philippines could be so important for the Japanese mourners. With over half a million Japanese war dead there (518,000 according to one of the government sources) including civilians (Koseisho Shakai Engo Kyoku 1997: 118), which was the largest number among the Southeast Asian countries occupied by Japan during the Second World War, Japanese memorial practices such as the recovery of remains, pilgrimage tours, and erection of memorials have been more widely held in the Philippines than any other country outside Japan since the mid-1960s (Nakano 2003).

The Japanese mourners could not be called melancholic as defined by Freud, since they knew what they lost all too well. They could be, however, as emotional as melancholic especially in the early years of bone-gathering and pilgrimage tours, largely because they felt collective guilt for the delay of mourning, which left the remains of their war dead in foreign soil for such a long time while the majority of the Japanese were obsessed with economic recovery. Their feelings of guilt for the loved ones sometimes turned to rage against the Japanese national government, which in their eyes, seemed neither sympathetic nor enthusiastic enough about carrying out the project of consoling the souls of the war dead. Here, we could find at least one thing the Japanese mourners of the Second World War dead share with the Filipino mourners of the lost revolution. They both had a sense of dissatisfaction, or even anger with the mainstream society's indifference to mourning.

In the mid-1960s, one of the most urgent issues for the Japanese mourners was to resume a government-sponsored bone-gathering mission which had officially concluded in 1958 after having sent one mission to each former battle site country. The Philippines was the last and largest site, in which the mission gathered and brought back 2,561 remains to Japan (ibid.: 349). The Japanese mourners, however, were far from satisfied. Air travel became rapidly popular after the government liberalized foreign travel in 1964. The era of high growth and the increasing income soon made foreign travel a craze among the Japanese. Under these circumstances, it was only natural for the Japanese mourners to think about their own travel for bone-gathering and pilgrimage.

In 1965, Nippon Izoku Kai (Japan War Bereaved Association, hereinafter JWBA), which then was one of the most powerful pressure groups and political bases to the governing Jiminto (Liberal Democratic Party), incorporated into its annual petition to the Japanese government the following: (1) resuming the recovery of war dead remains; (2) erecting memorials; (3) maintenance of cemeteries; and (4) providing financial and other assistance to the bereaved families' pilgrimage tours to the former battle sites and cemeteries. They also demanded the bone-gathering missions to be composed not only of government officials but private organizations and bereaved family volunteers (ibid.: 354). All of these demands were to be met within a few years. The 1967 Kagoshima mission, however, was organized in impatience with the indecision of the national government.

The mission was originated in the civic group organized in 1966 named "Hito Senbotsu Ikotsu Shushu Narabini Ireihi Konryu Kisei Kai (Association for the Promotion of the Bone Gathering of the War Dead in the Philippines as well as Erecting Memorial)." The association was composed of bereaved families and the veteran *seikansha* (survivors) in Kagoshima and Kumamoto prefectures and raised 15,523,217 JPY (43,120 USD), of which about 5.2 million JPY was subsidized by the local authorities of Kagoshima and Kumamoto prefectures. Kagoshima University, though it was a national university, belonged to the national government, and also collaborated with the project by offering its Faculty of Fisheries' training ship Keiten-maru and its crew to take the mission to and from the Philippines (Hito Senbotsu Ikotsu Shushu Narabini Ireihi Konryu Kisei Kai 1968). The Keiten-maru left the Kagoshima seaport on November 22, 1967 and came back on December 30 with 4,049 remains (2,495 from Leyte; 1,554 from Luzon) as well as several abandoned cannons, machine guns and 38 infantry rifles. As early as April the next year, the association erected the memorial on the site donated by Kaimon municipality government on the Cape Hanase beach, where on Saturday April 20, they held the unveiling of the memorial and the first memorial service with more than 4,000 attendees, in which the collected remains were dedicated.[6]

Why Kagoshima? In terms of the estimated number of the war dead in the Philippines, the Kagoshima prefecture (ca. 12,000)[7] does not outnumber other prefectures very much. No less important motive may have been attracting domestic tourists. The number of domestic visitors from outside Kagoshima to the Kaimon municipality's neighboring city of Ibusuki, known for its subtropical-like landscape and hot springs, jumped from 990,000 in 1965 to 1,550,000 in 1968 (Suzuki 1973: 23–32). Erecting the memorial on the Cape Hanase beach was thus an integral part of the tourism development projects for the local community to attract bereaved families and war survivors as tourists.[8] The lyrics of the *Kaimon Ondo* (Kaimon Dance Song) praises not only *Satsuma-Fuji* (Mount Kaimon) and *Somen Nagashi* (Flowing Somen Noodle), but Hanase Philippine View Park as follows:

> From the Cape Hanase, the Boom of the Temple Bell
> Echoes Around with a Hope that it will be heard by the Heroic Spirits
> Among Many Local Specialties of Kaimon
> Take Home Our Humane Hearts that Reach as far as to the Faraway Souls[40]
>
> (Kaimon-cho Kyoudo-shi Hensan Iinkai 1994: 739–41)

It was absolutely necessary for the bone-gathering mission to dedicate all the collected remains to the basement of the memorial, since the bodily remains, with which the souls of their loved ones were imagined to stay, were thought to be the key to attract bereaved families and the surviving veterans to visit the memorial. This, however, was a deviation from the national government's guidelines that required all the collected remains to be deposited at the Ministry of Health and Welfare (hereinafter MHW). The use of the national university's ship and bringing back the abandoned arms were equally problematic for the MHW, which was even forced to dispatch seven officials to join the Kagoshima mission in Manila to make it look like a national mission. In February 1968, shortly after the Kagoshima mission returned to Japan, the MHW issued an administrative guideline titled "About the Gathering Bones of the War Dead," stating they "will not allow any plans aimed at bone-gathering by the local authorities, private organizations, and so on in order to prevent troubles in the local communities as well as in respect for the true purpose of bone gathering." This document speaks for itself that the Kagoshima mission was a small "revolt" of the memories, carried out in defiance of the national government policy (Koseisho Shakai Engo Kyoku 1997: 513).

Logic of Bone-Gathering, Pilgrimage, and Viewing the Philippines

The *Minami Nippon Shimbun's* (*The South Japan Times'*) coverage of the mission indicates that the mission was surrounded by ample support and emotional expectation of the local communities. It was a big event. What is conspicuous here is the Japanese mourners' obsessive desire to connect with the souls of their loved ones in their own peculiar ways, i.e., gathering bones and/or visiting the place their loved ones died. Behind this obsession is the notion that their loved ones' souls are not free but bound to the bodily remains staying around the places they died. This makes it necessary for the mourners physically be as close as possible to the places where their loved ones had died. There, they may offer burning sticks of incense in front of the battle sites and memorials, call out the names of the dead, and weep aloud.

For example, a member of the Kagoshima mission carried the audio tape player he was asked, by the 84-year-old bereaved mother who could not join the mission, to play at the battle site.

> A mission's member raised his head and pushed the button ... the tape started and we heard the voice of a bereaved mother. 'Kesakichi, it was so unfortunate that you could not come back. I am now 84 years old. I will be going to your place very soon. Now please come back with the bone gathering mission' (Mrs. Asa Maeno of Miyanokura, Satsuma County).[9]

Not only the bereaved but also the veteran survivors or *senyu* (comrades) of the war dead joined the mission. The correspondent of the *South Japan Times* described the scenes:

> "Hey! Now I'm here to take you home! Let's go back together!" — Frenzy scream of the survivors echoed through the beach of Lingayen, the cemeteries of Clark Field, and the mountains of Baguio, as big drops of tears wet their faces.[10]

Even the *Manila Times* covered a half-page graphic story of a young woman in the mission, Atsuko Otsuka, who visited the Wawa Dam in Montalban, Rizal, where her father had been killed during the war. A free one-day trip tour to the Wawa Dam especially for Otsuka was offered by the general manager of the tourist company working for the Kagoshima Mission, who learned of her desire to visit the place which was not in the mission's itinerary.

> Tuesday afternoon, with clouds shrouding the Montalban mountains, Miss Otsuka bowed in prayer, dug the earth and burned letters she carried from her mother and brothers all addressed to her father.
>
> She improvised an alter and placed wooden markers and offered flowers she had hastily bought in front of a grocery store in Ermita before the trip. Then she cried.
>
> After a few minutes, she got up and strew more flowers all over the place and the river nearby.
>
> As she rode back to Manila, she kept on saying, 'I talked with my father!'[11]

Hanase Philippine View Park, where the collected remains were dedicated, is located at the scenic Cape Hanase beach facing the East China Sea at the base of Mount Kaimon, the 924-meter high conical-shaped volcano, which may remind anyone who is familiar with it of the Mount Mayon in Bicol. In spite of the name given to the park, it is of course impossible to get a view of the Philippine Islands from there. It is considered, however, that one can spiritually see the islands beyond the East China Sea from the park in the southern end of Satsuma Peninsula in Kyushu, i.e., the southwest end of mainland Japan. Then, one may connect oneself with the *ei'rei* (heroic spirits) of his or her loved ones, who are supposed to be unable to leave the faraway islands. The park's central memorial named *Shisei no Tobira* (the Doors to the Life and Death) was produced by a prominent local sculptor and the professor of Art at Kagoshima University, Shinya Nakamura, who was later to be commissioned to produce all the monuments in the park. The epigraph of the central memorial reads:

If it were permitted
We would have erected a memorial of grievance in the Philippines
Faraway islands where you, the unreturned spirits, still remain
And have prayed for you groveling at the monument
With no other choice we erect this memorial
At the southernmost land of Japanese Islands
Thinking about you and praying together
May your souls rest in peace
(Hito Senbotsu Ikotsu Shushu Narabini Ireihi Konryu Kisei Kai 1968: 2)

These scenes and the words of mourning may represent a melancholic aspect of the Japanese mourners, since in these cases, the lost objects are not dead in the mourners' minds but asking the mourners' help to free them and take them back home. The bereaved families talking to the dead and the melancholic survivors screaming in a mad frenzy might be diagnosed by psychiatrists as pathological as De los Santos and Pedro Calosa unless they know it is a socially accepted way of mourning in Japan, in which the living addresses the misfortune and discontent of the dead by speaking aloud to them.

"All the Same Bananas" or Not

The ways of connecting to the past is an interesting point of comparison between the narratives found in the Philippine popular movements of the early to mid-20th century and the Japanese ways of mourning for the souls of the Second World War. Like Atsuko Otsuka who said she talked with her father, Valentine de los Santos and Pedro Calosa both claimed they were communicating with the living personalities of the dead Filipino heroes. Particularly interesting is the interview Sturtevant conducted with Pedro Calosa in 1966, which was mentioned at the beginning of this chapter. It was too weird for the American scholar to use it as a factually reliable account in his own book, so Sturtevant put it in appendix instead. The interview, however, was so intriguing that Reynaldo Ileto quotes Calosa's account on his encounter with Felipe Salvador's "personality" in the next cell of the prison that he was jailed in Honolulu, Hawai'i, where he was an immigrant worker and the labor activist, as a vivid example of the *pasyon*'s reenactment in the Philippine life.

> It was true, he was captured by the Constabulary and he was hanged. But he did not die. His personality lived on and took different forms. I knew him in Honolulu. In Hawaii he was called Felipe Santiago. When I was in prison he was a crazy man in the next cell. I talked with him and he told me many things. He was Felipe Salvador. You understand! (Ileto 1979: 315–6; Sturtevant 1976: 272).

Vicente Rafael also examines the strange conversation between Sturtevant and Calosa in the opening pages of *Contracting Colonialism* published in 1988. What intrigued Rafael is that Calosa talked not only about his having been haunted by the dead Salvador, Bonifacio, and Rizal, but also about his having haunted the living Manuel Quezon, Aurora Quezon, and the American Secretary of War. To explain the spiritual world according to Calosa, Rafael presented a conception of "remembering-as-haunting," as one way of appropriation or "localizing what is outside of one" (Rafael 1988: 8–12).

Contrary to the Japanese souls of the war dead, these "personalities" seem to be bound neither to the bodily remains nor to any particular place, time, or anything. There even was no distinction between the dead and the living as shown in the episode where Calosa haunted Manuel Quezon and others. Here, the contrast between Japanese and Filipino ways to encounter the dead or lost-objects seem obvious. Japanese souls have some serious problems that make them unable to fly back to Japan, waiting for the rescue, while the Japanese mourners play the roles of desperate rescuers. Filipino souls, on the other hand, seem almost free-wheeling, having no problem flying to Honolulu, and daringly ignoring the border between the living and the dead. Does this show freedom of the Filipino souls and the straitjacketed personality of the Japanese even after their deaths? There could be other explanations.

Vicente Rafael argues that for Pedro Calosa, "the past appears metonymically as a series of names, dates, and events interspersed by moments of visiting and being visited by the spirits of historical personages" (ibid.: 11). The recurring experiences of being subdued by overwhelming powers in the numerous pasts *and the present* may have made the distinction among many pasts and present a nebulous one. In other words, the Filipino experiences of loss and defeat in the past *and the present* may have put all the different past events and even the present ones on the same plane, making not only the past and present Filipino heroes and victims to be imagined, but also those who imagine the encounters "all the same bananas." One should be reminded that the word was uttered by Calosa in 1966 when he was asked by Sturtevant if "the present movements" are like "the old ones like Colorums of your days, the Santa Iglesia of Felipe Salvador, and the Guardia de Honor" (Sturtevant 1976: 276). Such chemistry of interrelationship between the living and the dead or the imagining and the imagined as recorded by Sturtevant and reinterpreted by Ileto and Rafael may best exemplify Eng's and Kazanjian's conception of melancholia as "an ongoing and open relationship with the past" (Eng and Kazanjian 2003: 4).

On the contrary, the distinction between the roles played by the Japanese living mourners and the war dead is clear and not reversible. This indicates that Japanese war dead mourning, despite its melancholic appearance, in fact, allows the mourners to enter the work of mourning in the most classical definition given by Freud, which would eventually enable them to finish and conclude mourning and move on. The remarkable number of both the bone-gathering missions and the pilgrimage tours going to the Philippines since the 1960s shows how strong and long-lasting the desire was of the living, for the work of mourning, as well as how satisfactorily their aspiration was met. What made this possible is the transformation of post-war Philippine-Japan relations from one of hatred to reconciliation, which itself was the result of an interplay between the improvement of political and economic relations and the emergence of amity between the two peoples greatly enhanced by grassroots exchanges through war dead memorialization. Attention should be paid, however, to the fact that the Japanese mourners' satisfaction cannot be secured without quiet comfort given to them by their Filipino counterparts, who themselves are the living victims as well as the mourners of over one million dead victims of the Japanese aggression, oppression, and atrocities.[12]

The Filipinos' surprising generosity toward the pilgrimage tourists from Japan may largely be explained by an anthropological conception of reciprocity, which seems to have existed between the comfort given by the Filipinos and the gratitude shown by the Japanese in various ways, from the donation to the local communities to the massive ODA by the Japanese government. This relationship works, however, only as long as both parties share the understanding of the past events, for which Japanese mourners are expected to have feelings of apologies toward the Filipinos as victims of the Japanese aggression. It indeed was the case of the Japanese mourners visiting the Philippines especially in the early years. The same sense of regret and the gratitude toward the Filipino counterparts could be found in *Minami Nippon Shimbun*'s coverage of the 1967 Kagoshima mission as well as the mission's published report. Then, the first memorial service in April 1968 invited "Amante Lumiyas who helped bone-gathering."[13] In this way, Japanese mourners in their bone-gathering and pilgrimage tours were strongly aware of the Filipinos as "the others" whose help was indispensable for their work of mourning especially in their early years.

2004: The 38th Memorial Service

At noon on March 27, 2004, one year before the 60th anniversary of the end of the Second World War, I was holding a handycam among a crowd of people gathered at the Hanase Philippine View Park to attend the annual memorial service honoring "the Philippine Islands War Dead." There was a large attendance at the service, which was in formality sponsored by the Hito

Senbotsusha Irei Kensho Kai (Philippine Islands War Dead Memorial and Commemorative Association) but in fact managed by the municipal government of Kaimon.[14] The memorial service I attended was the 38th since its first in 1968. Although little is known nationwide, the Hanase Park's memorial service is one of the very few remaining annual services to honor the Japanese war dead in the Philippines. It definitely has been the largest one in terms of the size of attendance.

The memorial service was conducted by three priests from the nearby Hirasaki Shrine in a pure or even neo-essentialist Shinto religious rite style, which started with the purification and the mystic prayer to invite the heroic spirits of the war dead from *somewhere in heaven* all the way down to Hanase Park. After the heroic sprits were imagined to have descended to the memorial site, the priests left. Then traditional chant of a memorial poem was performed by five senior gentlemen accompanied by a *Shakuhachi* (bamboo flute), followed by women in white dresses singing in chorus a melancholic song titled *Hito Senbotsusha ni Sasageru Uta* (the Song dedicated to the Philippine Islands War Dead Memorial). Self Defense Forces (SDF) senior officers showed up and the Ground SDF military brass band played such military memorial tunes as *Umi Yukaba* (*If You Go to the Sea*). The climax of the whole program came when the Maritime SDF's P3C patrol aircraft flew over the park for three times, which the official program of the memorial service referred to as the *Kuchu Sampai* (Offering Prayers from the Air).[15]

The memorial service was honorably concluded in this way. What I felt there, however, was an atmosphere that could not hide the *hollowing out* of the memorialization among the attendants. What seemed absent among the crowd was the longing to connect with the souls stuck in the faraway islands, which should have constituted the basic concept of the memorial service. To some extent, it may be because there actually were not many bereaved families at the service (the majority were obviously the people of Kaimon neighborhood mobilized by the municipal government). It could be that years of satisfactory work of mourning in form of bone-gathering missions, pilgrimage tours, and annual services like this have taken that longing away from the hearts of Japanese mourners.

Many of the memorials erected by the Japanese outside of Japan during the 1960s and 1970s are reported to have fallen into a state of dilapidation.[16] This may have been as much the result of the downward trend in pilgrimage tours with the aging of the bereaved families and survivors, as a sign of completion of mourning work among them. The *ei'rei* or heroic spirits who once disturbed the mourners' minds so much by their cry for help from faraway islands, may finally have returned and peacefully settled in the mourners' inner selves. Thus, the Japanese mourners actually do not have to view the Philippines as a place quite as relevant for their mourning anymore. Instead, they do wave at the P3C patrol aircraft cheerfully, without being aware of or asking help of "the others."

Physical as well as rhetorical absence of the Philippines and the Filipinos in the Hanase memorial service was but another sign of amnesia in the Japanese's public memories of the war in the Philippines. This runs contrary to the fact that "History Issues" cause controversy between Japan and its Northeast Asian neighbors as they serve as a constant reminder of their contentious past.[17] If the gentle silence of the Filipino people has come from their desire to keep reciprocity and amity with the Japanese because Japan is a major donor country, it almost comes to the same as has been found in Philippine-US relations, in which Filipino former revolutionaries as the defeated in war and colonial submission had no other choice but to suppress their memories to survive and succeed in "the new era." Then, it will not be surprising at all if *we* face more revolts of the memories against amnesia in some way or another in the near future.

Conclusion

This chapter has tried to apply psychological conceptions of mourning and melancholia to the understandings of: (1) the

Philippine popular movements in the early to the mid-20th century as a revolt of the memories; and (2) the Japanese mode of memorialization of the war dead in the Philippines as shown in the 1967 Kagoshima mission for bone-gathering and the present form of mourning found in the Hanase memorial service in 2004. What is ironic is that in case of the Philippine-American War, whose memories were suppressed and forgotten, the dead heroes were still literally alive in the melancholic imagination of De los Santos and Pedro Calosa even six decades after the war's end, while completion of the Japanese mourning seems to have made the war dead really dead.

Equally important is the fact that the Lapiang Malaya's tragic end as well as the Pedro Calosa's final year interview stirred the imagination of Reynaldo Ileto and the following generation of scholars in their endeavors to reconstruct and recreate history in a totally different light from the previous scholarship. In this sense, 1967 marked as much the beginning of the next life of the war memory as the end of its first. Four decades have passed since 1967, and we find the historians livelily debating the Philippine-American War, as if they were fighting another memory war, which itself can be a very interesting subject of the Philippines-US history (Nagano 2004: 357–85).

Does this history of one war memory tell anything to another, which is going to be experienced the next four decades after the 60th anniversary in 2005? My answer is affirmative. The collaboration between Japanese desire to memorialize their own war dead and the Filipino accommodation to them may have prompted mutual amity between the two countries, while completion of Japanese work of mourning prompted the forgetting of the once so well remembered war in Japan, which may unsettle the bases of mutual understanding between the two countries. If Sturtevant's interpretations of Calosa and the Lapiang Malaya lack attention to the gravity of loss the Filipinos suffered in the lost revolution and war, he himself can be called a casualty of American amnesia. This episode can serve as caution to the Japanese scholars who are now vulnerable to the same failure.

How does one avoid the forgetting then? We probably can learn something from Pedro Calosa about function and utility of melancholic experiences of being haunted and haunting, dead or alive. We do not need a supernatural power today to haunt and be haunted, thanks to the Internet, as the verbal battles between Chinese, Korean, and Japanese nationalist bloggers show the 21st century's cyber forms of haunting games. I personally believe, however, it is still more desirable to haunt and be haunted "in person." Naoko Jin, a Japanese woman born in 1978, leads the "Bridge for Peace" project with Japanese volunteers of her generation, making video messages of both the Japanese war veterans and Filipino victims of Japanese aggression to be exchanged between the two sides (thus making them haunt each other!) in hope of seeking better mutual understanding and reconciliation. The single organizer of this conscientious project recalls she was motivated to engage in this project because of her own experience in February 2000 when she visited the Philippines as an undergraduate student, when she was emotionally confronted (or haunted, Calosa would say) by the victims who lost their loved ones by the hands of the Japanese during the war.[18] This episode tells, I think, that haunting nice people pays off. So I hope more "living personalities," dead or alive, will continue to haunt nice people of Japan, the United States, and the Philippines, to keep the venue for history as endless mourning alive and well.

Notes

1. More than 60, possibly 80, were killed and wounded according to the report of the investigation committee created by Marcos. "Casualty Toll Hits 60 in R.P. Battle: Report Blames Fanatics' Leaders," *Pacific Stars and Stripes*, May 24, 1967, p. 7.
2. "Ikotsu syusyu (pronounced as ee-ko-tsu Shoe-shoe)" can be translated into "recovery of the remains," while "bone-gathering" is a more direct translation which shows Japanese attachment to the bones of the loved ones. See Yamaori (2002).
3. "Aguinaldo, 94, Dies; Led Filipino Revolts," *New York Times*, February 6, 1964, p. 26; "Commander of Armies That Turned Back Japan Led a Brigade in World War I," *New York Times*, April 6, 1964, p. 26.

4. Originally, it was published as "Rizalistas" and reproduced in "Epilogue," in Sturtevant (1976), pp. 256–66).
5. US Embassy (Manila) to Dept. of State, "Joint Weeka #21," May 26, 1967. POL 2-1 PHIL: Central Policy Files, RG 59: Records of the US State Department, National Archives II, Washington, DC.
6. "Kyouri no Tsuchi ni Yasuraka ni [Rest in Peace at Home]," *Minami Nippon Shimbun*, April 21, 1968, p. 12.
7. The number is taken from the epitaph in the Hanase Philippine View Park.
8. Hanase Philippine View Park as a tourist development project was narrated in the following local history: see Kaimon-cho Kyoudo-shi Hensan I'inkai (1994), pp. 730–1.
9. "22 nenme no Taimen (3) [The Reunion after 22 Years (3)]," *Minami Nippon Shimbun*, December 26, 1967, p. 9.
10. "22 nenme no Taimen (6) [The Reunion after 22 Years (6)]," *Minami Nippon Shimbun*, December 29, 1967, p. 9.
11. "Japanese Girl Visits Father's Grave," *Manila Times*, December 8, 1967, p. B2-A.
12. For further discussion on this paragraph, see Nakano (2003).
13. "Kyouri no Tsuchi ni Yasuraka ni [Rest in Peace at Home]," *Minami Nippon Shimbun*, April 21, 1968, p. 12.
14. The municipality was merged with the more populous city of Ibusuki in January 2006.
15. Hito Senbotsusha Irei Kensho Kai [The Philippine Islands War Dead Memorial and Commemorative Association], "Dai 38 Kai Hito Senbotsusha Ireisai [Program of the 38th Memorial Service for the Philippine Islands War Dead]", March 27, 2004. The author published several video clips of the memorial service on YouTube including the following: "Hanase Annual Memorial 03/27/2004_01 Ringing the Bell," at <http://jp.youtube.com/watch?v=nG8w7V2ou5M>; "Hanase Annual Memorial 03/27/2004_03 Shinto Ritual (1)" at <http://jp.youtube.com/watch?v=JBnw4T0uT4o>; and "Hanase Annual Memorial 03/27/2004 _09 P3C Prayer & End," at <http://jp.youtube.com/watch?v=iKRLvVDNtwg> [accessed November 6, 2010]
16. "Kaigai Senchi no Ireihi Jittai wo Chosa: Hokai Sunzen no Hi mo [State of Overseas Battle Site Memorials are to be Investigated: Some of Them about to Collapse]," *Asahi Shimbun*, July 4, 2004, p. 15.
17. For further discussions on this paragraph, see Nakano (2006).
18. Naoko Jin, "Bridge for Peace: Objective," at <http://bridgeforpeace.jp/objective.html> [accessed November 6, 2010].

Part III:
Triangle Encounters — The Philippines, Japan and the USA

chapter 8

Baguio's Early 20th-Century Japanese Community: Culture, Society, and Work in an American "Hill Station" in the Philippines

Patricia O. Afable

Introduction

The origins and development of Japanese migrant communities in the Philippine Cordillera region were directly linked to the American project to create a mountain resort in the Spanish province of Benguet. Conceived while the Philippine-American war was still raging, this plan had as its models the colonial "hill stations" of South and Southeast Asia. In the last decades of the 19th century, the Spanish government had initiated a similar move. Thus, when the first official American exploratory mission arrived in 1900, they had precise information on the proposed location of a Spanish sanitarium at Baguio, some six kilometers south of the Benguet capital, La Trinidad and about 1,500 meters above sea level.[1]

Relatively uninhabited compared to the rice-growing settlements in the Trinidad valley, Baguio was the terminus on a trade route between the southern Cordillera and the Ilocos coast. The place name first appeared on an 1878 map by Manuel Scheidnagel, who was founding governor of the Benguet politico-military district in 1854. Most important for the new American government were the details in his and other Spanish surveys, not only of the salubrious climate, but also the rough estimates of the annual trade in gold from this isolated mountain outpost. The exploration of the region's mineral resources was an equally pressing colonial goal.

Within the first two decades of American rule, forging a region in the northern highlands involved setting up an administrative framework for the inhabitants, surveying and constructing highways into the mountains, and building a town at Baguio. From the beginnings of the city's creation, lowland Filipinos as well as Americans, Chinese, Japanese, and other migrants ventured there in search of gold, commerce, and wage work. Indigenous peoples from surrounding mountain areas arrived at the worksites, eager to participate in the new economy. As collaborators in the building of vehicular access into the mountains and an urban infrastructure for a summer capital, all these groups helped lay the foundation of Baguio as northern Luzon's economic and tourist capital.

The First Decades: Administering the Natives

The first American visitors found indigenous Ibaloy-speaking communities cultivating rice in irrigated fields and root crops in swiddens. For those in the environs of Baguio, a major component of their economy involved gold mining, whose products had been part of an active highland-lowland trade since pre-colonial times. In the second half of the 19th century, the gentle slopes of this high plateau became important as profits from the gold trade went into the acquisition of cattle by local people. The cattle industry was a sizable one: a 1908 statistic was 25,000 head of cattle for Benguet Province (US War Department 1909: 245). This declined as agriculture and city construction took up grazing land, and it was decimated in the Second World War.

Ibaloy-speakers shared the southern Cordillera region with Kankanaey, Kalanguya, and Karaw linguistic groups, and were classified by Spanish and American ethnology under the larger rubric of "Igorots." An early geographical description in the western coast for "mountain people," the term (as "Igorrotes" or "Ygolotes") was used in the historical records to refer to all the highland peoples of the northwest Cordillera, with the attached connotation of paganism and "savagery."[2] "Igorot" became the way local people identified themselves to outsiders, and the Japanese people and other outsiders in Baguio referred to them by this label.

The most familiar outsiders to Baguio people were from the Ilocos coast. In American ethnology, they were classed with other lowland Christian peoples as "Filipinos." Although most were traders, education in Spanish or the early American schools qualified many of them to fill the clerical levels of the American civil service in Baguio. Because of Ilocano dominance in public and commercial spheres, their language became the *lingua franca* of the many ethnic groups converged in Baguio. In the 1930s, Japanese children there spoke at least Ilocano in addition to Japanese, English, and their mothers' native languages.

The Philippine Commission's exploration of the Baguio-Benguet region in 1900 resulted in the early establishment of civil government there. Benguet Province, with Baguio as its capital, was formed in 1901. In 1908, the indigenous peoples of the northern highlands, organized into the Mountain Province, became the responsibility of the Department of the Interior's Bureau of Non-Christian Tribes. This ensured a separate status by which mountain people came under direct American rule. However, Baguio was separated from this organization and chartered as a city the following year.

The American Takeover of Baguio

As the American government proceeded to build the city center on the "Baguio Plain," they appropriated Ibaloy cattle and farming land in the best-watered higher zones of the plateau. It all happened overnight: considering the distance between Baguio and Manila — it called for two days' travel by boat, carriage, and horse — the decisiveness of the Americans was breathtaking. For local Ibaloys, it was all too familiar, for the seizure of rice lands for the Spanish capital at La Trinidad was still fresh in their minds. In the last years of the 19th century, the Spanish had sent the last members of Ibaloy resistance into exile for aiding Philippine revolutionary forces.

The American move was heralded by the erection of Constabulary headquarters and an Episcopalian chapel on the hill across from the Spanish-era municipal hall, next to the major cattle grazing grounds of what is today's Burnham Park. The census count of 1903, to which all local headmen were called to be enumerators, reinforced it; and the first sale of lots in the city center in 1906 clinched it. A young cattle-owner, Sioco Cariño, was made the first Presidente of Baguio, succeeding his father, Mateo, who had served in the Spanish period. Among other symbolic bows to the fledgling city's aborigines, community leaders were installed in a government Igorot Advisory Council, and the main streets leading away from the City Hall were given Ibaloy names. Subsequently, the cattle owners moved their herds out of the city limits into other parts of Benguet or to nearby provinces.[3]

By 1910, the American and European population of Baguio reflected the establishment of American civil authority. It consisted primarily of Constabulary officers, entrepreneurs, sawmill and mining technicians, and administrators from the central government, including doctors and their assistants. There were also a few industrial schoolteachers and Catholic and Episcopalian missionaries. Most Americans had been soldiers in the Philippine-American War who had stayed on to look for work after mustering out of the US Army. Dozens were prospecting for gold. Mining companies, all owned by Americans, began operations as early as 1906; however, most were small and did not become viable until the rise in the world price of gold in the 1930s.

Research Focus and Materials

In this essay, I will focus on the migrants from Japan and the community that they built in relation to this American enclave. My interest is in the work and employment patterns that they developed in the first decades of the 20th century. Construction, sawmill work, temperate-climate vegetable farming, merchandising, and contracting — these were the main areas in which Japanese arrivals responded to the social, cultural, and economic opportunities offered by Baguio's multicultural frontier. I will situate these specializations within local history and the distribution of environmental and geographical resources in the American regime.

United States archival documents and photographs and oral histories (Afable 2004: Chapter 1) contributed to this study. The background to the archival records lies in the intensive and self-conscious American government documentation of its infrastructure projects. These early reports, including photographs, projected the enthusiasm of its officials in the creation of their very own mountain retreat in a brand new colony.[4] The meat of the oral interviews consists of life stories; through particular examples, it becomes possible to locate persons and events in cultural space and historical time. In the interaction among narratives and textual and visual documents, the distinctiveness of Japanese work, as it was perceived in the wider community and fostered in Japanese homes, emerged as an important focus of Japanese-Filipino collective identity before the Second World War.

The first Japanese arrived in the Baguio area in 1903. Tens of thousands of others left Japan in search for wage work abroad, starting in the late 1880s. In 1906, on ships from Manila, the first organized group of Filipino laborers arrived in Hawai'i to work on plantations. In this first decade of the 21st century, we observe the centenaries of these events and place them squarely in the context of US colonial expansion. Through this study of the cultural, social, and historical dimensions of work among Japanese migrants, I chart their role in furthering the American project in the northern Philippines.[5] By focusing on the social dynamics — the adaptations, alliances, and intercultural accommodations — that their lives and work entailed, I present some of the cultural contextual and historical detail that contributes to a study of what Appadurai (1996: 182) calls the production of "locality." I hope to also show how Baguio's Japanese settlers were shaped by the history of their adopted region at the same time that they participated in its transformation.

Japanese Workers on the Highways

The establishment of communication links for the Baguio-Benguet region was very much a part of the early 20th-century history of transportation. To address the problems of high relief and difficult terrain, American administrators considered early experiments in the West in the form of rack and pinion railways and steam- and petrol-powered transport (Mohacek 2003a,b). The designation of the first access route in 1900, first called the Benguet Road and later the Kennon Road, was largely determined by the location of the port and rail terminus at Dagupan, in Pangasinan Province. However, from the beginning, the Kennon Road construction was troubled by a history of inadequate geological studies, a lack of knowledge of the climatic context, and woefully low estimates of costs and manpower. Escalating requests for more funds — the final cost in 1905 exceeded $2,000,000 — attracted controversy, and inevitably, fed into media portrayals of Baguio as an expensive American playground. A more stable second highway, the Naguilian Road, based on a well-graded "Spanish Trail" in the west, was widened and opened in 1914.

Japanese migrant workers participated in the construction of all access routes, including the failed ones. Their work on the Kennon Road has been well documented (Kennon 1906; Hayase 1989a; Yu-Jose 1997; Afable 2004: Chapter 1); for this reason, I will dwell on it only briefly. Beginning in 1903, about 1,500 Japanese worked on this highway construction, making up the largest group of foreigners (22 percent) in a workforce in which Filipinos made up 49 percent. In the laborers rolls, "Americans," including "[White] Americans, American Negroes, English, Australians, and white Europeans," contributed 18 percent. The Chinese made up 11 percent, and the rest came from some 40 nationalities, including hundreds of unemployed foreigners drawn to the possibilities of making a living in the new colony.

Early 1900s US immigration laws as well as Philippine labor unions had objected to the importation of unskilled labor. In 1903, however, Major Lyman Kennon, the road's head engineer, considered Japanese recruitment so essential to the construction that he was given a free hand to negotiate with the Japanese Consul for the arrival of over a thousand workers (Yu-Jose 1997). An informal agreement for the arrival of small lots of men to be staggered over many months ensured that their numbers did not attract undue attention at the docks. Thus, while the Japanese role in the Kennon Road was highly important in the memory of their community, the US records of the construction work initially downplayed their presence there.

By the time of Kennon's (1906) final report, however, he acknowledged their importance to the effort, although somewhat patronizingly: he described them as "superior" and "intelligent" workers, "fearless and active on cliff work," who "worked well when watched." Most importantly for their immediate future, Kennon made mention of Japanese carpentry and masonry skills that he had come to depend on. In contrast to this positive evaluation, however, there stood the Japanese's mortality rate on road construction (about 16 percent), which was the highest among the different national groups.

The completion of the Kennon Road in early 1905 was a tribute to the organizational ability of Major Kennon, his crew of overseers, and the men who built it entirely by hand. For the Japanese in 1930s Baguio, the work on that highway was an icon of their participation in the American effort to create the summer capital. Japanese studios in the city effectively publicized this, for large photographs of the road's most scenic portions decorated many Baguio homes and establishments before the Second World War.

W. Cameron Forbes and the Japanese Role in the Building of Baguio

Japanese workmen gained immediate employment upon their arrival in Baguio from the highway construction in 1905. An early official report from the Baguio Sanitarium (Thomas 1906) reported the presence of about 50 Japanese carpenters and workmen who were living on the premises and involved in its renovation and expansion. An important factor in guaranteeing employment for skilled workers was the government's decision in 1903 to make Baguio the official summer capital of the country. This involved the transfer of the national government offices to Baguio during the warmest months of the year.

William Cameron Forbes, the newly appointed Commissioner for Commerce and the Police who was to become the country's Governor-General (1909–1913), took on the assignment of building the city for this function. Through this appointment, the American official responsible for creating an infrastructure of roads, offices, official residences and transport facilities for this new town, became one of the largest employers of Japanese construction workers in that first decade of the 1900s. Warwick Greene, a young lawyer from Massachusetts, became Forbes' main assistant in the building of Baguio's infrastructure. He later became Head of the Bureau of Public Works. This guaranteed a lively interest in the Baguio public works projects at the highest official levels for another decade.

The task of creating Baguio could not have fallen into more enthusiastic hands. Affluent, cosmopolitan, and resourceful, Forbes launched into raising funds with great personal ambition as well as financial sophistication. In 1904, when the Philippine Commission invited Chicago urban planner Daniel Burnham, to draw up a plan for Manila, Forbes arranged for him to chart a design for Baguio as well. In publicizing his new role, Forbes made use of wide personal and professional networks, including his family's business associates in Massachusetts and Harvard University contacts. He also invited members of the American and Filipino business communities to join him with their ideas and investments. With American colleagues, he planned the labeling of Baguio's streets, parklands, and neighborhoods with pastoral names from his native New England.

Forbes saw to the survey of the choice, well-wooded sections of eastern Baguio into large lots, preparatory to offering them for sale to members of the Manila elite. The United States Army and the Navy surveyed their properties nearby, while in other high points of the city, Catholic Church orders staked out locations for places of retreat and worship. The Baguio Country Club opened in 1906 at Forbes' initiative and with some of his personal funds. That same year, he began the construction of his residence and extensive gardens at "Topside," an eastern location with magnificent views of the mining areas. A dozen Japanese masons, carpenters, and gardeners were involved in this project (Forbes 1904–1913).

Japanese-American Relations: Construction Work

Documents and oral accounts point to these Forbes-Greene projects as early sites of Japanese work. These included the first Episcopalian mission schools (one for White children and the other for Igorot children) and the Executive Mansion (later the Baguio residence of the Governor General and now of the Philippine President). The largest assignment was the Government Center, consisting of office buildings and accommodations for civil servants during the summer session in Baguio. Apart from Greene's responsibilities, the military reservation at Camp John Hay, the Bureau of Education's Teachers' Camp, and various Catholic religious orders employed Japanese artisans.

In these projects, Japanese carpenters established reputations for well-organized teams and high quality results that guaranteed them a viable niche in construction work. Their powerful first employers and the prestige of the building projects were crucial recommendations. It is clear that Japanese workers arrived in Baguio with the requisite skills at a most propitious time. From Japan, they were already familiar with working with pine; in this, they had an advantage over Filipino lowlanders. The highway experience had provided them with a merging of American tools and building traditions. Perhaps more importantly, it taught them how to interpret American construction blueprints quickly. This, along with the rudiments of English, Spanish, Ilocano and other northern languages that they picked up from the labor force, stood them in good stead in the first years in Baguio.

During the time that American energies were focused on building its government infrastructure, there existed a situation of productive negotiation and engagement between Japanese workers and American employers. Chief carpenters in Baguio gradually went into contracting, following a pattern that was apparently common in Japan (Goto, Sinoto, and Spoehr 1983) but not, for example, in Hawai'i. However, American contractors had the monopoly of government construction, although they took on Japanese chief carpenters as subcontractors, thus freeing them from the burden of raising bonds. Through these private arrangements, Japanese builders effectively cornered the market for the wide variety of construction work, from public works projects and plush residences to cheap market stalls and government housing. By many accounts, the contribution of Japanese builders to lowland northern Luzon infrastructure construction, including irrigation systems, schools, and municipal buildings, was also substantial.

Because of this expansion in job opportunities, carpenters from Fukuoka, Hiroshima, and other southern Japanese provinces sent invitations to members of their families to join them. Others came from military construction sites in

Manila. In the late 1920s, skilled carpenters from Pampanga Province arrived to work with Japanese builders, and soon, Kapampangan-owned firms gave Japanese builders their first taste of competition.

A vignette of early American-Japanese cultural exchange is afforded by W. Cameron Forbes's journal (1904–1913) and photographs of old Baguio. Forbes, one of the few Americans who singled out the role of Japanese artisans, described his house as an "Oriental" house with a "Japanese look." Japanese masons had constructed it and Forbes maintained a permanent staff of gardeners headed by a Fukuoka family named Tachibana. The representation of Japanese gardens using local materials is a well-known part of the horticultural history of eastern US and western European cities during that period. In Baguio, imitations of *torii* (Japanese shrine entrances) prominently marked not only Forbes's Topside and other officials' homes, but also such bastions of American authority and sensibility as the Country Club and Teachers Camp. Japanese workers constructed tea houses by man-made streams, arched bridges, and stone lanterns to conform to American idealizations of an Oriental landscape.[6]

The Lumber Mills

The other major source of employment for Japanese workers was in forest clearing and in the sawmills that supplied the pine lumber for construction. Hubert Phelps Whitmarsh, a journalist of English background who became the first Governor of Benguet, opened the first mills in the north side of the city (Halsema 1981). Herbert Heald, a businessman, who like Forbes, originally came from New England, eventually bought Whitmarsh's business and was to be the longest lasting employer of Japanese settlers in Baguio. He had been part of the Green and Brown Company that was contracted to build the Fort William McKinley barracks in Manila and employed some 600 carpenters there in 1905 (Yoshikawa 1998: 180).

The largest concessions held by Heald were in the forests of Mt. Santo Tomás, southwest of Baguio, starting in the 1910s. The early successes of sawmill technicians from Fukuoka, Hiroshima, Yamanashi, and Fukushima saw some of them pooling their money to set up small contracting companies. Large numbers of highland men were employed in these activities; few coastal people took on this kind of work. Eventually, Japanese contractors provided technical services at all levels, from sawyers and sawyer supervision, to builders of mills, installation and maintenance of machinery, and transporting timber and lumber.

The city's most affluent Japanese contractor in the 1930s, Kiichi Suda, had arrived from Fukushima in the 1910s to work as a sawmill hand. At the peak of his career, he was transporting lumber from the mills to the gold mines and is said to have fielded "one hundred trucks." Clearly, he was among the biggest customers of the local Chevrolet sales agency, which catered primarily to American companies. Suda built his home next to the Heald Lumber Company premises, at the edge of eastern Baguio — the most prestigious address a Japanese could have. Descendants often referred to him as "Heald Lumber's partner."

Residential Patterns and Forbes' Zoning Policies

The early settlement pattern of outsiders in Baguio was largely dictated by Forbes' zoning policies and the recommendations for the town center in the Burnham Plan. These allocated first, the large valley in the west to the municipal and government offices and facilities, to public parkland, hotels, churches, and a central business district. Second, they set aside the higher gently rolling land in the east as Baguio's prime real estate to be offered for sale. In the minds of local people, this eastern zone, with wide views of the southern Cordillera ranges, belonged to the "upper class" of Baguio. It included US government reserves, the Country Club, and large properties purchased by wealthy Americans and Filipinos.

In the late 19th century, this high portion of the plateau had been part of cattle-grazing grounds for a small number of Ibaloy families.[7]

In this evolving hierarchy of neighborhoods drawn along class and ethnic lines, less wealthy Christian Filipinos found themselves small lots in a space west of the commercial district. A narrow strip of land along Naguilian Road north of Burnham Park became known as "Campo Filipino." (At that time, the category "Filipinos" did not include "Igorots"). The first Catholic parish after the Cathedral was built here; it was settled mainly by Ilocano and Pangasinan traders and civil servants. A few Japanese families who were involved in the construction of Catholic missions lived in this vicinity.

The social divide between the east and west sides of town broke down in the weekend market, which was already a much-photographed gathering place in the 1910s. In the 1930s, townspeople mixed with the wealthier residents of the eastern district in church, in the movie theaters, and the American- and Chinese-run restaurants and cafes.

A few Japanese merchants had been able to buy land from Ibaloy owners and to establish general stores in the city center during the early 1910s. However, most Japanese found themselves locked out of lands reserved by American urban planning priorities. This was primarily because land in the eastern zone was not available for commercial agriculture. Forced to seek farming land during the slowdown in the Baguio building boom after the First World War, Japanese construction and sawmill workers found an accommodation with the other landowners, the Ibaloy residents of northern Baguio. Slightly lower in elevation from the central zone, these rice- and sweet-potato-growing areas in Guisad and Lucban belonged to Ibaloys named Kampulet, Karantes, Piraso, Daroan Pucay, and Sepik, among whom were early converts to Christianity. In time, and with the enthusiastic efforts of prominent Ibaloys, the exploitation of the Balili headwaters for vegetable production would become a third

Japanese occupational specialty, after construction and forestry work.

The Early Japanese Farms

The construction in Guisad Valley of the Episcopalian mission's Easter School marked the first colonial space deliberately produced with Baguio's native people in mind. Here, the coming together of a small network of American missionaries, recent converts among the Ibaloy landowners, and Kagoshima and Hiroshima sawmill workers and carpenters fresh from the Kennon Road project, resulted in the first land leases to Japanese for vegetable cultivation. With these first lessors, Japanese farmers laid the foundations of what is today a multimillion *peso* industry in the production of mid-latitude vegetable crops, especially cabbage, potatoes, beans, carrots, celery, and peas.

The expansion of vegetable crops into the Trinidad valley's Balili basin became possible in the early 1920s. Baguio's Mayor Halsema, who was concurrently the Benguet provincial engineer, hired 200 Japanese workmen to build an irrigation system in the low-lying areas of the valley. This momentous change in the landscape and economy came to be interpreted in interesting social and ritual terms that celebrated the coming together of Ibaloys and Japanese. Descendants on both sides say that Clemente Laoyan, the mayor of La Trinidad and a wealthy and progressive Ibaloy landowner there (Clemente Laoyan I Foundation 2002), met Tadahiko Sugimoto, a vegetable farmer who had settled in Guisad with his Ibaloy wife, Isang Gomez. Laoyan had seen the lush and productive Sugimoto gardens, and deciding that his relatives should learn these new agricultural techniques, he offered Sugimoto favorable lease terms to move to newly-drained land in La Trinidad and employ local Ibaloys. Within a decade, Laoyan's son married Sugimoto's eldest daughter, in turn accelerating the arrival of more farmers from Sugimoto's prefecture, Kumamoto.

Japanese-Igorot Relations: Vegetable Farming

In the Japanese migrants' entry into commercial farming, they had no competition, except perhaps from a few Chinese gardeners. Neither the American nor lowland Filipino residents were interested in this kind of agriculture. For local people, however, commercial farming had unprecedented social and economic consequences. Hundreds of young men and women from mountain villages and speaking several different languages began trickling in to seek work on these farms, thereby participating in the technological exchange that is the main legacy of this period to Cordillera people. The migration included many Bontoc and Kankanaey people from the upper Chico and Abra Rivers in the north, who had been considered enemies by southerners only the generation before. The establishment of *pax Americana*, officially associated with schools, the Constabulary, and missions in the highlands, found equally enduring support in these frontier work sites.

Marriages of Japanese men to local women, some before 1910, facilitated an early move into truck farming. The Ibaloy, Kankanaey, and Bontoc wives brought relatives from their home villages, some of them a five days' walk away. It was common for a farm's workforce to consist mainly of people from one village or region. The stability of work teams depended greatly on the wife's management and mediation; ultimately, these were crucial to enabling Japanese carpenter-farmers to have second construction careers away from the farms.

The intercultural relationships involved in establishing and running these farms were multifaceted and not without inherent social tensions. First of all, indigenous highlanders were at the bottom of Baguio's social hierarchy and Japanese-Igorot marriages were looked down upon by everyone, notably other Japanese. Within the Japanese community, these unions were regarded, at best, as marriages of convenience by the earliest of the settlers who could not afford to send home to Japan for brides. On the other hand, by marrying Japanese or other outsiders, local women faced the risk of being ostracized and disinherited by their families. In the memories of descendants, however, Japanese men were sought after for their prestige as farm bosses, skilled carpenters and good wage earners.

Childcare, trading between farms, and the cooperative labor needs for house-building, land clearing, irrigation, and the transport of produce were organizational problems that women rose to daily. It is not surprising that wives often promoted marriages between their relatives and their Japanese husbands' colleagues and relatives. In this way, extended kin networks, the most important sources of mutual support, evolved around sets of related women who were married to Japanese men. These highly adaptive arrangements were also drawn along the women's ethnic lines and old regional loyalties. On the other hand, prefectural affiliation and occupational links determined men's friendship groups.

In general, the local women did not join the Japanese society of their husbands except in the privacy of their homes and farms. Few spoke Japanese with any fluency and communication in the home was in an Ilocano pidgin that incorporated elements from Spanish, Japanese, English, and mothers' languages. Attendance at the Japanese School enabled children to play increasingly important roles as interpreters in the family, farm, and market.

Japanese men and other outsiders were ritually incorporated into indigenous society by way of community-wide feasts that called for the slaughter of pigs and sometimes of cattle. These celebrations marked life transitions and served to validate marriage in the presence of the women's kin circle as well as her ancestral spirits. To be able to convince a prospective Japanese (or other outsider) husband to co-sponsor a large wedding feast raised a woman's status in her kin group. Copious amounts of rice wine flowed during these occasions; in fact, narratives point metaphorically (and humorously) to rice wine as bringing Japanese migrants and native women together.

Japanese representations of native highland cultures and their participation in commodifying and commercializing them are worth mentioning here. Much of the tourist promotion of Baguio has centered on the exoticization of the region's indigenous cultures and peoples. In this respect, the Japanese businesses were not far behind in extolling a Noble Savage image for their highland neighbors. Their photo studios displayed handwoven "Igorot costumes" and ornaments that clients could wear along with props of spears, shields, and musical instruments.

Postcards from the 1910s show main street bazaars selling native artifacts from all highland groups, especially wood sculptures, baskets, weapons, textiles, and ornaments. A major Manila writer, A.V.H. Hartendorp (1951, quoted in Ellis 1981) took Baguio merchants to task for encouraging "mass-produced" art objects in non-traditional styles. He singled out Japanese "curio dealers" before the Second World War as being responsible for introducing "picturesque" and "realistic detail" in the human figures and animals produced by Ifugao wood sculptors coming from the northeast. These "traditions" in local woodcarving for the tourist market continue today.

The 1920s and 1930s: Consolidation and Expansion

In the 1920s, Baguio joined the list of the most prominent tourist destinations in Asia. The Japanese community came into its own as transportation improved, the expansion of tourism required new construction, and the export of highland vegetables to the Manila market became a reality. Japanese entrepreneurs moved into new levels of capital investment. Both Hideo Hayakawa and Sanji Nagatomi, who had started bazaars side by side on Session Road in the 1910s, brought close relatives over from Yamanashi and Fukuoka respectively, to man their expanding businesses.The Hayakawas founded a hospital and pharmacy and added a photography studio and a transport company to their Japanese Bazaar. Fukushima migrants, after working in sawmills for most of a decade, began to make their mark with investments outside the central district and in the provision of lumber for mine and sawmill construction.

The northern railroad had reached the west coast of La Union Province. Citing the benefits of American civil government and a national police, tourist brochures promoted Baguio and the nearby mountain region as a safe and relaxing adventure (Arnold 1912; Cámara de Comercio de las Islas Filipinas 1920). An invigorating climate, unparalled views of mountain valleys, well-tended gardens, walking and motor trips, as well as "studies of native life" offered a unique vacation in this American "wonderland." In 1916, Baguio had 8,000 visitors; and in 1927, there were 22,000 travelers to Baguio (Halsema 1991). This was at a time when the city population was 8,000. Another ten years later, the tourism reports showed six times as many people visiting the city (Afable 2004: 54).

The Japanese Association and the Japanese School

The Baguio Japanese formed a Japanese Association (*Nihonjin-kai*) in 1921 and established the Japanese School in 1924. In the first, the settlers instituted a mutual help organization for its growing community. In the second, they made provisions for the continuity of Japanese language and culture in their adopted city. These moves reflected a commitment to a continuing Japanese presence in Baguio as well as in the country's international community. Toyohei Hayakawa, a Yamanashi merchant who served as Baguio *Nihonjin-kai* president for most of the years until the end of the Second World War, led a small sophisticated group of central city merchants with strong links to the Manila Japanese commercial sector. Membership of the Association was boosted to over 400 at the height of the gold rush in 1936 to 1937, from about a third of that number in 1921.

Through the 1920s, the leading merchants in the city center rotated the high positions in the Japanese Association among themselves. The division between these business families and the farming and carpenters' families, many of whom had native wives, was well demarcated socially and geographically. This situation appeared to be mitigated in the 1930s, with the growing affluence of farmers, most of whom were heads of large Japanese-Filipino families living in Trinidad. They successfully made their voices heard in the Association, especially in the powerful education committee.

In bringing together various occupational, regional, and entrepreneurial groups in support of a school, Japanese community leaders not only sought to ensure language and culture maintenance but also to prepare the next generation for life in Baguio's international milieu. Instruction in English started in the fourth grade in the Japanese School, and totaled 15 hours per week for the higher grades. The first enrollment of 25 pupils drew from offspring of the Japanese-Filipino marriages of the 1910s and before. It is of interest that the three English-language teachers at the School came from Igorot backgrounds.

Official public celebrations, especially on July Fourth and Rizal Day, were day-long affairs during which the Japanese flag flew alongside the American and Filipino flags. In the 1930s' city parades, distinctive Japanese community floats, festooned with banners of many nations, displayed artistic pageants of Filipino, Japanese and American historical symbolism (Afable 2004: 50).

The "Salad Bowl" of the Philippines

Baguio's renown as the country's one source of temperate climate vegetables became firmly established by 1930. Some 200 Japanese and Japanese-Filipino families in Baguio and La Trinidad cultivated a total acreage of about three square kilometers. A 1932 issue of the *Baguio Bulletin*, a weekly supplement of the *Manila Bulletin*, reported that cabbage production in Trinidad was close to 20 tons per hectare. (At the present time, this yield is exceeded only in closely supervised experimental plots, where 30 tons per hectare are reached, with petrochemical fertilizers.)

With three crops a year and prices per kilo swinging between P0.05 and P0.25, Trinidad vegetable farmers were described as carting home "sackloads of money." The stability of Japanese-Igorot marriages — most of them lasted until the Second World War — testifies to the support they eventually enjoyed within the community as well as the general prosperity in the region in the 1920s and 1930s.

Work Specialties and the Japanese Community's Last Decade

Japanese migrants, as part of a workforce that was defined by ethnicity, immigration, wage labor, gender, and technology, developed distinctive occupational lines that were essential to the American-initiated projects in southern Cordillera. Their maximization of the social, technological, and economic resources available to them centered on a few initiatives. Settlers' remittances back to Japan, which are reported to have greatly increased in the 1930s, would have been a major focus of these decisions.

One initiative had to do with the selective migration of people from Japan. The men who arrived in Baguio in the first decade of the 1900s represented many prefectures, mainly in southern Japan and a few northern areas. However, this picture shifted dramatically in the second decade. The successes of a few Yamanashi, Fukuoka, Kagoshima, and Hiroshima people led to an increase in their numbers with the arrival of relatives and townmates from these regions. The late 1910s saw an influx of young Fukushima men arriving to join relatives who had quickly risen to supervisory positions in the sawmills.

Thus, by the end of the 1930s, Baguio's Japanese society had been augmented primarily along a few regional and family lines. These "boundary-maintaining" practices were such that people could point to a Fukushima faction, a Yamanashi faction, a Kumamoto faction, a southern faction of loosely-connected Fukuoka, Hiroshima, and Kagoshima pioneers, and so on, whose memberships were based on their leaders' individual career histories and kinship ties.

A second direction was the channeling of profits into contracting. This resulted in a small number of efficient broker-contractors who represented well-organized work teams. This level of organization became important during the Baguio goldmining boom in the mid-1930s. While the Japanese did not work as miners, they filled the great demand for mining installation builders and technicians. Also, several decades of association with Heald Lumber put them in a most advantageous position for logging and transport contracts, for filling the mines' need for massive amounts of lumber. Thus, by the 1930s, the long history of Japanese-American collaboration had paid off handsomely; it buttressed what was ultimately the handmaiden role that the Japanese played in relation to American interests.

These initiatives have to be seen in the context of Japanese-Chinese competition, which came to a head during the boycotts of the 1930s. They represent the Japanese community's closing of ranks and a shoring up of gains vis-à-vis the Chinese, as the groups competed for patronage from American commercial interests. The 1939 census reported closely similar numbers for the two: there were 1,114 Chinese and 1,064 Japanese in Baguio. At that time, the city's population was 24,000 (*Census of the Philippines* 1940). There were 755 Americans and Europeans.

Bilingual education in the Japanese School was important for the community's competitiveness. The English skills of people like Sempei (Henry) Hayakawa and Shonosuke Furuya, who attended Philippine universities, and the School alumni, were crucial to the community's multicultural relations. Kiichi Suda, who brought many young Fukushima people to Baguio, made it obligatory for them to attend classes in the local public schools, to learn English from children.

American capitalist goals in the Baguio region defined the limits on ownership of forest and mineral resources and local people's and non-Americans' access to them. However, by developing work specializations close to the highest technical levels in the construction and forest industries, including mining installation, Baguio Japanese were able to make themselves indispensable to the exploitation of these resources. Marriages with native women, a direction some took in the early years, effected a winning balance between construction work and commercial farming. Women's support networks ensured an ethnically diverse range of cooperative and paid labor arrangements. By the 1930s, these alliances, which had encountered much community opposition initially, had resulted in large, prosperous farming families, especially in the Trinidad valley. At the end of that decade, the hopes for continuity of a Japanese community in the Baguio-Benguet region lay in the hands of its highly bilingual, locally well-connected, and enterprising Japanese-Filipino membership.[8]

In the first four decades of the 20th century, fruitful social and economic accommodations between Japanese and highland peoples on the one hand, and Japanese and Americans on the other, set the geographical and technological stage for the second half of the century. After the war and with Philippine independence, the commercial exploitation of southern Cordilleran environmental resources passed into the hands of Filipinos, Chinese, and Americans. Meanwhile, the rapid rebuilding of Baguio after the Second World War was made possible by the technological heritage of the 1920s and 1930s workplaces as well as the formal educational opportunities they had engendered.

A Historical and Cultural Postscript

About two-thirds of the Baguio Japanese community described here perished in the Second World War. Most died of starvation and illness in 1945, in the mountains of southern Ifugao. With some exceptions, all Japanese who survived the Second World War in the Philippines were repatriated to Japan from US military internment camps at the end of the war. Most Filipino wives and their Japanese-Filipino children remained in the Philippines, to endure many years of intense anti-Japanese feelings from the general public. Few ever saw their husbands or fathers again. Most Japanese-Filipinos changed their identities, and the stories of a Japanese community before the Second World War circulated only in small family circles. The memories recorded here are primarily of elderly children, mostly female, of Japanese-Filipino marriages.

The patterns of intercultural accommodation that evolved in the multiethnic Baguio frontier created what Richard White (2006) has called "mutually comprehensible worlds." A glimpse of the Japanese-Filipino descendants' view of these worlds is instructive in its implicit expressions of agency and sociality. When speaking confidently of a "partnership" between Kiichi Suda and Heald Lumber, narrators invoke a local model of Japanese-American relations in Baguio on the eve of the Second World War. It is one that elides the historical specificity of Suda's background as a migrant worker and claims a bond with the American managers and capital owners based on work, production and mutual need. Similarly, in describing the notable transformations to land and environment in Benguet Province, the ritual expression of Japanese-Igorot relations ignores the great social and cultural divide between migrant Japanese and indigenous Filipinos in the early 1900s. Phrased in terms of marriage bonds between Sugimoto and Laoyan and emphasizing technological and labor exchange, this model rejects a marking of highlanders as peoples of tradition who were outside the realm of the modern. In this study of Japanese life and work in Baguio, I make a preliminary attempt to ethnographically and socially contextualize these discourses.

Notes

1. On the history of Baguio as a hill station, the definitive source is by cultural geographer, Robert R. Reed (1999 [1976]). This includes a section on the cultural construction of disease and health in the tropics.
2. For the early American ethnic classifications, see Worcester (1906). From different perspectives, Scott (1962) and Finin (2005) cover the long history of discussion and controversy of "Igorot" as an outsider's

and insider's label; Finin also sets forth the American administrative foundations for a Cordillera consciousness. For a trenchant comparison of American policies toward Philippine highland peoples and Japanese adminstration of Taiwan aborigines, see Barclay (2003).

3. Tapang (1985) gives an economist's view of the socio-cultural background to this cattle industry. In the Philippines, the legal discussions of what constitutes "ancestral land" have a long history and they make reference to the landmark 1909 case of Mateo Cariño vs. the Insular Government in which the United States Supreme Court recognized native title over a 146-hectare land parcel on the basis of native custom and long association.
4. This enthusiasm on the part of US officials did not go unnoticed by descendants being interviewed for this project: pictures of old Baguio, showing the places where their fathers had worked, allowed some introspection into the whole "archival" process. The fact that photographs and documents referring (even if only indirectly) to their fathers' work were preserved in Washington DC took on special meaning: it validated their association with these sites and gave authenticity to their childhood experiences. Thus, within the research process itself, we found the "American shadow" being reiterated in an unexpected way.
5. For studies of the Japanese settlers' role in furthering American interests in the southern Philippines, see Hayase (1984, 1989b).
6. See, for example, the first annual edition of the *Manila Times*, February 1910, for a spread of Baguio photographs featuring some of these gardens and *japanoiserie*. It is said that Forbes's brother held an interest in the newspaper.
7. For a map showing this distribution of Baguio land by 1928, see Afable (2004), p. 39.
8. Thus, for example, bright children of mixed marriages were encouraged to further their education in Japan. Also, Toyohei Hayakawa, the "big boss" on Session Road, is said to have tried his hand at matchmaking newly arrived Japanese men with daughters of Japanese-Igorot marriages. It appears, though, that the generation gap between the fathers who came in the 1910s and the young men who arrived 20 years later was large enough that fathers did not encourage their daughters to marry them. One reason given was that aging fathers had decided to spend the rest of their lives in Baguio, and they did not want their daughters to follow their husbands to Japan. Some of the issues raised here in regard to inter-ethnic marriage are given a historical dimension in Barclay's 2005 study of Japanese colonials and aborigine women in Taiwan.

chapter 9

Competing Shadows: Japan and the USA in the Filipino American Imagination

Augusto Espiritu

In the last few decades, scholars of the Philippines have shed increasing light upon the Filipino and Filipina diaspora. As a result of post-colonial, global, transnational, and more recently, empire studies, historians in particular have shown that the Filipino diaspora has always provided a transformative supplement to the fundamental events of Philippine history, from the emergence of Filipino nationalism to the era of globalization (Ileto 1998; Rafael 1997; Choy 2003; Manalansan 2003; Espiritu 2005). Similar to these studies, this paper attempts to shed light on the diasporic dimensions of Filipino national discourse about Japan and focuses upon several paired texts, which reflect the views of Filipino transmigrant and immigrant men and women. These include two political tracts written during the US colonial period, *America, the Philippines and the Orient* by Hilario Camino Moncado (1895–1956) and *Mother America: A Living Story of Democracy* by Carlos P. Romulo (1899–1985); two post-war and post-colonial novels, namely *The Bamboo Dancers* by N.V.M. Gonzalez (1915–1999) and *Villa Magdalena* by Bienvenido Santos (1911–1996); and lastly, two late 20th-century immigrant novels, *When the Rainbow Goddess Wept* by Cecilia Manguerra Brainard (1947–) and *When the Elephants Dance* by Tess Uriza Holthe (1966–) (Moncado 1932; Romulo 1943; Gonzalez 1993a; Santos 1986a; Brainard 1999; Holthe 2003). One caveat — this paper is not meant as a definitive study, but a preliminary exploration of recurring perceptions of Japan and Japanese among Filipinos in the USA.

I argue that there are two strands of thought that emerge from these writings, which for heuristic purposes, I label "pro-Japan" and "anti-Japan" thinking. On one hand, one notices a recurring pattern of pro-Japan thinking that although not unmindful of problematic Japanese actions in war or diplomacy, continually presents Japan and Japanese in a positive light. This line of thought tends to be "anti-US," or critical of US imperialism in Asia and racism in the USA, and layers the cultural and spiritual values of the "East" over the "West." On the other hand, anti-Japan thinking connects "negative" memories, anxieties, and historical experiences centered on the Japanese Occupation of the Philippines with the unstable relations between Japan and the Philippines in the post-war period. While such a view might be critical of the United States, in the end, it is content with a "pro-US" or pro-Western orientation. Hence, one might say that the tropes of "Japan" and "America," as competing shadows in the determination of Filipino lives across the oceans, provide two powerful renderings of the past and equally compelling visions of the future for Filipinos in the diaspora.

The Colonial Era: Moncado and Romulo

Positive Filipino American views of Japan have their roots in earlier Filipino diasporic appraisals of Japan at the turn of the 20th century. *Ilustrados,* like José Rizal and T.H. Pardo de Tavera, were inspired by Japan's rapid modernization, constitutionalism, and military ascendance (Constantino 1985), unparalleled in Asia, as well as by its pan-Asian racial ideology, which drew anti-colonialists from China, India, and Southeast Asia into Japan. From the beginning of the Philippine Revolution against Spain and the subsequent Philippine-American War, the Philippine Republic sought Japanese intervention on behalf of the Filipinos through its principal representative in Japan, the ilustrado Mariano Ponce (Karl 2002: 168–74; Rafael 2000: 103–21; Ponce: 1932). Given Japan's concern for renegotiating unequal treaties with the West, Japan maintained neutrality toward the Philippines' anti-colonial conflicts. This did not mean, however, that the Japanese were unsympathetic to the Filipino cause, as indeed key individuals provided moral support and some material aid, although the actual material support remained rather minimal (Anderson 2005: 150–2, 213–18; Saniel 1973: 241ff).

Still, Japanese intervention lingered in the minds of Filipinos, no less because "El Víbora" (the "viper," the *nom-de-guerre* of revolutionary leader General Artemio Ricarte) went into exile in Japan rather than acknowledge US colonial rule. Indeed, pro-Japan sentiment remained a vital part of popular protest ideology against the American occupiers and the Filipino elite collaborators, from the conspiracies of the early 1900s to the Sakdal revolt of the mid-1930s (Ileto 1998: 135–64; Goodman 1967b: 133–94), even as Japan's imperial ambitions became manifest with the occupation of both Korea and Manchuria and the maturing of Japan's strategy of the "Greater East Asia Co-Prosperity Sphere" (Limqueco 1991: 89–106). Benigno Ramos, the noted Tagalog writer and leader of the Sakdals, provides an important link here, as he traveled to Japan during the 1930s to meet with Ricarte and likewise journeyed across the Pacific to meet Filipino migrant leaders in the USA to oppose passage of what he regarded as the sham independence promised by the Tydings-McDuffie bill (Goodman 1967b: 138–9). Among elite leaders like Jose P. Laurel and Benigno Aquino, Sr., pro-Japan sentiment and collaboration with Japan during the Second World War provided the basis for attaining the long-sought after Philippine independence that the USA and Philippine colonial elites had been unwilling to provide (Joaquin 1983: 153–69).

Negative Filipino appraisals of Japan, on the other hand, derive from both anti-"Oriental" agitation in the USA as well as a growing Filipino uneasiness with Japanese imperial ambitions in the Philippines (Saniel 1973; Yu-Jose 1999; Terami-Wada 1991; Ikehata and Jose 1999), both of which helped fuel Filipino nativist reactions. While the US government maintained positive diplomatic relations with Japan (LaFeber 1994), American popular opinion in the US rejected the Japanese. There, a widespread anti-Oriental movement led by the trade unions, which had but recently gained passage of an exclusion law against Chinese "coolies," now turned against Japanese migrants and succeeded in gaining passage of laws that limited Japanese immigration, property rights, and US citizenship rights (Daniels 1969; Ichioka 1988).

Racially-inflected class conflicts between Japanese and Filipino migrants in Hawaii and California also reinforced negative Filipino American perceptions of Japan. Indeed, certain Japanese migrant leaders in the USA regarded themselves as colonial pioneers who remained loyal to the Japanese Empire (Azuma 2005: 89–110). Meanwhile, Japanese community attitudes of superiority toward other Asians tended to reinforce negative perceptions of Japan and the Japanese, even as individual leaders among Japanese and Filipinos sought to transgress such borders and establish intercultural solidarities. In Hawaii, for instance, the charismatic Filipino labor leader Pablo Manlapit formed a close friendship with Fred Makino of the *Hawaii Hochi* newspaper on the basis of interracial unionism, a relatively novel concept for the US territory at the time, which was ethnically divided by the overarching sugar plantocracy. However, in the 1920 sugar strike, most Japanese labor leaders refused cooperation with Filipinos, deciding to submit separate petitions to the Hawaiian Sugar Planters Association, for no ostensible reason other than their disdain for Filipinos as an ethnic group, thus weakening the strike (Kerkvliet 2002; Jung 2006).[1] Likewise, in northern California, an interracial liaison between a Filipino man and an American-born Japanese woman who had eloped was thwarted by the Japanese family's fear of racial and sexual impurity, especially from darker-skinned, mostly working class Filipino men. Filipinos resented this public insult and launched a boycott of Japanese stores, which lasted several weeks (De Vera 2002: 68–70). In the Central Valley as well, labor conflict between Japanese contractors and Filipino laborers struck California's San Joaquin Delta, providing the basis for expressions of Japanese racial supremacy and stereotypes of Filipinos in the Japanese-language press (Azuma 2005: 187–207). Lastly, Filipino workers and Japanese community leaders in Los Angeles differed over perceptions of what constituted morally legitimate and respectable recreation, in particular on the question of gambling (Maram 2006: 63). It should be noted that Japanese American entrepreneurs and nationalist leaders became targets of similar boycott actions by other Asian groups, notably Korean and Chinese groups especially in the wake of the Japanese annexation of Korea in 1910 and the invasions of Manchuria in 1931 and that of China in 1937 (Yang 1984; Ichioka 1990). These pre-war developments would contribute to the anti-Japanese climate among Filipinos during the Second World War. Long-held Japanese stereotypes of Filipinos as the "Other," or as violent criminals and sexual predators have in fact influenced Japanese-Filipino American relations down to the present day (Fujikane 2000).

Meanwhile, in colonial Philippines, with these US developments in the background, negative views of Japan gradually began to develop. For instance, Catherine Choy provides an interesting example of early 20th-century nationalist feminism, which distanced Filipinas from Japanese women. In words that reflect the growing impact of Americanization upon Filipino elite women and men, two Filipina educators in the early 1920s attempted to differentiate modern Filipina feminists from their "Oriental" counterparts, including Japanese women, by depicting Filipinas as "liberated" and Asian women as remaining imprisoned by regressive traditions of wearing kimonos, foot binding, and usage of the veil (Choy 2003: 35–7). During the late 1920s, as Japanese leaders pondered the value of issuing a "Monroe Doctrine" for Asia, Claro M. Recto, a member of the National Assembly, declared in a public debate his opposition to any such unilateral declaration for Asia. Moreover, he warned Filipinos of Japan's imperial ambitions, citing its takeover of Korea and its increasingly belligerent moves toward China (Recto 1930). Finally, the hitherto minor Japanese migration into Manila and the small Japanese colony in Davao, where 14,000 Japanese came to dominate the hemp industry, began to raise suspicions of Japan's colonial ambitions in the Philippines (Goodman 1967a). Grant Goodman is at pains to present the circumspection and restraint with which Filipino political leaders like President Manuel Quezon and the Japanese Consul General's office in the Philippines handled the tensions over land titles in Davao. However, with international tensions rising between Japan and the United States during the 1930s, waves of anti-Japanese opinion began to wash on the issue, spurring US and Philippine colonial government investigations of Davao and widespread rumors of "illegal entry of [Japanese] immigrants, smuggling of arms and ammunition, and fortification of strategic locations," in what appeared to be a Japanese colonization scheme, or "Davaokuo," in the making (ibid. 1967a: 11, 19ff, 51, 77).

With these influences in mind, it becomes clear how Moncado's *America* (1932) and Romulo's *Mother America* (1943) provide paradigmatic views of Japan among Filipino transmigrants to the USA. Moncado was the ambitious head of the Filipino Federation of America (FFA), a controversial, mystical group — part mutual aid society, part religious confraternity — founded in Los Angeles, which subsequently spread to Hawaii Territory and the colonial Philippines (Cullinane 2000; San Buenaventura 1990). In his book, Moncado explores the complex interrelationship between the United States, the Philippines, and East Asia. With the European powers "exhausted" by the First World War, the future of the Philippines for Moncado would depend upon recognizing the new powers in the "Pacific era," the United States and Japan (Moncado 1932: 16). In this context, he advocates for Philippine independence from the USA, the neutralization of the Philippines, and the establishment of friendly relations with Japan to protect the Philippines from attack in case of war among the belligerent powers. Moreover, he sees an independent Philippines as a crucial mediator in the problems that beset China and Japan, Asia's presumptive leaders (ibid.: 7–10).

Moncado heralds the "awakening of the East," centered on Japan's arrival on the world stage as a power to challenge the West. Echoing Rizal and Ricarte and his contemporary, Benigno Ramos, Moncado preached love for Japan for two reasons. On the strategic level, it was Japan that had made tremendous sacrifices for all Asia during the Russo-Japanese War of 1905. Had Russia won, he reasoned, nothing would have stopped Britain, the USA, and other powers from dismantling China and consolidating Western colonial control of the continent. Because of this unquestionable leadership, Moncado was willing to make some startling allowances to satisfy Japan. He believed, for instance, that China was indebted enough to Japan to allow Japanese concessions in Manchuria for the needs of her industrial economy.

But Moncado also identified a religious reason for sympathizing with Japan. Moncado believed in an overarching spirituality that unified Asia. Quoting the Japanese thinker, Kakuzo Okakura, he highlights the common emphasis in Asian religious thought for the love of the "Ultimate" and the "Universal," as against the West's love for the "Particular" (ibid.: 211–3). Such a philosophical view of Asia, which we might label today as "Orientalism," corresponds with Moncado's own fascination with Philippine animism and mysticism and his incorporation of the *pasyon* into the rituals of the Filipino Federation of America. For Moncado, such spiritualism provides a strong foundation for an overarching pan-Asianism, which values peace among Asian neighbors and mutual defense against the encroachment of foreigners: "Yes," he writes, "Asia is one, racially, spiritually and politically" (ibid.: 213; see also San Buenaventura 1991: 169–93).

With respect to the USA, Moncado turns distinctly anti-American, arguing that "America's pretension to altruism in the [colonial] Philippines is untenable" for it is no more than a ruse for "economic advantage" and imperial expansion into the Asian continent (Moncado 1932: 7–10). While he notes the marked decline in Japan's relations with its Asian neighbors because "she has become too much like Western Powers in her dealings with weaker nations" (ibid.: 29; see also 135), Moncado reserves his ire for the USA's actions in Asia and white racism in America. For instance, he rebuts US arguments for an "Open Door," exposing the self-interested nature of this pronouncement in light of already existing European colonial spheres of influence in China. Moncado correctly observes that the US accepted colonialism in its various legal pronouncements (ibid.: 164). Moreover, while it pronounces the "Open Door" in Asia and insists upon equal treatment of its citizens in Asia, the USA in fact has a closed door policy toward Asian labor migrants in the United States, practices racial discrimination toward them, and deprives them of civil rights (ibid.: 166–74).

While Moncado rejects the unilateral pronouncement of an American Monroe Doctrine for Asia, he nonetheless leaves the door open for a Japanese Monroe Doctrine. He quotes the representatives of several Latin American countries to show that while the Monroe Doctrine may have had a beneficial, anti-imperial, anti-European effect in the beginning, it has over time only engendered "Yankeephobia" because it has become the selfish means for asserting US hegemony throughout Latin America (ibid.: 134). Nonetheless, in the case of Japan, Moncado makes some startling allowances. While he rejects a unilateral pronouncement of an Asian Monroe Doctrine, he does recognize Japan's unchallenged power in Asia and welcomes the possibility of a Japanese Monroe Doctrine if it is done in consultation with other Asian countries (ibid.: 134–6). Such favoring of Japan becomes obvious in his rationalizing of Japan's conquest of Korea and Manchuria as necessary expansions to offset Japan's densely packed population and to provide the raw materials for maintaining her industry. Moncado likewise believes that Japan would have no reason to attack the Philippines, for she does not have the natural resources for which Japan invaded Manchuria (ibid.: 8).

Perhaps what accounts for Moncado's bias toward Japan as opposed to the United States was his personal experience with virulent US racism toward Filipinos. Filipinos, like earlier Chinese migrants, were victimized by pogroms, beatings, and murders by white racist mobs during the late 1920s and early 1930s. Meanwhile, the US government provided no relief for Filipino migrants as a result of racism and official neglect and because Filipinos had no political representation of their own (Moncado: 132, 172–4; Quinsaat 1976).

In the meantime, Romulo's *Mother America*, at least on the surface, has a striking resemblance to Moncado's *America*. Both books reveal similar concerns about US imperialism, the emergence of Japan, and the colonial histories of the Philippines. Both authors draw substantially from the missionary and historian Sidney L. Gulick's *The White Peril in the Far East* (1905). But the differences between the two emerge in their views on Japan and their attitudes toward the USA. Romulo's historical circumstances differed from that of Moncado's for *Mother America* was published after Pearl Harbor and the Battles of the Philippines, after Bataan and Corregidor and the infamous Death March, which marked not only the defeat of an America that had been deemed invincible, but also the death of numerous Filipino troops and the destruction of much of the country. Like Moncado, Romulo, who was exiled to the United States for the duration of the war, is attempting to chart an independent course for the Philippines. He believes in the extension of the Atlantic Charter to Asia, indeed the drawing up of a Pacific Charter that would prevent future invasions and create a security arrangement that would prevent smaller countries from attack. Like Moncado, Romulo too believes that the United States is not without its faults in the Philippines even though his discourse is infused by a quasi-religious faith in America's redemptive and regenerative capacities. Finally, for Romulo as for Moncado, the Philippines has a great future role to play in

Asia as an impartial broker between East and West, as well as between China and Japan.[2]

The differences between Moncado and Romulo, however, become sharper in relation to the subject of Japan and the Japanese. For Romulo's stridently anti-Japanese propaganda, the Japanese are both a "problem" and a "menace." Romulo rehashes common racial stereotypes of the Japanese (common in the USA where Romulo had spent quite a bit of time) — that is, as sneaky, dishonest, cruel, and treacherous, especially in infiltrating and subverting Philippine society from the *apa* vendors of Manila to Baguio's highway workers to Davao's hemp entrepreneurs. Japanese culture, he writes, is based upon the insecure foundations of honor or face, which he describes as "the lowliest inferiority sense in the Orient" (Romulo 1943: 69), masked by a bristling air of superiority and an inexorable warrior or bushido code (ibid.: 65–71).

In agreement with Romulo, Filipino labor migrants in the USA expressed much of the same view during the war, no less for being exposed to these ideas from Romulo's lecture tour throughout the United States. Indeed, not only did Filipinos in the USA make liberal use of the racial epithet "Jap" to describe the "enemy" in the Philippines, many also unreservedly expropriated the agricultural lands formerly held by Japanese Americans incarcerated by the US government during the Second World War (Buaken 1948: 291, 324; Nomura 1986-87: 99–117).

Romulo sought to focus attention upon the work of a benevolent US Empire in the Philippines, which brought the benefits of "Filipinization," the Jones Law, and the setting of an actual date for independence with the Tydings-McDuffie Act, all of which inoculated the Filipinos from the virus of Japan's "Greater East Asia Co-Prosperity Sphere," to which Indonesia, French Indochina, and British Southeast Asia had succumbed (Romuro 1943: 7–11). (By contrast, Moncado points to issues Romulo leaves out — the problems of independence with strings, the continuation of US bases that infringe upon Philippine sovereignty, and the unequal rights between

Americans in the Philippines and Filipinos in the USA (Moncado 1932: 172–4, 213–4). Indeed, Romulo's post-war vision for Filipinos is as Occidentalized Orientals, America's ally in Asia not only strategically but also in terms of shared values. Romulo might have countered Moncado's evocation of the "spiritual oneness of Asia" with his preaching of the "spiritual pattern." If Moncado celebrates the East, Romulo celebrates the West. Instead of collective life and the contemplation of transcendent values, Romulo valorizes a secular religion that unleashes self-interested free enterprise, gives free play to liberal politics, and preserves "the moral sanctities of the *individual*" (Romulo 1943: 140–1, 146; italics, my emphasis).

The Post-War: Gonzalez and Santos

In the first two decades after the Second World War, the Japanese Occupation continued to provide the subject of fierce divisions in the Philippines, particularly on the question of the meanings of Filipino collaboration with the Japanese. Related to this issue, the question of war-damage reparations from Japan also remained a thorny issue in post-war Philippine-Japanese relations, especially in the context of the Philippines' dire need for reconstruction funds, the weak economic state of occupied Japan, and the US' Cold War strategy for Asia (Abaya 1946; Steinberg 1967; McCoy 1980; Rafael 2000; Meyer 1965). These historical issues found their way into Philippine literature, from Stevan Javellana's pioneering wartime novel of Iloilo, *Without Seeing the Dawn* (1947), to Estrella Alfon's Cebu stories, to Edilberto K. Tiempo's novel, *Watch in the Night* (1953). Likewise, pre-war Japanese experiences in Baguio found a voice in Sinai C. Hamada's "Tanabata's Wife" (1973) (Javellana 1947; Moore 1994; Tiempo 1953). Taking in historical and literary influences, trans-Pacific, Filipino-American writers, N.V.M. Gonzalez and Bienvenido Santos, expressed their views of Japan in compelling ways. While rejecting stereotypes of the Japanese, they still continued to reflect the pro- and anti-Japan divisions of the pre-independence period.

Gonzalez avoids direct engagement with the violence of the Japanese Occupation in his fiction, but he does in some stories evoke the lingering tensions of the war.[3] Gonzalez' experience of war, as told by his wife Narita Manuel Gonzalez, was largely positive even though he and his family were forced into domestic exile in Mindoro. Narita Gonzalez credits the occupation for encouraging Gonzalez to write his first Tagalog short story during the Japanese-sponsored literary events during the war. After the war, sponsored by two Rockefeller Fellowships, Gonzalez toured not only the USA, but also traveled to various Asian countries, including Japan, twice. The mundane but poignant experiences he had there provided the basis for his second novel, *The Bamboo Dancers* (1959) (N. Gonzalez 2000).

The key theme of the novel is the rehabilitation of the Filipino and Filipina intellectual disillusioned by the emptiness of war and American education. The modern-day scholar-protagonists do not find enlightenment in America. Indeed, America seems to create the conditions for Filipinos to become confused of their true identity. Instead, the novel in effect represents the recovery of self as a return to the Philippines, especially by way of Asia and Asian values, so to speak. And Gonzalez has his leading characters, especially Ernie Rama, spend a long time in Japan, especially Tokyo and Hiroshima, though avoiding the rather crass Filipino men who talk endlessly about reparations *and* Japanese red-light districts (Gonzalez 1993a: 169). At the same time, Ernie becomes engrossed in fulfilling an errand for a white American missionary who is connected to a charitable rest house for atomic bomb survivors in Hiroshima. Through encounters with everyday Japanese, from A-bomb survivors to the Japanese bellhop, with whom he goes fishing, and from the anti-nuclear demonstrators to Mrs. Ishikawa, a Nisei woman from the United States, he discovers the meaning of genuine human contact. As he listens to their stories of war and their newfound sense of solidarity, something awakens Ernie's sense of compassion (ibid.: 165, 175ff, 23–240). The image that emerges of Japan and the

Japanese is that of a benign co-participant and instrument in the self-realization of the Filipino or Filipina, far from the "face"-obsessed stereotypes of Romulo's "The Japanese Mind" ("Serenade" in Gonzalez: 1979).

While Bienvenido Santos, like Gonzalez, rejects stereotypes of the Japanese, he does paint more negative views of the Japanese than Gonzalez. Santos was a *pensionado* during the Second World War, trapped in the USA and separated from his wife and daughters in the Philippines. Hence, he never directly witnessed the war, except through the eyes of Filipino labor migrants in the USA who had become exiles.[4] Many of his post-war stories reflect the expatriate's sense of guilt for having assimilated into American life and harboring a secret desire to return to America. When Santos does touch upon Filipino experience during the Japanese Occupation, as in his short story, "Early Harvest," he presents Japanese characters less as rounded figures than as discrete obstacles, which Filipino villagers must overcome through cunning, determination, and the help of the supernatural (Croghan 1975: 173–82).

In his longer works, Santos reveals an unflattering view of Japan and the Japanese and a searching, though still positive, appraisal of the USA. In his novel, *The Volcano* (1965), which explores three decades in the lives of a US missionary family in the Philippines, the sole Japanese character named in the novel is Soda, a pilot whose plane has crashed in the forest. Soda subsequently becomes a prisoner of the community of Americans and Filipinos hiding out in the Bicol jungle and is portrayed as a helpless victim, if not a caricature. His first appearance is as an injured airman badly in need of the attention of the American protagonist, the missionary doctor, Paul Hunter. Even though Soda endears himself to the villagers by planting vegetables, he is bereft of nobility, always hunching and fearing for his life, especially during the closing years of the war when the Japanese were in retreat from the advancing American army (Santos 1986b: 179–91).

In a different sense from *The Volcano*, Santos' other novel, *Villa Magdalena* (also 1965) presents a likewise negative view of

Japan that contrasts with the regenerative Japan of Gonzalez' *Bamboo Dancers*. The story, much like *Bamboo Dancers*, concerns the alienation of the Filipino, this time from corruption. In this case, Don Magno Medallada, a tycoon, initiates a poor orphaned child, Fred Medallada, into his corrupt empire and his familial home, Villa Magdalena. Don Magno Medallada has drained not only the wealth of his wife Magdalena but also the spiritual energies of her family, the rich Condes. The Japanese Occupation of the Philippines attains importance in the novel not for any positive return to indigenous culture as in Gonzalez' experience. Instead, the Japanese are notable for having killed Fred's teacher, a close friend of the family. Moreover, Japanese soldiers humiliate both Don Magno and Fred by slapping their faces at a checkpoint and create the adverse conditions (uncontrolled violence, hyperinflation, and food shortages) for Don Magno to swindle fellow Filipinos and rise to power (Santos 1986a: 140–9).

Isabel Conde, the niece of Doña Magdalena, attempts to flee from Villa Magdalena by eloping with Sol Gomez to Japan. For the two lovers, Sol and Isabel, Japan is a lonely place of exile, bleak, far from home geographically and culturally. It is a place of refuge that despite everything, is still not far enough to protect them from the corruption and tyranny from which they are running. Indeed, their escape is fleeting for Fred soon arrives on behalf of Don Magno. Fred manipulates Isabel into signing away her properties to the magnate, which proves his loyalty to his adopted father (ibid.: 213–27).

One final factor makes Japan unappealing to the Filipinos of *Villa Magdalena*, which Fred notices. While he, Isabel, and Sol are eating in a restaurant in Tokyo, two Japanese, a censor in the war and another whose father had died in the Philippines during the war, ask the Filipinos for advice, presumably on how to search for the remains of his father. This question makes the Filipinos uncomfortable. Fred realizes that it had reopened wounds of war that had not yet healed, and these Japanese had assumed a familiarity they could not reciprocate. Fred connected this awkward moment to his bitter experience of seeing downtown Tokyo (several years after the end of the American Occupation) completely rebuilt while the Philippines remained in ruins (ibid.: 213–27). Such a view resonates with post-war Filipino resentment toward Japan, which many in power felt should have been further disciplined for its conduct in war by paying substantial reparations. But US Cold War strategy overruled this approach, regarding Japan as an important Cold War partner, and protected Japan from substantial Philippine war claims (Meyer 1965: 132–40). (Interestingly here, Fred's bitterness is directed toward Japan and not to the Americans who had created the conditions for post-war reparation diplomacy.)

The Late 20th Century: Brainard and Holthe

From the 1960s to the 1980s, especially after the repeal of discriminatory legislation in 1965, Filipinos, especially a greater proportion of women, began to immigrate in large numbers to the United States (Chan 1990; Takaki 1989). Many of them had been born after the Second World War. Despite this, a sizable number had either lived through or lived with relatives who had experienced the Japanese Occupation of the Philippines. Certainly, this number increased during the late 1970s when family reunification provisions supplanted occupational categories as the preferred mode for admitting Filipinos into the USA and subsequently brought into the country more elderly Filipinos, for whom vivid memories of war remained (Posadas 1999: 36–43). Toward the end of the 20th century, wartime biographical accounts were published, including Maria Rosa Henson's *Comfort Woman* and Alfredo Roces' *Looking for Liling*, that focused Filipino American attention on the war, this at the same time when Filipino and Filipina global migration to Japan, the Middle East, and other parts of the world was becoming more and more prevalent (Henson 1999; Roces 2000; Tolentino 2001: 7–10).

Filipino American fiction joined this developing wartime discourse with the publication of Cecilia Manguerra Brainard's novel of the Second World War, *When the Rainbow Goddess Wept* in 1999. A few years afterward, the much younger, US-born Filipina, Tess Uriza Holthe, published her lengthy novel of the war, *When the Elephants Dance* (2003). Remarkably, despite the passage of decades since the end of the Second World War and the vast distances in time and culture across the Pacific, the same dual perceptions, of pro-Japan/anti-US and anti-Japan/pro-US sentiment, which haunted the colonial period and the first 20 years of the post-war period, continued to persist in these Filipino immigrant and Filipino American texts. Perhaps at the same time, the advantages of distance, time, and gender have allowed both of these women writers to face the war directly and provide expression to hitherto ignored voices of women and children.

A rather complex view of the Japanese emerges from Brainard's luminous and underwritten novel, which effortlessly weaves together history, myth, and memory through simple, suggestive prose. Brainard combines all three through the recollections of a young girl, Yvonne Macaraig, who witnesses the transition from pre-war to wartime Ubec (fictional Cebu) through her family household's experiences among the guerrillas, especially that of her father, Nando, and her mother, Angeling, and the stories of their indigenous maid, Laydan. Laydan enigmatically enjoins Yvonne to "become the epic," and she fondly recites the exploits of her hero, Tuwaäng, who battles to save the rainbow goddess from the clutches of an evil giant.

To say that this novel is "pro-Japan" is an obvious simplification because the narrative holds nothing back in portraying Japanese soldiers as killers, torturers, and destroyers. At the same time, the novel refuses to dehumanize the entire Japanese people. As Nando tells Yvonne, "[A]ll people are alike." They are both good and bad, even the Japanese who are their enemy. Faithful to this insight, the novel portrays sympathetic Japanese characters before, during, and after the war, inside and outside of the military. Among the closest pre-war friends of the Macaraig household (which include Yvonne's grandfather, Lolo Peping, her aunt, Tiya Lourdes, and her cousin, Esperanza), is a Japanese family, the owners of the local *sari-sari* (or small convenience) store, especially the mother and daughter named Sanny and Mica. Both are kind to Yvonne. Indeed, Sanny trusts Yvonne and her cousin Esperanza enough to allow them to take her daughter to the movies. As the war draws near, Yvonne defends the family from the growing hostility of those lashing out at anyone Japanese. In the wake of the Japanese invasion, neither Yvonne nor the members of her family are prepared for the news that a fire, said to be arson set off by rumors that Sanny's husband was a Japanese spy, had razed the store, killing both mother and child (Brainard 1999: 15–24).

A second sympathetic character might be the Japanese military. During the war, the guerrillas capture no less than the Japanese military's chief of staff in the Philippines, Admiral Yoshida. In response, the Japanese army razes several villages and creates havoc for the inhabitants of Ubec. The guerrillas, including Yvonne's father and Tito Alvarez, (the popular governor of Ubec who before the war had been attracted to Japan's Greater East Asia Co-Prosperity Sphere, until the Japanese killed his wife and children when he refused to collaborate), decide to save the rest of the villages from Japanese violence by negotiating a truce with the Japanese in exchange for the release of their commanding officer. This is resolutely opposed by the vengeful and racist American, Martin Lewis, an insubordinate guerrilla, who is portrayed as having a sordid past, having murdered his own Filipina wife and a peasant father who had attempted to block Lewis from raping his daughter. The Filipino leaders, nonetheless, overrule Lewis and return the Japanese admiral to his troops. When Lewis kidnaps and tortures the Filipino leaders for this act, Admiral Yoshida's men, for reasons of honor or indebtedness, risk sending operatives to free the captured Filipino guerrillas (ibid.: 194).

A third sympathetic Japanese character is an unnamed doctor. Toward the end of the novel, in the emotional reunion of the Macaraig household, which had been divided between the tightly controlled city and the guerrilla countryside, Tiya Lourdes grieves the disappearance of a Japanese doctor, who at great personal risk, had took her as partner and provided for her and Esperanza, while protecting the Macaraig home from destruction.[5]

Alongside of this many-sided portrayal of Japanese, the novel displays a critical attitude toward the Americans. Both Lolo Peping and Laydan, their maid, regard Americans as enemies. Both were old enough to remember the Philippine-American War and the atrocities committed by the Americans, including the genocide in the island of Samar presided over by General Smith. (Everytime the senile grandfather hears talk of war, he blurts out anti-American slogans, which shocks Yvonne's initially pro-American father) (ibid.: 9, 18–9). The often-heroized General MacArthur, for whom Nando owes allegiance, is pictured as a somewhat distant figure. While he rallies Philippine guerrillas to him, American and Filipino, and eventually returns with American GI's, the length of time he takes to respond to the sufferings of the Filipinos leads the guerrillas to some painful conclusions. Indeed, Nando realizes this after much soul searching. A pensionado who had lived among Americans before the war, Nando comes to realize that his Americanization, expressed in consuming everything American and an unmitigated pro-Americanism, had been badly misplaced. The tortures he suffers under Martin Lewis and the self-interest that leads America to save Europe first and sacrifice the Philippines, awakens in him a newfound sense of nationalism (ibid.: 198).

Neither criticism of America nor complex views of the Japanese, however, pervade Holthe's *When the Elephants Dance*. Holthe's immigrant parents told her numerous stories about the war that have been infused into her novel, and which take a decidedly grim view of the Japanese. Holthe's novel has some notable similarities with Brainard's: both narrate the experience of war from the experiences of everyday people. Both write lyrically of the stories that people told each other to forget the dangerous circumstances in which they lived or simply to relieve boredom. Like Brainard, Holthe too utilizes haunting legends and animist folklore, even Tagalog expressions, albeit marred by many jarring linguistic errors. And both present relatively sympathetic Japanese individuals. In Holthe's novel, this is not incidental, as a Japanese mother and daughter (Mrs. Yoshi and Mica; Mr. Yoshi having been taken into an internment camp after Pearl Harbor), come to share the entire war experience with the Filipino protagonists that huddle together in the cellar of the Karangalan house to hide from the Japanese toward the end of the war. Neither the mother nor the daughter, despite being of Japanese ancestry and appearance, escape the brutality of Japanese soldiers (Holthe 2003: 28, 359).

Still, Holthe's novel betrays a subtle bias against her sympathetic Japanese characters. While Mrs. Yoshi and Mica experience the war together with their Filipino neighbors, they are nonetheless set apart from the Filipino families. Holthe's novel is built out of chapters in which each of the different families narrates the tragic incidents and legendary occurrences that brought them to their present plight. The Japanese family is excluded from this narration of family history. The Japanese family, so to speak, has no roots that can allow it to be identified as Filipino or Filipina.

Beyond these individuals, the image of the Japanese becomes even more one-dimensional as Japanese military atrocities encompass the book, reminiscent of Javellana's *Without Seeing the Dawn* as well as numerous portrayals of the Japanese in Philippine film and television. The opening chapter, based upon the real-life experience of Holthe's father, is a stark torture scene told from the voice of the young protagonist, Alejandro Karangalan. This is followed by a second long chapter in which Alejandro's sister, Isabelle, helps the injured guerrilla leader, Domingo Matapang, only to get captured by Japanese soldiers who rape her (reminiscent of comfort women stories). The third chapter tells the story of the guerrilla leader Matapang, which includes a battle scene with Japanese soldiers who had discovered the meeting place of two competing guerrilla groups. There is also the story of Alejandro Karangalan's father who is captured by Japanese soldiers and is nearly executed in a killing pit filled with beheaded Filipinos (Hartendorp 1964: 417). He escapes death only when he overwhelms a Japanese soldier who set him aside with the aim of sodomizing him. The final chapter results in the capture of the entire Karangalan family, their forced march through the streets of Manila, flanked by mutilated, charred, and bullet-ridden bodies of men, women, and children, and the group's bloody escape from a warehouse after a brutal struggle with two Japanese sentries.

Unlike Brainard, Holthe seems indifferent to US colonization or the faults of American leaders, as well as the indiscriminate bombing of Manila, which elicited severe reproach from Filipinos after the war (Nakpil 1967 in Brands 1992: 209–10, 370). Indeed, the novel derives its force from what appears a life-and-death struggle between Filipinos and Japanese, between good and evil, between a people that are imprisoned and their oppressive and inhuman captors. As though innocent of all this, America stands outside or above the fray, only in the end to return (like a *deus-ex-machina*) to aid in freeing the family captured in the Manila warehouse (Holthe 2003: 357–63). Perhaps the only mitigating factor in this inexorable portrayal of the Japanese is the bevy of divided Filipinos themselves — the willful and disobedient daughter, the cowardly neighbor, the guerrilla leader who plays god with people's lives and is also an adulterer, and the former Makapili (a notorious collaborator with the Japanese), who despite his change of heart, is undisturbed by all the fellow townspeople that he put to death. Toward the end, one is left with a community that, while hopeful for the future, seems emotionally and morally spent.

Conclusion

This chapter then has presented the persistence of divergent attitudes toward Japan and Japanese among Filipinos in America through a representative selection of political tracts and fiction from three generations of Filipino transmigrant and immigrant men and women in the United States. This chapter includes as well the ways in which Japan and the United States have acted as "competing shadows" shaping the lives of Filipinos and commanding their allegiance. While these works grapple with the ever-present problems of Filipino independence, identity, material well-being, and place in the world, their narratives of Japan reveal the outlines of two recurrent world views.

In sum, the pro-Japan/anti-US view valorizes Japan's political leadership in Asia and its Eastern spiritual qualities; admires its sense of solidarity in the aftermath of war and nuclear nightmare; and recognizes the nobility of individuals who were honest neighbors, honorable enemies, and self-sacrificing lovers. This view also demystifies the USA as a colonial power with selfish motives like any other colonizer, feels unease at the spiritual emptiness of American civilization, and reacts with revulsion at the crudity of American racism, sexism, and self-interest. The second, anti-Japan/pro-US view, however, condemns Japan's imperial ambitions upon the Philippines and toward Asia, locates Japan's aggressiveness in its insecure racial character; rejects, or perhaps defers, friendship with the Japanese on the basis of the unfairness of Japanese progress and continuing Philippine ruin; and reviles the almost unmitigated cruelty of the Japanese military in causing the unforgettable traumas of an even now distant war. Moreover, this view sees the USA and Western liberalism in general as the political and spiritual hope of the future, aspires for and is attracted to Americanization (despite the seemingly disloyal nature of this desire), and at the same time, regards Americans as being above or outside the violent conflicts that have shaped the relations between the Philippines and Japan.

These then represent the complex emotions that both inspire and trouble Filipinos in the USA when they look back and look forward to the future of Filipino, Japanese, and American relations.

Notes

1. Once the strike was underway, however, a bond of suffering, disease, and labor repression tied Filipinos and Japanese alike. See Kerkvliet (2002), pp. 22–5, 34.
2. For background, see Espiritu (2005), pp. 19–26.
3. See "The Blue Skull and the Dark Palms," in Gonzalez (1963) and "The Flight of the Gentle Folk," in Gonzalez (1993b).
4. For background, see Espiritu (2005), pp. 139–44.
5. Brainard (1999), p. 212. See also the Japanese doctor who treats Yvonne's grandfather, p. 76.

chapter 10

Singing of Modernity and US Shadow: Bodily Aesthetics and Ideology in *Salidummay* and *Shoka*

Michiyo Yoneno-Reyes

But the new wine must be put into fresh wine-skins.

Luke 5:38

Introduction

Two central issues of ethnomusicology in the 1990s were identity politics and cultural hybridity.[1] Benedict Anderson's *Imagined Communities* (1983) provided a handy framework for ethnomusicological studies in seeking the arena of music in the construction of national consciousness or in the projection of a particular ethnicity. In due course, a number of studies unraveled the cases where "tradition" was *invented*. One of the pioneering works with such a discourse was Christopher Waterman's study on *juju* as Yoruba's syncretic "master tradition." It demonstrates the process of making of *juju* by the Yoruba nationalism movement by incorporating a variety of musical styles found in the Yoruba land such as African, Middle Eastern, Afro-American, and European (Waterman 1990). T.M. Scruggs' study on the use of music on the construction of

Nicaraguan national consciousness marks a model example of the penetration of Andersonean framework in ethnomusicology (Scruggs 1999). He examines the process of the national-consciousness building of Nicaragua as a multi-ethnic nation in the 20th century. Scruggs emphasizes the incorporation of various musical elements from remote areas within Nicaraguan state territory into the aesthetics of the metropolis, middle-class population. Scruggs suggests that development of radio technology in the 20th century is an aural equivalent to movable typewriter, which Anderson claims, had crucially contributed to the rise of national consciousness in Europe. Therefore, it is natural that in a number of former colonies that experienced the rise of national consciousness in the 20th century, music played a significant role worth studying.

In contrast to the music-as-identity-marker discourse of the 1990s under Andersonean framework — that tended to emphasize the ideological invention of "tradition" — ethnomusicology in the 2000s shifted its focus into performance as bodily experience, following the path of the anthropological trend. Excellently unraveling the paradox of the "invented tradition" practice, Rebecca S. Miller shed light on the aspect of collective memory/sentiment and selfhood, rather than ideology, in revealing "cultural ambivalence" the Kayaks of a Caribbean village experience with *quadrille*. The *quadrille* is a dance-music-song of a European-American creole, which is "neither wholly embraced nor completely rejected" by the Kayaks while retaining popularity particularly at a local festival; it was once associated with the whites, but today, is received well as "local culture." It presents the nuance of elite culture within a village and it evokes in village folk the collective traumatic memory of enslavement by European colonizers, but at the same time, it indicates the pan-Caribbean identity (due to its creole nature) as well. Pointing out "a rupture of a historical understanding of community and self, Miller suggests that the Kayaks "negotiate the forces of modernity that inform and transform a developing post-colonial identity" (Miller 2005: 435).

This paper closely traces the process of the making of the so-called *salidummay* songs as a folk song genre in the 20th century in the northern Philippine highlands. The *salidummay* is a group of songs often performed to symbolically express the collective ethnic identity of the northern Luzon highlanders. Some dozens of rather simple tunes, most of which characterized by refrain words "dang dang ay si dong ilay, insinalidummay" or its variations, are customarily recognized as tunes for *salidummay*. These are characterized by meter rhythm, and pentatonic, hexatonic, or diatonic pitch systems. Words are mostly either in any of the dialects of the northern highland communities or in Ilokano, the *lingua franca* of the region. The words deal with a wide variety of topics often succeeding the words of "traditional" chants for life passage rituals, and non-ritualistic ones such as courtship and epics. Manifestation of collective ethnic identities, activists' messages of social concerns, as well as Biblical messages, are also sung with the tunes of *salidummay*. The words may be composed extemporarily or quickly written on a piece of paper for one-time performance in village contexts often based on the existing formulae. Several variations of *salidummay* songs — mostly published ones either in the form of song books or in cassette tapes or CDs — have fixed words to particular tunes.

This paper examines the impact of the US shadow on the process of the formation of the *salidummay* as a modern folk song genre from the perspectives of body and aesthetics. In so doing, this paper seeks the socio-historical meaning of modern unison singing, the action observed prominently in the performance of *salidummay*; namely, its bodily and aesthetic contribution to the rise of the sense of belongingness to a community at various levels. The rapid progress of the historical investigations of *sambika/shoka/gunka* (hymn/school song/military song) in the process of reception of Western music in modern Japan has inspired me to approach the *salidummay* songs generally known of the northern Philippine highlands as comparable phenomenon while embracing differences.

Among a number of excellent studies on body in recent anthropology, the concept of the "mindful body," as summarized by Nancy Scheper-Huges and Margaret M. Lock, paved a way to this study (Scheper-Huges and Lock 1998). Critically reflecting on the assumption of dualism of modern science, that tends to dichotomize mind/body, spirit/matter, nature/culture, Scheper-Huges and Lock suggest the holistic concept of the mind-body-society interaction. In my response to the "cultural ambivalence," as I myself observe in *salidummay*-making, I seek the inseparability between senses and actions, beyond ideological constrains. Robert Desjarlais further introduces the concept of aesthetics into the study of society and culture, beyond the conventional domain of the word in artistry genres, in order "to grasp (and tie together) the **tacit leitmotivs** that shape cultural constructions of bodily and social interactions" (emphasis mine). He argues the values and practice as the aesthetics of the everyday are the embodiment of the "visceral experience of cultural actors (rather than articulated through concrete artistic or philosophic tenets)" (Desjarlais 1992: 65). As I empathize with Miller's "cultural ambivalence" in connection with *salidummay*-making, I ask how a newly introduced manner of music-making — rather than music text itself — at the advent of modernization in the Philippines, like in Japan, both forced by the power of the United States, has molded the musical senses of the common populace and affected music-making in the succeeding decades.[2]

The discussions in this paper will include the aspects of signers' adjustment to the particular musical elements (particularly metric rhythm, pentatonic and diatonic pitch systems) as aural/oral experience, the changing musical tastes by generations, the centripetal force of "traditional" epics/ballads as common knowledge, the impact of development of media technology, and the affect of nostalgia and intimacy. Owing largely to the arguments on the Western impact on the musics of the world by Bruno Nettl, I relate *salidummay* and *shoka* songs to the trinity of church/school/military, the three modern institutions that played a crucial role in the rapid spread of Western-folktune singing in the non-Western world at large. That shall reveal the US shadow in the process of modernization in the Philippines and Japan, though in different manners. Nettl suggests that Christian songs were often the first encounter with Western music in many non-western societies, as he summarizes the situation among the "native" Americans.

> In many instances, the first intensive exposure of non-western societies to Western music was through church music. Certainly this was true in the Americas, and although the sound of military music may fleetingly have preceded, it was religious music that various groups of Indians were first persuaded to learn ... Learning the music quickly was surely more a function of desire or pressure than simply of ability. But the speed with which Western music was added to the indigenous repertory, or replaced it, was indeed amazing, for Torquemada, the Franciscan chronicler, quoted by Harrison (p. 48), tells us that, within a few decades of the conquest, traditions had developed that included polyphonic singing of masses and Vespers — even in small settlements, and local building of European instruments, organ among them (Nettl 1985: 7).

My data shows that the Second World War was the crucial historical event for the emergence of early forms of *salidummay* songs sung by anti-Japan guerrilla soldiers in northern Philippine highlands. They belong to the first generation who had bodily acquired skills to sing metric and pentatonic/diatonic tunes through schools as well as Protestant churches both led by Americans during the first decades of the 20th century. This was particularly so in the northern highlands as a specially treated colony.[3] Even in the second half of the century, the bodily aesthetics of the highlanders allowed post-colonial schools, churches and cultural-milieu to further contribute to the making of *salidummay* as the Cordillera (pan-highland) identity-marker. Meanwhile, the recent rapid progress of the musicological/historical studies on Japanese *sambika/shoka/gunka* leads us to a comparable perspective. Led by painstaking studies by Yasuko Tsukahara (1993) and Rihei

Nakamura (1993), a series of recent studies on the history of reception of *yogaku* (literally "western music") in modern Japan have unanimously revealed the significance and interconnectedness of those three song genres that by themselves underwent the vital course of transformation (Kyo [Kan] 1998, 2002; Gottschewski 1998; Teshirogi 1998, 1999; Matsushita and Teshirogi 1998; Yasuda 1993; Oba 2002). When the word "modernization" (*kindaika*) was to general public a synonym for "importation of the western civilization" in the late 19th century, the influence of American counterparts to those three song genres was remarkable.

Original data on *salidummay* performance and its sociocultural background in this study are largely based on my participant-observation in my intermittent fieldworks in Mountain Province, Kalinga, Abra, Ifugao, as well as in Baguio City since 1993. Among the nearly 40 villages and towns that I visited, the most recent major fieldwork site was a Banao village at the crossroads of the Provinces of Kalinga and Abra. My six-month main fieldwork during the dry season of 2003–2004, including derived short visits to eight villages in Kalinga and Abra, was preceded by three preliminary short visits in 2002 and 2003, as well as four-month fieldwork in Baguio City in the rainy months of 2003. My exposure to other approximately 30 towns and villages in northern Luzon highlands marked the significant prelude for this study. Spatially comparative perspectives were nurtured in this study. Archival/bibliographical research, which forms a substantial part of this study, was primarily conducted at the following institutions: the University of the Philippines Main Library Filipiniana Collection, the University of the Philippines College Baguio Cordillera Studies Center, the St. Andrew's Theological Seminary, among others.

In this paper, I use the term "northern Philippine/Luzon highlands" when referring to the physical highland areas in northern Luzon where the people conduct "mountain/hill life," as a term primarily for space, regardless of the administrative grids (such as Provincial borders for Cordillera Administrative Region, or CAR) and "ethnic" connotations (Figure 1). As we shall see, this paper integrates the inconsistent usages of the term *salidummay* and its numerous variations, and presents that *salidummay* is a word established with such a spelling only in the early 1990s. Yet, I have chosen to use the word *salidummay* throughout this manuscript, because it is so far the most acceptable compromise. In this connection, I would like to note at the outset that the term *salidummay* in this paper must always be read with the "so-called," or as "a group of songs, usually associated with the term *salidummay*."

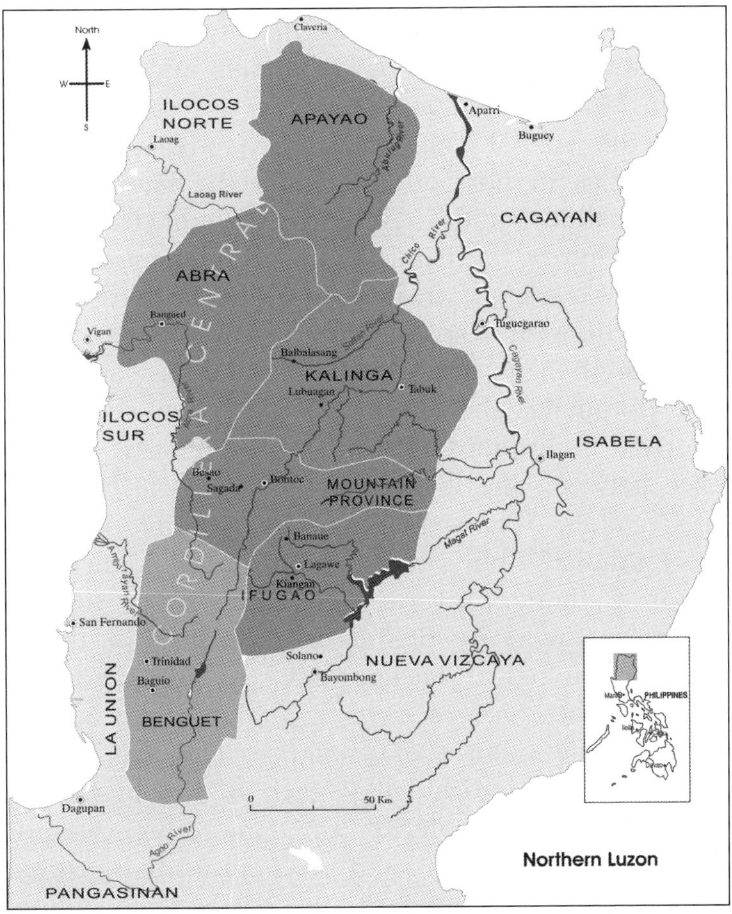

Figure 1. Map of Northern Luzon Highlands (Based on Afable 2004: xvii)

Formation of "Mountain Province"

Vicente Rafael piercingly analyzes that the 1903 Census conducted by the US colonial administration was the first step of categorizing the peoples of the Philippine archipelago in connection with the place of residence and language with assumption of the tempo-spatially static concept of ethnicity (Rafael 2000). Gerald Finin illustrates in detail that the creation of the "old" Mountain Province in 1908 by the US administration as a "contoured" reservation-like space (consisting of the sub-provinces of Apayao, Kalinga, Bontok, Lepanto, Ifugao, Amburayan and Benguet) that further spurred molding the sense of belongingness of both lowlanders and highlanders as such (Finin 2005) (Figure 2).

While the spatial continuity of Spanish Politic-Military Commandancies in northern Luzon in the late 19th century and municipalities under American administration in the early 20th century is explicit, the fundamental difference is that the Americans treated the highlanders as though they were different "spices" from lowlanders. Thus, the "isolation myth" of non-Christian tribes as an American invention dominates the Filipinos' imagination even today in post-colonial Philippines. During the Spanish period, the difference between the lowlanders (*Indios, Infidels*) and highlanders (*Igorottes, Tinguianes* etc.) was not perceived as that of race or ethnicity, but simply as that of residence. Because the Roman Catholic converts were often made to converge in the coastal towns by Spaniards regardless of their place of origin or biological background, the highland dwellers inevitably meant "non-converts," if not runaways, subsequently with the nuance of prejudice. However, a number of Spanish records indicate that each of the highland communities was hardly isolated from the other. Despite the scarcity of transportation and communication technology for our contemporary standard, the barter trade among the highlanders-midlanders-lowlanders was more common than

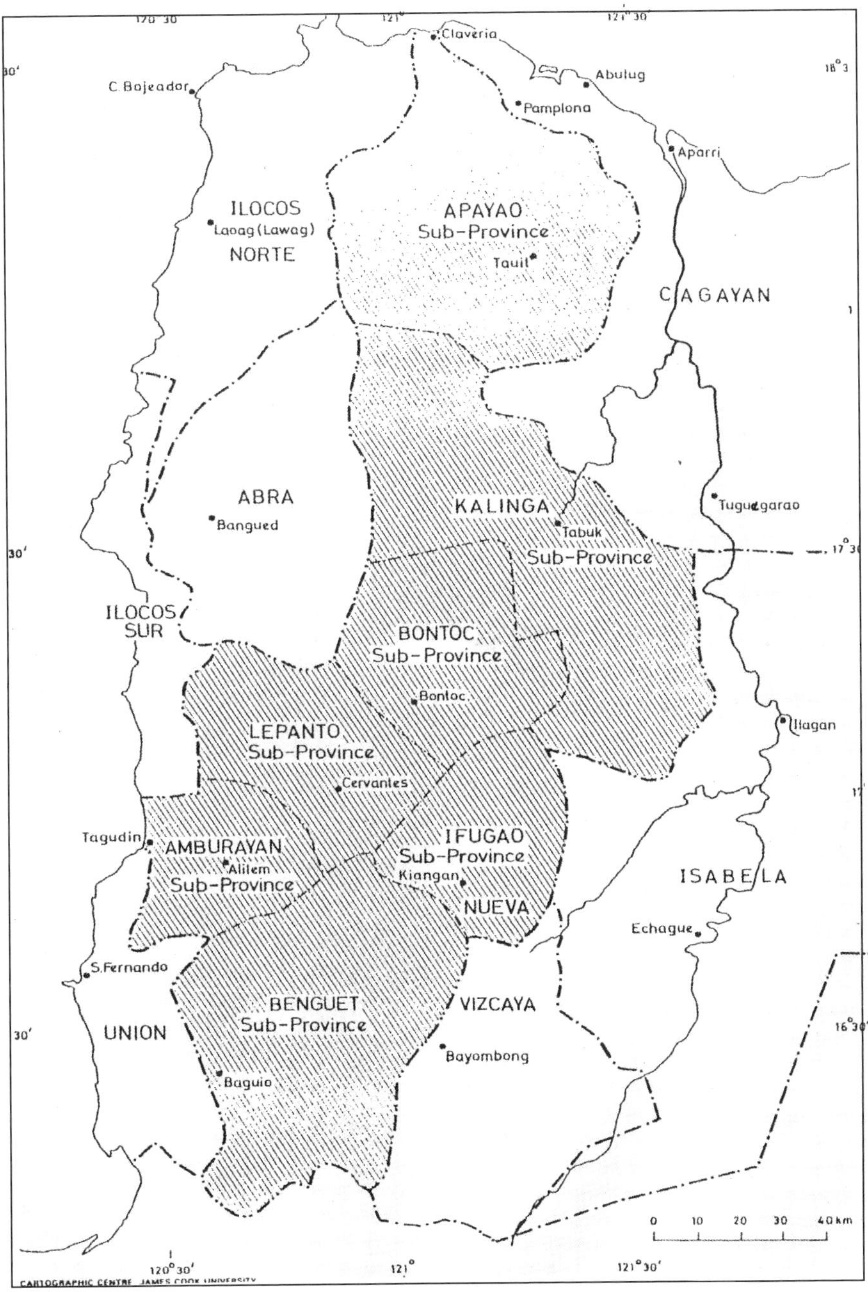

Figure 2. Map of the "old" Mountain Province 1908 (Fry 1983: 50)

we may think today, through rivers, ranges and trails. Their physical ability to travel long distances (sailing and hiking) far exceeds what we can imagine today. Similarly, as legends and oral history inform us, the migration from/to distant areas was frequent. The population of upstream and that of downstream of the same river were often in close ties; i.e., relatives, clans or *kailian*s (village-mates). On the other hand, they could hardly get in touch with other highlanders who lived along the other river systems. Careful observation of the contemporary patterns of migration/movement, facilitated by the spread of kinship network at each household level among the northern highlanders, as well as cultural continuity and gradational variations in space, allow us to imagine the past as such (Afable 1989, Azurin 1991, Austin 2001, Finin 2005, Keesing 1962, Panabang 2006, Scott 1969, 1974 [1977], 1982, 1993).[4]

Americans overlooked such fluid mobility and socio-cultural dynamics among the highlanders-midlanders-lowlanders, and set an artificial boundary to sum up all the different highlanders into one by separating them from their fellow tribesmen residing in the mid/lowlands. A series of policies, projects and incidents thereafter (i.e., *Cañao*, Trinidad Agricultural School, employment at mines, etc. See Afable 1998a; Finin 2005: 77–106) provided the opportunities for the highlanders from different places to get to know one another and contributed to the formation of the concept of fellow-*montañosa*. But I argue that formation of such a concept was rather limited to the "official" settings, namely the imagined domains. To each individual, it has had little realistic impact to daily life. The indigenous sentiment of the intimacy with one's co-villagers and emigrants, as well as that of the estrangement from the "enemy tribes" that occurs more often with neighboring groups of people, remains persistently strong. I suggest it is more appropriate to emphasize a sort of "dual (or even more multiple) sentiment" of belonging among northern highlanders.

The 1900s–1930s: "Grounding" and Introduction of Education

Any genre of performing arts in the world — from opera to jazz, or to *kabuki* — experiences considerable formal transformations until the genre gets "established," after producing vast variations of performing texts in multiple styles. The *salidummay* too gradually *became* a genre after several decades of transformation since the emergence of its embryo in the first half of the 20th century.

The US colonial administrators as well as civilians in the early 20th century paid special attention to the northern Luzon highlands for various reasons.[5] The development of technology of road construction in the 19th century, while sailing rivers still remained significant, had already made a large area of the highlands accessible to Spaniards and allowed them to establish politico-military commandancies. Concurrently, the establishment of ethnology/anthropology under the prominence of evolutionism in science prompted scholars and non-scholars alike, including some European nationals, to write about the newly discovered "primitive" people(s) and their society in the region. Thus, a great amount of literature containing the ethnographic accounts of the northern Luzon highlands was produced in the early decades of the 20th century. The authors included scholars, administrators, and missionaries, among others. Similarly noteworthy is a research program on Philippine folk music and dances conducted by Filipino researchers/artists in the 1920s that led to the production of several literary and art works using "native" motifs (Santiago 1931 [1957]).

In spite of the abundance of the literature on the northern Philippine highlands, however, published accounts on *salidummay* hardly exist in the early decades of the 20th century.[6] Given such a situation, I infer that the *salidummay* did not exist in this era, but its ancestors did as older folk chants, as relevant terms appear as chant forms. For example, Faye-Cooper Cole, an American ethnologist who conducted fieldwork in the old

Abra Province in 1907–1908, presents staff notation of two ostensibly relevant songs: *Dang-dang-ay* and *Diwas* (Cole 1922). The transcribed tunes in Cole, however, scarcely resemble any of what we know as the tunes of *salidummay* today.[7]

Works by Lawrence L. Wilson and Morice Vanobervergh on Apayao respectively, are another set of important literature. Two song lyrics, among six, by Wilson (an American mining prospector and writer) (Wilson 1947 [1967]), are of particular importance to this study. *A Feast Song* is remarked with "Tune-*salecdomoy*," implying the presence of a tune known in the locale/then as *salecdomoy*, though there is no way for us to know from this information how that tune may have sounded like. The presented wording of *A Feast Song*, with rhymed lines, seems to have little to do with what we know as the wording of *salidummay* today. Another song lyric *Salindumay*, includes refrain words: "salindumay duma-ay," "salindomay domiwas," and "salin dewas domiwas." On the other hand, Vanoverbergh (1960), a Belgian priest who informs us of his penetrating observation of the highland Apayao in the 1910s, illuminates *salen dumay*, *dewas* and *dandan-ay* of Apayao: the first two as an alternating song-dance primarily between men and women — or *utagaki*, to appropriate the Japanese term which itself is a comprehensive cultural concept and has been established as an academic term, with no equivalent in Western/Asian languages; and the last one as a story-chant by old men.[8] Some dozens of examples of lyrics of those by Vanoverbergh indicate that these words hardly resemble those of what the northern Luzon highlanders call *salidummay* today. But in terms of performing style (story chant or call-and-response), it is plausible that these forms had preceded the *salidummay* of the coming decades.

In the early decades of the 20th century when various chants were the principal vocal repertoires in the entire area of the northern Luzon highlands, the colonial education greatly influenced the musical senses and ability of the children. In those decades, many children began to attend elementary school at least for a few years. Children were exposed to American (predominantly Irish and/or Scottish-American) folktunes through children's songs as a part of official curriculum. Besides, in the Protestant communities, American Protestant hymns were taught at schools and Sunday schools.[9] Boy Scout and Girl Scout activities were also the venue for informal education where singing American songs played a significant part in implanting American values and senses into the children's minds and bodies. A letter of an American female missionary recollecting her early days in late 1925 in a village at the border of the present Kalinga and Abra Provinces informs us how highland children got along with "America" through singing hymns.

> It was 24 years ago today that I arrived there to live. And the next day I visited the school and talked briefly about why the mission had to come there at the request of the people, and what we were going to try to do. And everyday there after I talked to one of the grades ... Fr. Walcott arrived on December 5th, escorted by Fr. Sibley who had been there twice before, and at once we started teaching Christmas carols & getting ready to give the Christmas pageant ... I never shall forget the beauty of the plaza that Christmas Eve ... the lovely stable and the nice pagan children taking the parts so [well?] and [?] [?] the old carols that were so new to them. [I] know you [managed] to sing [well][even][though] the words were pretty hard for you.[10]
>
> (the words in [ ] are the author's attempted reconstruction of the faded photocopy of the original letter.)

The "school" in the letter refers to the public elementary school established in the village a few years earlier. Thus, both the church and public school got engaged in education conjointly in realizing the civilizing project. The colonial education produced the youth, who would in the following decades contribute to the emergence and wide spread of the early form(s) of *salidummay*.

1940s: Emergence of *Salidummay* as Guerrilla Song

A number of written accounts on *salidummay*, though mostly written in the 1970s and 1980s, as well as local oral accounts, state that *salidummay* emerged as anti-Japanese guerrilla's songs during the Second World War. It is said that it spread throughout northern Luzon, both in highland and lowland areas, through mobile guerrillas who were locally recruited. These songs were not necessarily perceived/entitled as *salidummay* at that time, though. These songs must have sounded novel, because of the locally-modified American tunes, characterized by double-meter rhythm and pentatonic or diatonic pitch systems.[11] But in other elements, those songs largely retained conventional features. The words often followed those of older chants (epics and lyrics including courtship song-debate); and "traditional" call-and-response performance style (alternation between solo-verses and a group-refrain) continued; and as for the context of performance, the early *salidummay* during the Second World War were performed in the conventional setting of courtship singing as well as that of personal ballad chanting. They were dialogically rendered between a troop of guerrillas and a group of maidens of the village where the troop stationed in the open air at dusk — presenting the features of *utagaki*.[12] Young guerrillas in the midst of hardship of soldering life also sang ballads to themselves for comfort, with "traditional" wordings and "modern," namely American influenced tunes: these were to become the early *salidummay*s after the war (Figures 3a, 3b, 4a and 4b).

Bruno Nettl suggests the distinction between westernization and modernization of changing musical forms of the non-West as follows: when a musical text changes into western style while retaining the context of performance, it is westernization; while it more or less retains its musical text while changing the context of performance, it is modernization (Nettl 1985). To apply Nettl's model, the *salidummay* emerged as "westernized" style of existing vocal practice. At its early stage, such a new singing practice was not considered a new "genre"; merely a variation of the existing vocal forms that was modified in accordance with the new *taste* of the youth, especially metric rhythm and pentatonic scales. They had learned and bodily internalized them unexpectedly quickly under the extraordinary socio-cultural pressure of colonialism. Aural/oral exposure to metric and pentatonic tunes soon became the youth's ability of rendering them, while tending to lose ability to improve more melismatic or syllabic chants with various vocal ornamental techniques. The new ability and taste decisively oriented the direction of *salidummay*-making in the following decades.

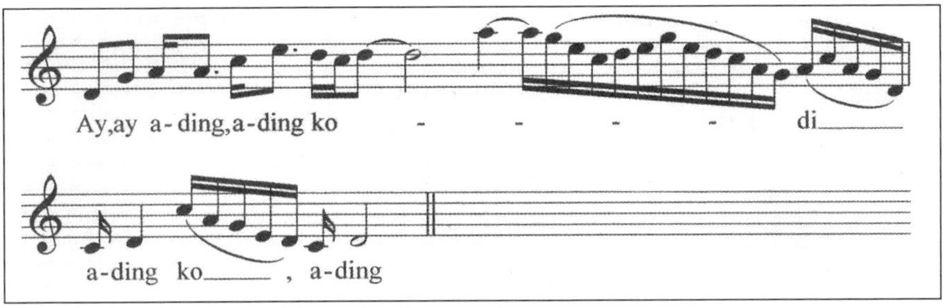

Figure 3a. A Kalimusta

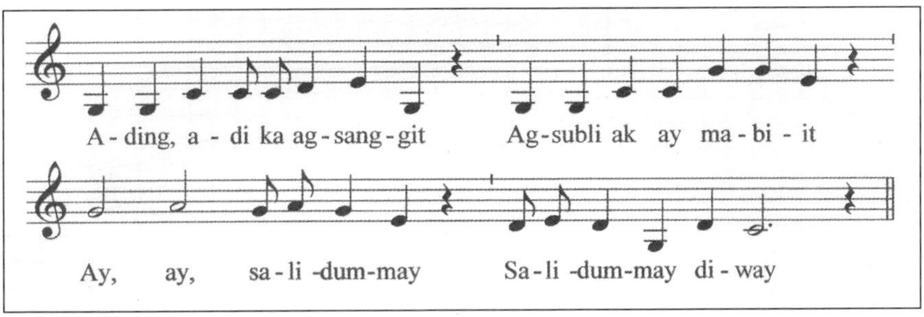

Figure 3b. *Ading di ka agsangit* (*Don't Cry My Dear*) (Original tune of *Ay ay salidummay*)

Figure 4a. *Bury Me Not on the Lone Prairie*

Figure 4b. *Adto takon na-olnong* (*We are All Here Gathered*). This tune was learned from GIs during the Seond World War by Filipino soldiers. It was adapted to the words of a pre-existing work song, and later, the work song with this *salidummay* tune became a song to be presented during festivals (Saboy 1990).

The 1950s–1960s: Re-enforcement of Colonial Taste

The earliest published account on *salidummay*, in my investigation, appears only in 1966 (Dozier 1966). Dozier's mentioning of *salidummay* marks the beginning of the massive accounts, though each is fragmental, on the *salidummay* songs in the literature in the 1970s–1980s. As anthropologist Dozier distinguished the "*salidómay* or diwas" from the *dangdang-áy*, yet indicating all of these terms imply the multiple features of the contemporary *salidummay*: the ethnic-identity symbol among the highland students, women's presentation number, courtship singing (*utagaki*). His distinction of *diwas* and *dangdang-áy* reflects the pre-war category of chants where the two existed as different forms. These chants at the crossroads of Kalinga, Abra and Apayao Provinces, which used to have distinctively different tunes of their own, were adapted with novel tunes, and it is likely that eventually, the distinction of the two became blurred.

> Most popular of these songs is the pan-montane *salidomay* or *diwas*. Some of the melodies of the *salidomay* are known by all the major ethnic groups of the Mountain Province. While the melodies appear to be limited in the songs of this group, there is constant improvisation of words to fit the occasion, as for example in the case of serenading a girl friend, the words are

> made to suit the appearance and personality of the girl. The singer attempts, at least, to adjust the choice of his words to conform to the time, circumstances, and the person or persons involved (168).
>
> *Dandang-áy*. Women's group song sung in large festive gatherings like weddings and peace-pact celebrations (267).
>
> *Salidómay* or *diwas*. Pan-montane songs for all festive occasions and for gatherings of young people from the mountain tribes of north Luzon in cities away from home. These songs may be sung by either a man or woman as a solo or by groups of either men or women alone or by mixed groups of both sexes. When young students return home on vacations from Baguio and Manila it is common for them to join in singing one version after another of the *salidómay* as they ride the jolting Dangwa bus from Baguio to Tabuk (268).

To integrate various available oral and written accounts, the 1950s–1960s was the period when *salidummay* became more popular especially in the provinces of Abra and Kalinga as youth's song. Youth did *utagaki* (courtship singing-debate) with Americanized tunes; most of which are considered as *salidummay* tunes today. Also, it is reported from northern *lowland* provinces that "ay ay *salidummay*" as jest song was widespread then (Figure 5).[13] Teachers let grade school pupils sing the words they composed (but presumably not significantly deviated from the existing words of various chants) with those "new" style of tunes too. The youth of this period turned out to be the generation of the most significant agents (singers) of *salidummay*-making. It is through this generation's performance that *salidummay* became elevated as "authentic" songs in some localities in the coming decades when the youth then reached adulthood. It must be reminded that the youth always leap at something fashionable, especially when it comes to courtship and entertainment. The youth of this period also adopted *salidummay* tunes in work songs — often in the form of call-and-response — such as in rice pounding (especially that for community affairs), planting, harvesting, etc.

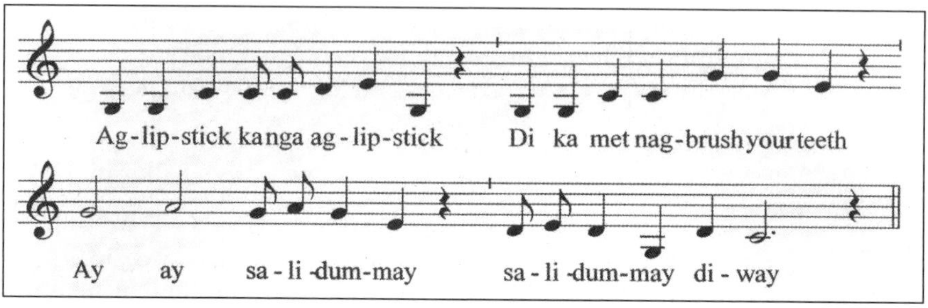

Figure 5. *Aglipstick ka nga Aglipstick* (*Ay ay salidummay tune*)

The 1970s–1980s: Height of Popularity

The 1970s–1980s largely overlap with the regime of President Marcos (1965–1986) whose administration played an idiosyncratic role in national culture building. It was also in this period that written accounts on *salidummay* peaked in number, though still variously spelled and termed, and mostly fragmental and inconsistent.[14] These two historical facts are closely related when viewed from the point of the "US shadow." Ostensibly irrelevant variations of *salidummay* songs in the 1970s–1980s — "women's song," as "NPA song" as protest song, and as "indigenous hymns" — are all foreground that reflect, though indirectly, the post-colonial socio-cultural milieu, where the US had variably made an impact in both ideology and bodily-aesthetics.

I begin the disassembling of this complex with the problematique of the Mountain Province. In 1966, the old Mountain Province, established by American colonial administration as a reservation-like contoured territory, was dissolved into four (later five) independent provinces. However, the phantom of the old Mountain Province, as collective mental framework of the Filipinos that views the highlands — their people, society, and culture — distinctively different from the lowlands, remained. Marcos administration called highlanders "cultural minorities," and treated them as important resources to represent "genuine" Filipinoness. This is merely the opposite side of a coin of the US colonial administration that called them "uncivilized/non-Christian"; both on the assumption that these highlanders were never colonized.[15] For the promotion of "genuine Filipinoness," under the slogan *"isang lahi, isang bansa, isang tadhana"* (One race, one nation, one destiny), as well as "unity in diversity," anthropological studies about the "cultural minorities," like during American colonial period, made a leap in those decades after silence of post-war recovering years. Mostly conducted by American and US-trained Filipino scholars, a series of anthropological studies in those post-colonial decades were not free from the phantom of the old Mountain Province framework. They even reinforced such an American discourse in the milieu of *"Bagong Lipunan"* (New Society) ideology. Further to mold such a framework was Summer Institute of Linguistics (SIL), an American semi-academic/religious institution mandated for linguistic research and Bible translation into "minority" languages. Anthropologists, linguistics, post-colonial administration, and churches worked hand-in-hand to produce a number of ethnolinguistic maps of the Philippine archipelago, that provided visually static images of ethnic categories. That led to the establishment of the sense of ethnic identity as such among the northern highlanders themselves, namely in terms of tribal names and collective identity. Establishment of such a sense of belonging marked the beginning of the era of co-existence of modernity and pre-modernity, in Canclini's term (Canclini 1995). That is to say, the northern Luzon highlanders began to obtain a sort of bi-cultuality where they code-switch between two domains of sense of belonging: that of bodily aesthetics and that of ideology.[16] The former normally presents the concentric-circular gradation of density of intimacy in space, while sensitive relationship may be experienced with neighboring communities, and kinship ties are consistently emphasized. If the former is more or less a "face-to-face" community, in Anderson's definition, the latter is a domain of "imagined" community.

The *salidummay* is the very song-genre that crosses the borders between the two domains. There is an absence of serious studies on *salidummay* in the 1970s–1980s but a large cohort of fragmental accounts indicates its locus outside the domain of "authentic" rituals. Simultaneously, frequent albeit fragmental mentioning of *salidummay* in a large quantity of data on "traditional" culture and people of the cultural minorities in this period makes us assume the height of popularity of *salidummay* then as the music-making activity in the domain of everyday life in a number of northern highland villages. The 1970s–1980s was the transitional period when *salidummay* as unauthentic songs gradually became authentic. That was because the agents, prominent performers of *salidummay*, those who were youths during the Second World War, had grown old enough by then. They became duly recognized as mature members in each community, where seniority and marriage with children mark a significant qualifier for one's entry to adulthood. That symbolically indicates the growing domination of the northern highland communities by the children of colonial education. This is the factor that connects multiple faces of *salidummay* songs; as "songs of women," as "indigenous hymns," and as protest songs. All of these variations are rooted in the domain of everyday village life, but given new faces as the Cordillera identity marker, when made to adjust to the code-switching of the agency.

Being assumed "traditional" for their popularity and lyrical/contextual/performative rootedness, the SIL's initiatives of indigenizing the liturgical materials, in parallel to Vatican II (1968), largely incorporated *salidummay* songs as "indigenous hymns."[17] However, the choice of *salidummay*, among a number of *more* indigenous vocal forms, I argue, is attributed paradoxically to its very "modern" musical features introduced by Americans: metric and pentatonic scales that facilitate group, unison singing. Concurrently, it was due to the popularity of *salidummay* as a youth/courtship song that it *became* an "NPA song," as rural guerrillas in their tender age sang *salidummay* songs; first for self-consolation in the forest, but gradually with militant words of communist ideology. Here too, the "modern" musical features were the driving force for their adoption to wider repertoires of protest songs. As the anti-Chico dam movement grew from that of village folks to that of cause-oriented groups toward the Cordillera Autonomy Movement in the second half of the 1980s, *salidummay* as NPA soldiers' personal songs became protest songs suitable for group singing. At another scene, village "women" (married with children) began to publicly "present" prepared *salidummay* songs — pre-composed lyrics for each particular occasion set for any of the familiar *salidummay* tunes to be sung — often in groups — during communal "programs."[18]

In these new loci of *salidummay* performance as group-singing/presentation, performers sometimes came to wear uniformed costume; most commonly a wrap skirt of woven materials for women with a plain T-shirt or a blouse. Consequently, a costume would indicate the oneness of the group of agents, while its difference from others gave the distinction of a sense of belongingness, which was often defined by space, as imagined through ethnolinguistic maps. Benedict Anderson aptly implies the organic correlation between the action of unison-singing and modernity, epitomized by the establishment of nation state, as he pays attention to the bodily meaning of singing of a national anthem, like recitation of the *Book of the Common Prayer*, an "experience of simultaneity" as "occasions for unisonality, for the echoed physical realization of the imagined community" (Anderson 1983: 132).

Much as the national culture building of the post-colonial Philippines had to depend on its conceptual framework of the American colonial administration, *salidummay*-making of the 1970s–1980s also implicitly anticipated the era of US-led globalization. I attribute the facile acceptance of the so-called Country and Western songs in the northern Luzon highlands to the bodily aesthetics, beyond ideology, of the northern Luzon highlanders; their nostalgic memory of the intimacy with American individuals — nurses, missionaries, etc. — during the colonial period, as well as their aural/oral familiarity with Anglo-Saxon folktunes in addition to other common tunes such as hymns, school/children's songs, scouting songs etc.. The spread of Country and Western songs in the northern highland communities, primarily through radio, boosted by the development of the cassette tape technology of low-cost and handy mass production in the 1970s, can be seen as the embryo of the era of globalization where the popular culture of the United States penetrates the world. Indeed, the 1960s was the decade when the world came to have the common popular music repertories more eminently than the previous decades, owing to the development of popular music industry. Except for The Beatles and a few others, American artists thoroughly began to dominate the international market of the music industry. The continuing popularity of Country and Western songs in northern Luzon highlands until today is manifested in daily local radio broadcasts, countless illegally produced and locally circulated cassette tapes/CDs, and endless productions of vernacular songs in the Country and Western style.

However, the access to electric media was still greatly limited to a large portion of the highland population until recently. The popular songs once learned through electric media were transmitted orally, and eventually, some of those were added to their local singing repertoires with considerable variations. For example, vernacular lyrics were adapted to the tunes of *Don't Cry John* and *Tom Dooley*, among others. The *Tom Dooley* tune did not only become a new/modern tune of *Siya Obpay Dis Dis Damo*, a northern Kankana-ry ballad of a rejected lover (the older tune is by now almost completely neglected), it was even once used in 1995 for a *salidummay* song whose lyric was composed particularly for the occasion of a homecoming of a local elementary school. I dare categorize this variation for one-time performance as *salidummay* because of an added phrase "ay ay ay ay salidummay diwas diway diwas diway salidummay" to each stanza. Concurrently, the tune of *Green Beret*, an American patriotic song popularized during Vietnam War, was modified and later established as a *salidummay* tune (Figures 6a and 6b).

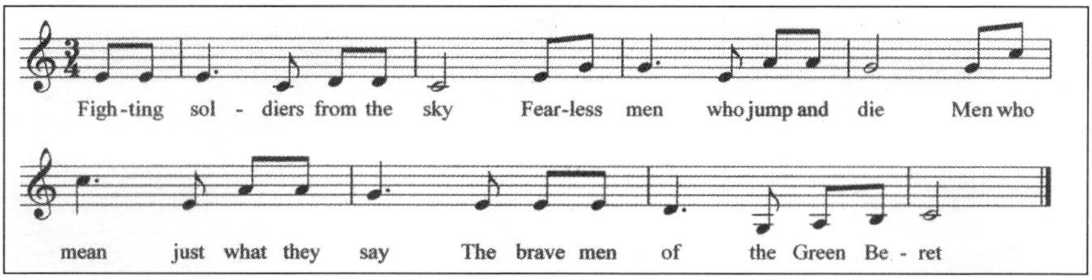

Figure 6a. *Green Beret*

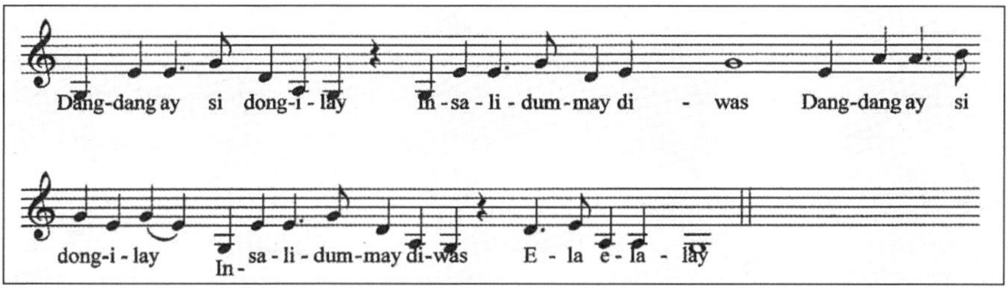

Figure 6b. Dangdang-ay with *Green Beret* tune as women's song

The 1990s–2000s: Establishment of the Term "*Salidummay*" as a Folksong Genre/Globalization

It was only in the early 1990s that the term "*salidummay*," with such a spelling, became more or less established as terminology of a musical genre. I consider the publication of a cassette tape album — entitled *SALIDUMMAY* by a singing group named "Salidummay Group" in c.1989 — a leap. The Salidummay group is one of the activities of Dap-Ayan ti Kultura iti Kordilerya (DKK), a cultural sector of the Cordillera People's Alliance, a cause-oriented group based in Baguio. The album was overwhelmingly accepted within and without the northern highland region, in the ambiance of relief from the dictatorial politics: the group itself became upper ground then. The word *salidummay* spread in print with its jacket, and so did the refrain words (i.e., "dong dong ay si dong-ilay") added to various tunes compiled in the album, including the tunes that otherwise may not be considered as *salidummay*. Since then, the literature that contain accounts on *salidummay*, from academic to journalistic ones, almost unanimously began to adopt the spelling of *salidummay*. Teresita Maceda's reference to various vocal forms in her account on protest songs of northern Luzon highlands in the 1970s–1980s makes us aware that the songs we vaguely presume as *salidummay*, particularly those in the albums of the DKK Salidummay Group, were *not* perceived as *salidummay* in those decades, but were termed by various refrain words.

> The song form was also converted by the New People's Army or NPA into a news bulletin to facilitate the transmission of news which would otherwise take three weeks to disseminate. Set to a simple folk melody, the news is learned by heart and disseminated to the people much faster. Among the peoples of Kalinga, Abra, and Bontoc, song forms like the **salidummay, donglala, oynasi, balasebasem,** and **idi mid** were recast: to narrate significant events in the struggle of the Cordillera people against the Chico Dam project and the militarization of the area; to discuss issues affecting the people in verbal joust form; and to situate the tribal problems in the context of the Cordillera struggles as a whole. In recent years, some of these songs have been recorded and performed by the group called Salidumay [sic.] (Maceda 1994, vol. 6: 121).

The *salidummay* until today continues to be the symbol of regional ethnic identities. It is often sung at the scenes related to "modern institutions," such as schools, churches, Local Government Units, NGOs, etc., and in highland villages and towns, being more broadly accepted in this period than ever. On the other hand, it is noted that the *salidummay* has come to be less frequently performed today at the domain of "non-modernity" in highland villages and towns; particularly in the arena of "daily" (non-ritualistic) private singing activities. In this relation, I further point out that the rituals have been rapidly secularized in these decades. Communal rituals of different natures such as wedding feasts and peace-pact celebrations, and harvest celebrations (particularly in Ifugao Province), have now come to present a quintessentially uniformed ritualistic text, analogous to that of town fiesta, which itself has succeeded the *cañao*-style programs, the American colonial legacy, in one way or the other. A scene of the *cañao* in Bontoc (around 1906) described by Lt.-Gov. Samuel Kane (quoted by Finin 2005) as a feast of a sub-province of the old Mountain Province, strikingly resembles a provincial and/or municipal fiesta today.

> Weeks prior to the scheduled arrival of American officials from Manila, invitations were sent to out to subprovincial villages by runners, telling residents of the impending feast, and asking villagers to bring their musical instruments, most important of which were the *gangsa*, or gongs. Ample amounts of meat, rice, and other goods were amassed for the events that were supposed to last two days. However, because delegations sometimes came early and stayed late, the event could extend several days beyond the planned schedule. Supplies for the Bontoc cañao included 200 sacks of rice, 10 carabaos, 20 large hogs, 100 bundles of leaf tobacco, as well as the fermented drinks that were transported from many different villages (Finin 2005: 53).

At another angle, it is also possible to reckon the projection of various levels of regional identities by northern highlanders, the emergence of locality, as response to the globalization (i.e., Appadurai 1996), or another locus of "US shadow" where the post-colonial Philippines is more prone to fall prey to than many other nations, as the only country the US has ever colonized. In correspondence to the growing significance of *salidummay* as the ethnic symbol of the northern Luzon highlands, the *salidummay* has further been used in some cases at national and even international scenes as a handy tool to express the sense of national identity. For instance, *salidummay* songs have attracted attention in the field of music education. Some recent music textbooks/reference books for grade schools include considerably modified *salidummay* songs (Enriquez and Del Rosario 1968: 119 *Salidommay*; Rivadelo 1992: 21 *Isneg: Ballad*; 36 *Dongilay*; 58 *Salidomay*; Prudente *et al.* 1998: *Salidummay*). In this relation, Buenconsejo informs us of the employment of a *salidummay* song "Danum" from a DKK CD album *Salidummay Diway* (2000) at a fiesta in Davao for dance accompaniment by the Agusan-Manobo pupils in Mindanao (Buenconsejo 2005). Largely influenced by the DKK's *salidummay* repertoires, the motif of *Ay ay salidummay* tune (the refrain portion of Figure 5) has become popular material for the so-called "Pinoy pop music" repertoires (by Yoyoy Vellarme, Grace Nono, Pinikpikan, Tribu, etc.). Similarly, the same motif has been used in the field of art music composition (i.e., *Amianan (North)* by Perfecto De Castro, a guitar quartet work, 2004).[19]

Conclusion: Toward Comparison with *Sambika/ Shoka/Gunka* in Modern Japan

My data on the making of *salidummay* through *salidummay*-making resonate with Bruno Nettl's ethnomusicological assumption that the trinity of church/school/military are the major modern institutions that have played the foregrounding role in rationalization of music in the non-West at large. Similarly, a series of recent, excellent archival researches on the history of reception of *yogaku* (western music) in Japan have almost unanimously presented the significance of such a trinity. As the American cultural impact has been the significant leitmotiv at every corner of the process of *salidummay*-making, meticulous archival studies have uncovered the shadowy underlying intimacy between American protestant churches and the introduction of music education into Japan in the early years of its history (c.1870s–1890s). It is shadowy because it was more at the personal level than institutional/systematic one, as only the meticulous archival researches could reveal (Yasuda 1993; Teshirogi 1998, 1999).

For instance, Eben Tourjée (1834–1891)'s life reflects the atmosphere of Boston, the center of music education in the US in the second half of the 19th century, where music education was not separable from the Protestant mission. Being the first President of the Music Teachers National Association, and as a strong Christian, he held significant positions in Christian organizations in Boston (such as President of the Boston YMCA, President of the Boston Missionary Society, etc.). At the New England Conservatory of Music, which he founded, the board members consisted of the representatives of the overseas mission division of different denominations. In the summer of 1872, while taking a vacation, he was, incidentally and personally, consulted by Arinori Mori, Japan's Minister to the United States who had a strong interest in Christianity, about the direction of music education of Japan. Tourjée stated that progress of Japan would not be realized without the Japanese's learning of music, and through music, the essence of Christianity as most important spirit of Western civilization. Tourjée had earlier expressed his opinion that music must be introduced to public school curriculum in the United States in order for pupils to learn basic musical skills, so as for them to be able to serve during Sunday services (Tourjée 1871, cited in Teshirogi 1999).

Luther Whiting Mason (1828–1896), vice-president of Music Teachers National Association, who too had a strong desire for Christian mission, was dispatched to Japan by Tourjee (1880–1882). To him, to be dispatched to Japan, was "God's Will" and was to spread Christianity to Japan through music education — reflecting the ideal of New England Conservatory that music education was for Christian mission. Through his intimate contact with two Japanese students of Harvard, Shuji Izawa and Tanetaro Mekata, the three submitted "Suggestion on Shoka Education by Japanese Language" to the then Vice-Minister of Ministry of Education Fujimaro Tanaka in 1878, including the wall charts of the suggested 15 Japanese *shoka* notations: nine of which were taken from American textbooks, and one which had a Japanese lyric adapted to a hymn tune *HAPPY LAND*, made of anhemitonic-pentatonic scale said to be of "Indian Air."[20]

In the worldwide trend of the Westernization of music culture in the past centuries where the "trinity" played a significant role, both Japan and the Philippines experienced the opening to modernization forcibly by the Unites States of America, and subsequently submitted to an unequal treaty and colonization, respectively. Differences between the two countries, however, were: a) monopoly of American powers in the Philippines versus the prominence of other Western empires (Germany, Great Britain, France) as well in Japan: as manifested by the use of American music textbooks in the former and that of edited textbooks — so as to compromise with Japanese cultural elements to some extent — in the latter; b) Spanish vestiges as pre-American legacy and its limited cultural impacts in the northern Philippines highlands versus that of the Netherlands and the strong cultural background of Chinese tradition in Japan; and c) Japan itself was to become an empire (in colonial Korea and Taiwan, modernization/westernization of music was brought through Japanized "Western" music such as *shoka* and *gunka*).[21]

Junko Oba's study on *gunka* is enlightening. She, like my approach to *salidummay*, traces its process of making as a song genre that has "strong influence of Western military song and Japanese folk songs" (Oba 2002). In its early stage, *gunka* used to depict the stories of soldiers in the Sino-Japan War and Russia-Japan War whose wording was in the *gunkimono*-ballad style of the middle-age epics of sad warrior heroes with popular folktunes of that time. That reminds us of the early stage of *salidummay* as *dangdang-ay*, a chanted story. During the Pacific War years, *gunka* was indistinguishable from *shoka* as incorporated in patriotic education. After the Second World War, *gunka* became a genre of popular folk songs engaged with a growing music industry. Reflecting on such a process of making on one hand and recalling her own childhood observation on the other, Oba asks, why her father and male relatives used to sing *gunka* when drinking during family gatherings in the years of Japan's high economic growth. She concludes, "gunka has become a personal and collective nostalgia property from their war-period youth" (ibid.).

Comparing the making of modern folk songs in the northern Philippines with that in Japan — though the former is done primarily through ethnographic research and the latter primarily through archival research — from the point of view of aesthetics of bodily experience, I point out the "shadows," or the "tacit leitmotiv," a term by Desjarlais, at two levels: "America" and "modernity"; the latter was to be realized through the former's ideal of "civilization project." At one level, modern folk songs in both countries (*salidummay*, *sambika/shoka/gunka*) are a form of bodily-aesthetical "surrender" of the "Igorrots" and Japanese to Anglo-Saxon musical tastes. At another, it is their being swallowed by modernity, where musically speaking, the music of the Western rationality rules — epitomized by the system of tonality and meter, which theoretically peaked in the Vienna School in the 18th century; the two principal musical elements that surpassingly dominate the contemporary pop music. Thus, this ethnomusicological/anthropological study leads to an essential question of "what is *the* Western music?", implicitly questioning the current division of labor in musicology.

Notes

1. I am deeply indebted to Dr. Eufracio C. Abaya of the University of the Philippines for the conceptualization of this paper. I am also greatly thankful to Dr. Belinda A. Aquino, Dr. Hiromu Shimizu, Fr. Resurreccion B. Reyes, Jr. as well as anonymous referees, for their constructive comments on earlier versions of this paper. The major fieldwork for this study was funded by the Toyota Foundation (01-D-555) and the University of the Philippines Local Faculty Fellowship (2003–2004).
2. For instance, Flores (2000) is a work which applied such a concept of aesthetics in social studies of the Philippines.
3. See Finin (2005); Fry (1983); Jeninsta (1987); Sullivan (1991); among others.
4. Such an idea of the author is indebted to (Cannel 1999), which develops constructive arguments on the highland-lowland relationship in Bicol.
5. The economic stake on the gold mines in the region was one of them. Another was the public opinion over the colonial responsibility to "civilize" the "Indios"; the Spanish term for the lowland native population. It was interpreted by Americans with the images of the Native Americans, and thus came to signify to Americans the "kind" of people found in the Philippine highlands. See Finin (2005), p. 25.
6. The following literature I investigated did *not* include any reference to *salidummay* or its relevant terms, despite their dealing with vocal music within the region in one way or the other: Schadenberg (1887), Cole (1907–1908), Meyer (1882), Jenks (1905), Barton (1949), Santiago

(1931 [1957]), Reyes-Tolentino (1946 [1990]), Romualdez (1932 [1973]), Buenventura *et al.* (1966), Moss (1920a, 1920b), Moss and Kroebar (1919), Vanoverbergh (1978), Reid (1961 [2009]), *The Progressive Music Series* (1919, 1932, 1948, n.d.), *Philippine Music Horizons* (1953).

7. In early ethnomusicology in the early 20th century, the subject of research was usually limited to the tonal aspects of music. Little attention was paid to the lyrics in vocal music. No lyrics are provided in Cole (1922).
8. Billiet and Lambrecht passingly mention that *dangdang-ay* of the Tinguians of Abra of the early 20th century was epic singing. This statement was denied by my Banao informants who claim themselves a sub-tribe of the Tinguians. Meanwhile, an oral account that the Maengs of southern Abra sing epic with *salidummay* tunes may be relevant. Billiet and Lambrecht (1970 [2001]) and personal communication with Hallen Sumingwa.
9. So far, I scarcely have had access to the Roman Catholic communities.
10. A photographic copy of the late Charlotte G. Massey's letter to late Fr. Theodore T. Saboy, dated on "St. Andrew's Day" (which is November 30) in 1949, available at St. Paul's Parish Office, Balbalasang, Balbalan, Kalinga. The original copy was not found in the personal collection of the Saboy family in the search in 2005. Fr. Saboy was one of the "children" referred in the letter.
11. Since the early years of comparative-musicology/ethno-musicology as modern science, the pentatonic scales have been often associated with "Oriental"/Asian musical features. While it is true that great civilization of ancient China produced sophisticated musical theory of pentatonicism and it significantly influenced the wide area of Asia, my data show that most of the older vocal forms/styles in the northern Philippine highlands — folk culture in nature — use two-, three- or four-pitch systems. Musical instruments of the region are mostly designed to produce five pitches in an octave but except for flutes, they usually produce a drone and/or resulting melodies, if any, of repetitive short motives of two-, three-, or four pitches. I consider the pentatonic scales in northern Luzon highland as examples of the American influence for two reasons: a) it is possible that pentatonic tunes were shaped in northern Luzon highlands in the early 20th century as natural adjustment in learning Western diatonic tunes for those who were familiar with fewer-tone-scales; b) most of the Anglo-Saxon folktunes that are largely Irish or Scottish in essence are pentatonic, and it is probable that they were easily internalized by the young population. Researchers must be extra cautious to the speed of changes of tunes. As one of my informants clearly presented, for example, the *liwliwa* (chant) tune of the so-called Northern Kankana-

eys in western Mountain Province has been changed from four-tone to pentatonic (the latter the informant described as "more elegant" than the former) in the last several decades, while the *liwliwa* has been believed in Philippine ethnomusicology to be an "indigenous/traditional/archaic" vocal genre on the assumption of unchanging continuity.

12. Personal communications with Soledad Killip in 1997, Maria Carmen Domingo-Kuk in 2006, FGD in Nacagang, Sagada, Mountain Province in 2002, among others.
13. Personal communication with Drs. Carolyn Sobritchea, Raul Pertierra, and Prospero Covar.
14. The term *salidummay* was not very established yet at this time. Literature presents different spellings and terminologies such as *salidomay, salidommay, salidumay, ilalay, elalay, dangdang-ay, dongdong-ay*, etc., and what these terms signify may vary from one to the other, depending on the observation/understanding of researchers/writers, as well as the communities they studied.
15. Such an assumption, however, is not accurate. Historical documents convey that Spaniards had obtained a certain extent of access to the highland areas and their people(s), i.e., Politico-military Commandancies, some Roman Catholic missions, etc. See Afable (1989); Keesing (1962); Scott (1974 [1977]).
16. Finin points out that a sort of pan-mountain identity existed as early as the 1930s among students in Baguio and mining workers (Finin 2005). I consider that such a historical background surely contributed to the establishment of the post-colonial pan-Cordillera identity, which northern highlanders themselves utilized as weapon in proactively projecting themselves.
17. Here, I define *salidummay* hymns: a) the hymns with a so-called *salidummay* tune and English Christian lyric; and b) those with a conventional Western hymn tune and vernacular lyric to which a *salidummay* refrain is attached.
18. I suggest that that was due to the loss of opportunities for "women" to expose their selfhood, as the result of decline of shamanistic/domestic rituals, i.e. healing, witch crafting etc., which were used to enable them to execute their social power (over men who would do the same in communal rituals). I infer that the genderly-egalitarian inclination of each community prompted women to seek alternative loci, to metaphorically negotiate with men toward balancing, who otherwise may overpower women in communal ritual settings in *gangsa* (flat gong) playing, as well as in solo chanting (*oggayam*, etc.).
19. This contrasts with the previous generations (Anton Molina, Kasilag, Jose Maceda etc.) who never used *salidummay* as motif in art music

composition in the fad of integrating "native" tunes to the Western compositional technique.

20. Shuji Izawa (1851–1931) was soon to be in charge of the Music Management Division under the Ministry of Education, the forerunner of Tokyo National University of Fine Arts and Music. Meanwhile, Tanetaro Mekata (1853–1926) was a government bureaucrat who was dispatched to study music education then, though upon his return to Japan, he developed his career in the Ministry of Finance and Ministry of Justice.
21. Among the studies on the reception of "western" music through Japan in former colonies of Japan (Kyo [Kan] 2002), though as a non-fiction essay, it excellently depicts the predicament of elderly Koreans and Taiwanese who find their strongest nostalgia in Japanese songs (and other forms of Japanese popular culture such as Norakuro comics they were familiar with during a tender age). Kyo [Kan] likewise emphasizes the significance of church/school/military as the front doors of the entry of western music to Japan (probably without being familiar with Nettl's "trinity" theory), as well as the prominence of double meter and anhemitonic-pentatonic scales in modern folk songs in Korea. To rephrase this in anthropological terms, this is the matter of bodily aesthetics and memory. (An elderly Korean's recitation of the multiplication tables in Japanese even today is likewise a matter of bodily memory. In this relation, Filipinos doing the same in English until today may be a more serious matter of the continuous US shadow in the country.)

chapter 11

Love Triangles: Filipinos, Japanese, and the Shifting Locations of American Power

Nobue Suzuki

In December 1995, when I was still a graduate student at the University of Hawaii, one of my Filipina research informants, Julie,[1] asked for my business card and I gave her one written in English. She however asked for one printed in Japanese. Julie reads Japanese fairly well and so I assumed that she wanted to study the language. Later, I realized that she was always carrying the card in her wallet and when she met some Japanese, including her in-laws, she selectively showed my card around, implying, "My *ate* (big sister), is a 'professor' at an American university." In August 2006, she again asked me, "*Ate*, now you teach at a new university [in Japan] and so you must have a new business card. Give me one. One in Japanese, you know that, right?" Julie also talked about me to her Filipino friends and occasionally arranged for them to call her at home when I was scheduled to visit her. After exchanging greetings over the phone, she passed the receiver to me and said, "*Ate*, speak in Tagalog!" Soon after my brief chat with the caller, Julie took the phone and said, "Now you believe me. She really can speak Tagalog. She's the one who wrote a book[2] about me in English!"

While for Julie, my affiliation with America — via my competence in English, educational training, and marriage to an American — together with my job as a college professor and ability to speak Tagalog are usually drawn upon to enhance her social standing, different instances triggered various responses from my other Filipina informants. Imee, for example, insisted that I should have a child because "You can hire a babysitter easily in America. That's what everybody does in America, right? So childrearing is not a problem [like it is in Japan]."[3] She was not convinced that my meager income then as a language instructor with a semi-dependent graduate student husband living in the high cost city of Honolulu would not allow us to enjoy such a lifestyle. Instead, she looked at my hands and said, "See, your hands are telling me that you're not doing much housework, are you? After all, your husband is American. Life is hard for me in Japan [with my Japanese husband]." She refused to accept the fact that my hands were cleaner not because of my American partner but because of my skills and philosophy to skip whatever chores I deemed "unnecessary."

Today, one's identity is understood not as something that is fixed but as a process, relational and constituted within shifting relations of power. It is a contingency that reflexively arises in encounters and interactions with others. By associating with someone or something else, we also forge new identities and acquire new social positionalities. Thus, Julie's insistence on having my business card in Japanese is not intended to help remember my contact information, but to present herself to other people as having a "big sister," a quasi-kin who enjoys multicultural attributes and high cultural capital: she is a "professor" at American and Japanese universities who writes "books" in English and Tagalog. The manner in which Julie mobilizes my (inflated) status and occupation has thus worked to steer the ways in which interlocutors conjure up her identity through her association with the deployed images of her "*ate*." Imee, on the other hand, saw in me an "America" and its clichés and complained about her "hard" life and "low" social positionality.

Reflecting on these ethnographic encounters, this paper explores how intermarried Filipinas and Japanese men shape their intimate relationships by translating their interlocutors' identities and by doing so translocally, that is, with regard to somewhere else not bounded by Philippine and Japanese contexts. My interests revolve around the question: what happens in the encounters between two sets of people — Filipinos and Japanese — who are one way or another "hybrid?" This question may sound odd because I identify the Japanese as hybrid whereas the nation is popularly known for its racial-ethnic homogeneity. Seeing Japan in a different light however, besides the actual presence of ethnically diverse people there, we do find some miscegenous attributes in Japanese society: it is the only Eastern nation-state which is also recognized as a full member of the North and First World. Moreover, Japan is also seen as *hankai*, or half-civilized, located between the "civilized West" and "barbarian Asia" (Komori 2001). This positionality has situated the Japanese between the "civilized" and "uncivilized." Japan's national identity is thus not settled but amphibious, moving between multiple sets of racial, national, geopolitical and economic spheres in the global terrain. In the unfolding of the marital trajectories of Filipina-Japanese couples, Japanese men's amphibious attributes have come to wrestle with Filipinas' mestiza and hybrid backgrounds, colored by the legacies of Western colonization.

In what follows, I analyze the particular ways in which something "American" enters the lives of these women and men. The work of translating each other's identities makes what is irreducibly alien into something familiar, intimate and respectable, and enables the translators to anticipate and create better futures. Simultaneously, however, such attempts also produce botched knowledge, which hopelessly sows seeds of betrayal and vengeance. I begin by delineating the social and historical routes in which these particular translational acts became shaped.

Border-Crossing and Fixed Identifications

The increasing number of cross-national, cross-ethnic marriages worldwide is a corollary to women's global migration. Conversely, conservative gender and sexual ideologies in most societies continue to construct women as not (too) mobile geographically and economically. When women actually do cross national borders, they tend to be discussed in particular ways. During the last quarter of the 20th century, Filipinas have migrated abroad for various reasons. Although many do so as professionals and skilled workers, it has usually been working-class people and especially women domestic workers and entertainers who have been the topics of popular discussions.[4] Distinguished from elite "expatriates" and male workers, these female workers are given particularly classed and nationalized identifications, and their sexualities and moralities are quite commonly seen as suspect (Suzuki 2002a). Though this tendency partly reflects observers' concerns for the abuses that occur at work sites and in the process of migration, this suspected sexuality has ideologically stigmatized women workers in the globally circulated discourse.

After large numbers of Filipinas began migrating to Japan in the 1970s, they have been situated in peculiarly bounded social locations because the majority of them work as entertainers in nightlife businesses.[5] Despite the professional title of "overseas performing artist," the women commonly work as bar hostesses. Though their most important task is usually to talk to customers, bar women seldom receive social respect and are commonly equated with prostitutes.[6] The observers of and speakers "for" these workers — such as lawmakers, activists and scholars — have justified this equation with the assumption that the women are paupers from a Third-World country who must do anything they can in order to earn an income. Indeed, there has been a tendency to view non-white-collar migrant women within these sexualized, classed and nationalized positionalities. By underscoring the women's alleged Third-World-ness and eradicating the presence of elite "expatriates" from the discourse, observers — who tend to come from materially and nationally higher standings in Japan, the Philippines and elsewhere — skillfully exclude themselves and veil their own privileges. This has resulted in the domination of particular clichés about global women migrants.

Likewise, the growing number of intermarriages between women from the Third World and men from the First World has been discussed in sexualized, classed and nationalized terms. These wives or "brides" incite popular, academic and advocacy discussions and are usually considered victims of male power and various forms of inequality in both their home and host societies. Correspondingly, their partners are characterized as men whom local women reject because of their anti-social behaviors — such as violence and alcoholism — and they are often located at the edges of geo-economic and masculine hierarchies in their societies. Emblematic are stories of "mail-order brides." In the case of Filipina-Japanese marriages, the men are similarly caricatured, with the Japanese men dominating the Filipino women with more abundant money that the men have as members of the North. However, Japanese husbands are also distinguished from the Western husbands of Third-World women because the Japanese are negatively marked as being "backward," "traditional" Asians. Especially when associated with "victimized prostitutes," Japanese men are thought before marriage to coercively demand Filipinas' sex at bars, as these establishments are allegedly operated by *yakuza* gangsters, and upon marriage to command other gendered services.[7] The women are identified as "poor women of the South," where the word "poor" carries the double meaning of pauper and pitiful. Unlike Filipina-Western men relationships, which are seen in terms of East-West differences and associated gender and geopolitical power disparities, Filipina-Japanese marriages are discussed along a North-South axis. Their relationships thus tend to be seen as based not only on gendered and sexual submission but more explicitly on money than East-West associations, and the social locations and personal positionalities of both women and men are commonly portrayed as fixed and their power relationships unchangeable.

These fixed identifications have prevented us from imagining other subversive spaces and moments. Yet, since identification is not reducible to identity, it is important to consider the gaps between them and the incompleteness of identification. Once we realize (from our own experiences) that marital and familial relationships are never as loving and together as we would wish, we begin to nurture different imaginations through which to view these intermarriages. And we see that in practice, these women and men transform their gendered, classed and national identities and positionalities in daily lived negotiations.

Translational Spaces

In order to animate the fixed identifications of Filipina-Japanese couples, in this essay, I draw on recent discussions of translation. In translation, we try to overcome the historical and structural differences that lie beyond surface-level linguistic discrepancies (Nagano 2006). To make sense of differences, we attempt to mobilize and appropriate the diverse pieces of knowledge and discourse that are available at a particular time and space and assemble them to create something intelligible (Sakai 1997a). Recall the ways in which Julie and Imee, described above, variously put together my marital, educational and cultural relations to America and created two different versions of a person named "Nobue Suzuki." Translation is thus a fortuitous articulatory practice and its contingent nature prevents it from being fixed. As in the ways Julie and Imee explored my identity, some of the pieces of knowledge assembled in the processes of translation may remain external to the "translated" person. Nevertheless, the knowledge produced in this way still engenders meanings to those who are translating.

Given the ineluctable foreign origins of their nation, translation and the imaginations it conjures were quite pervasively deployed in Filipinos' quotidian experiences under the Spanish regime (Rafael 2005). For them, translation involves a "double process of appropriating and replacing what is foreign while keeping its foreignness in view" (ibid.: xvii). Although many people make claims to their nations by forging an autochthonous origin, Filipinos often do so by exploring their foreign roots. This practice allows them to revise their national foundation so as to project a new filiation. In contemporary Philippines, translation continues to be part of their subject formation as well as a source of empowerment. They usually accomplish these by approaching "America," which signifies wealth, education, beauty and leisure and by bringing its power into their everyday lives (Cannell 1999). In other words, for Filipinos, such a translation constitutes a process in which "becoming foreign [is] associated with the experience of modernity" (Rafael 2005: 5).

On the other hand, Japanese also use "American" references, though the degrees to which and ways in which they relate to this symbol are different from those among Filipinos. In the minds of many Japanese, the sense of an inferiority complex is the effect of American military intrusion and conquest — the end of samurai feudalism in the mid-19th century and defeat in the Second World War — as well as of skewed images circulated through capitalist practices and media representations of the USA as the center of modernity, advancement and affluent lifestyles. The Japanese tend to see America as the juxtaposed yet un-coalesced other to its own nationalist sentiments as a unique nation-state. At the same time, however, in dealing with its Asian others and post-colonials, Japan has exercised a strategy of "the strange coexistence of an uncritical identification with the West [and America] and an equally uncritical rejection of the West [and America]" (Sakai 1997b: 135) in order to justify its domination in Asia. Given the above, what happens and what relations emerge when Filipina wives and Japanese husbands with their differential histories make reference to "America" while negotiating interactions and interrelations with each other?

To tackle these questions, I find Leo Ching's work useful (Ching 2001a). He analyzes Taiwanese subject formation in the context of Japanese military and cultural rule from the 19th century on. In two related ways, Ching helps us imagine the shifting terrains where these women and men build their quotidian experiences while invoking and translating their partners' particular identities. One is his extension of Homi Bhabha's notion of "not-white, not-quite," in which Ching identifies Japan as a nation-state that is "not-white, not-quite, *yet alike*." Bhabha (1994) argued that colonials' mimicking behaviors resemble the behaviors of white colonizers, but their mimicking is not quite the same as the colonizers because of the former's status. For the Taiwanese, however, the domination of the Japanese is like that elsewhere of white Western colonizers. After all, the Japanese are members of the North, wannabe Westerners and in some cases, "honorary whites." Indeed, one of my Filipina informants recently confirmed this by saying, "Remember, Japan is America of Asia." Conversely, however, the Japanese are not granted full membership in the West and are often excluded for their nation being "traditional" situated at the edge of the "Far East." These conceptualizations reverberate with Komori's concept of *hankai* and with Sakai's remark on Japan's ambivalent global positionalities.

The other way Ching is useful is that he locates Taiwan not simply against Japan but between Japan and Mainland China, two domineering nations in Taiwanese subject formation. These multiple and shifting axes of analysis help us see the "American" presence in Filipina-Japanese relationships and to more dynamically situate their associations in a new perspective beyond static binary relations of power, such as North-South, East-West, First World-Third World, male-female and so forth. The real and imagined presence of America adds the new referential axis of the West to the previous North-South and East-South relations in which Filipinos and Japanese are normally located.

Furthermore, the "America" conjured up between Filipinas and Japanese further complicates Ching's triangular space precisely because the US is a "real" Western country, which creates a hierarchy based on global power as well as unsettling relations among the parties involved. Thus, for Imee, I was an "uncanny double": I am at once a Japanese and a metonymic American and so am "not-white," "yet alike." As shown below, for Japanese husbands, in certain contexts, their Filipina wives become "American" and therefore "Westerners" wrought by their colonial legacies. Filipinos' acts of approaching and appropriating the American symbol have offered them a certain *generative* link to this global power. At the same time, by referencing their colonial history in dealing with Japanese, Filipinos can also establish a *genealogical* filiation to America without actual belonging. Conversely, precisely because of such filiations, Filipinas have come to suffer from violence, similar to that of their ancestors during Spanish rule, and have been faced with Japanese men's betrayal and vengeance. Below, I begin my description of the ways in which Japan became a substitute for "America" in these women's pre-migration phases.

Tracing "America" in Roots and Routes

Light My Fire

When women, especially those from the so-called "Third World," migrate abroad to work or marry, prevailing allegories suggest that they do so out of their "traditional" sense of selflessness, filial piety and sacrifice in order to earn money for their families. This view is compounded by the idea that the women are considered to come from the impoverished sectors of poor societies. Such an argument may be valid in some ways. However, when most people in the world live under global capitalist economies, it offers a rather weak explanation of migration as such. Most of us, both rich and poor, work for money and for our families and increasingly more people relocate overseas for better pay, "quality of life" and career opportunities. Furthermore, recent scholarship has shown that women migrate for a variety of reasons, both including and exceeding upward economic mobility (Constable 2005; Suzuki 2002b). Moreover, those belonging to the poorest segment of a society largely remain immobile (Cannell 1999: Chapter 1). Among women's complex reasons to move, in this section, I focus instead on some of the ways in which my Filipina informants made reference to "America" and the "modern" as important components that enticed them to go abroad. One way in which they were attracted to Japan began in their immediate living environment.

Since the 1970s, the development of the global economy has changed local socio-cultural sceneries and people have increasingly become exposed to numerous material and symbolic foreign things. Filipinos who grew up from the late 1960s were situated amid the Marcos (1965–1986) and Aquino (1986–1992) governments' heavy reliance on foreign loans and investments. After the fall of the Marcos dictatorial regime in 1986, the amount of Japan's official development assistance (ODA) to the Philippines rose sharply, providing billions of dollars through international agencies. Currently, Japan is the primary ODA donor for the Philippines, and the country's landscape and media are filled with Japanese images, projects and goods. Meanwhile, Japanese cultural products (for example, anime) have flooded into the Philippine market and Filipino homes. In addition, the development of tourism in the Philippines from the 1970s began attracting large numbers of Japanese visitors, who spent significant amounts of money there — in 2001, an average of 250 dollars per day (Go 2001). As post-war anti-Japanese sentiments weakened, Japan became associated with wealth in the minds of many Filipinos, as follows:

> There were lots of Japanese coming to Manila. I got used to seeing them. Cassette-radios, cameras, color TVs and those things … I thought there were money-bearing trees in Japan … When you go to the black market … the dollar and yen are really strong. America is far away. So, naturally Japan is the place [to go for work] (Diowan 1986: 114).

For this woman, a wealthy Japan is an easy substitute for America.

For many Filipinos, their fantasies about "Japan" are drawn from international brand goods ("made-in-Japan") and images of Tokyo as a cosmopolis, in which scenes of the countryside and poverty do not occur. Japan is *like* "America," endowed with the conviviality and sophistication of a global city. Thus, Japan does not offer just "money-bearing trees" but other signs of "America," in its modernity and "good life." Japan is conceived as a "culturally advanced country" with scrumptious food products (Nakano 1999), Tokyo Disneyland and the "push-button world of technology." Light skin color is another feature of modernity that Filipinos regard highly. Light skin color signifies beauty and a leisurely life associated with "Americans" and upper-class Filipinos (often believed to be of white mestiza origin), who unlike farmers, can live without exposing themselves to the tropical sun. Since the 1970s, when Marcos established the labor-export infrastructure, Filipinos began to notice this feature among relatives and neighbors who had gone to Japan to work as entertainers at nightclubs. Upon their homecoming, the returnees' skin having grown lighter was positively remarked upon, if not envied, as in Julie's comment: "Their skin has grown light ... Why did they become beautiful? Well, I should go [to Japan] after all and I'll become pretty too." Besides their lightened skin color, these return migrants from Japan also appear in trendy fashion, sexy dresses and designer goods; all of which speak socially unspeakable, material and sexual desires to their observers. Moreover, their homecoming, often accompanied by life-sized stuffed Disney dolls, serves as "proof" of their return from "America."

Together with their night work at Japanese bars, such styles have invited other people's strong objection and damnation, but these are not mere reflections of the materialism embraced by these young women alone. In fact, their behaviors suggest these young working-class women's impossible relation to the neoliberal economy while inside their homeland. They also point to the modern space the women attempt to locate themselves in and to their fantasies to participate in global consumerist culture on par with Filipino elites who have been enjoying "America-in-the Philippines" (Cannell 1999) and with people in the global North (Go in Go and Jung 1999). It is generally true that these women express their wishes to provide a better life for their families and to be good Christians to their fellow countrymen through individual and group donation projects. Simultaneously, they also personally board the airplanes to migrate to Japan to enjoy overseas travel, another sign of modern and middle-class life, and to immerse themselves in what is conceived as a modern life. Filipinas' desires for "America" should thus not be hastily collapsed simply to a "colonial mentality" or a residue of the past. Concomitant to the colonial presence, the wealth and modernity projected by Japan's capital, goods and tourists as well as Filipina return migrants in everyday scenes in the Philippines, are also the effects of today's global capitalist structures and market economies which have been translated into new fantasies of modernity among Filipinos that light their fire to move to "yet-alike" Japan, the "America of Asia."

Malambing Men as "American"

Upon arriving at marriages with Japanese men, many Filipinas however find that Japan and the Japanese are not so "modern" as they imagined: they do not hire maids or nannies, as seen in Imee's comments above, and their husbands are not *malambing* (sweet, affectionate).

According to many Filipinas I talked to, Filipino men are *malambing*. Asking questions like "Have you eaten?" and buying a small gift of sweets on the way home from work are *malambing* expressions men use to show to the women in their hearts. Such behaviors resemble, they say, those of "American" men. When talking to me, Leah asserted that my partner "must treat you like a lady. Americans are known for their 'lady first' and expressions of love to their wives, aren't they?" Similar to numerous other Filipinas, Leah compared such mannerisms with those of Filipinos as follows:

> Filipinos do things as if to follow American ways ... In the Philippines, not only women but men too serve. The husband asks his wife, "Would you like some coffee?" I like people who follow American ways. [Americans] are romantic, aren't they?

This kind of idealization of *malambing* "American" and Filipino-turned-"American" men may be a way to establish grounds on which these Filipinas attempt to influence their Japanese husbands.

Contrary to the women's expectations, in most cases, the Japanese husbands I talked to respond to my question, "Do you tell your wife '*mahal kita*' (I love you)?" by either saying flatly "No" or things like "*Mahal*? I'd say to her our water bill is *mahal*" (high, expensive). However, some Japanese husbands do try meeting their wives' expectation that they should follow "American" ways. For instance, at the social hall at church, Shibata often holds his wife, Fanny, around her shoulders or waist while sharing one chair — though there are many empty ones around. Fanny also asks him to hold her hand while walking and he does so unless his hands are full with grocery bags. Shibata, like some other husbands, has learned to tell her, "*Aishiteru*" (I love you), though they tend to do it rather ritualistically and tell me that they say it so often that the practice has become "like air" (non-emotional; taken for granted). While men appear to remain aloof when talking to me, a Japanese observer, they nevertheless verbally express these words as instructed by their wives. This happens in a culture where numerous Japanese husbands think of their wives in terms of their gender role such as "she is the mother [of our children] and not a woman." Moreover, in ordinary Japanese conversation, if they ever express affection, they would use the stative verb, *suki* (literally, "I like you" but pragmatically, "I love you") more commonly than "*aishiteru*" largely because their wives have trouble with the difference between the literal and pragmatic meanings. These suggest that such an expression is not simply transferred from a Japanese expression, but that the Japanese husbands of Filipinas are making efforts to accommodate their wives' wishes to enjoy *malambing* relationships. As such, for these middle-aged Japanese men, even uttering the one phrase alone is significant and remarkably "American." These men can then be elevated to being "gentle-hearted husbands (*yasashii danna-san*), like 'Filipinos.'" At the homes of Filipina-Japanese couples, "following American ways" not only transforms Japanese husbands into being gentle-hearted, but engenders subversive moments of power and disturbs the prevalent gender and national order.

Although many husbands were attracted to their Filipina wives whom they assumed to be traditional "women of the past," others were stunned by the women's ability to speak English. Lorna graduated from a highly regarded university in the Philippines and once aspired to work at the Department of Foreign Affairs (of the Philippine government) in order to use her skills in English. She speaks and sings well in English and her linguistic competence and confidence captivated her trader husband-to-be at the bar she was working. Many Japanese husbands learn from their Filipina lovers and wives or from reading that "in the past, the Philippines was a colony of America" and that "Filipinos got American education." Some others think that because of US colonization, "Filipinos are Westernized." Here, Filipinas can assert not only a generative claim by speaking English, but also genealogical claim to America: Filipinos are "Americans." Having made their foreign filiations clear to their husbands and noticing their husbands' admiration and related sense of inferiority complex, some wives effectively use code-switching from Japanese to English and tell their husbands, for example, to restore their paternal *rights* — a concept the Japanese have recently imported from the West — to attend to their children's needs. Said in English, such a message also comes with other notions associated with "America," such as equality and democracy. Such an exchange for Filipina wives is a way to remind their husbands of their "Westernized" upbringing. Some husbands witness these notions to be enacted among Filipinos in statements like "husband and wife are partners!" Others have come to even take pride in their wives' Western attributes and abilities to speak English, saying emphatically, "My wife speaks English effortlessly (*perra pera*)!" For most monolingual Japanese who cannot really judge their wives' varying levels of competence, their wives' proficiency is something that is "cool" (*kakkoii*) and that they admire. One husband, a former amateur rock 'n' roll musician, even remarked, "They speak the international language. That was my yearning! I was like a frog in a well. [But associating with Filipinas,] I could hop out to beyond the seas."

What is significant in all these is that in their everyday exchanges, Filipinas appear to embody and enact "America" and emerge as the metonymies of the US presence in their Japanese husbands' eyes. The "America" the women conjure and cite transforms the couples from being simply men of the North and women of the South, and realigns them within the current but differently composed global national-linguistic hierarchy. In this newly emergent repositioning, Filipinas are translated into being not-white, yet-alike "Westerners," rising above their husbands. Furthermore, by speaking the language of power and globalization, Filipinas occupy the realm of the "international," while Japanese husbands remain in the "well" deeply rooted in the local terrain, immobile. Only when associated with Filipinas, are these Japanese men able to fantasize about a life beyond the "Far East."

"America" Betrayed

Philippine history has also shown that translation does not always establish cordial filiations with the foreign and modernity and that mistranslation and thus misrecognition can lead to suspicion, conflict and violence. As translation is an articulatory practice, such detrimental responses may appear to arise out of the blue. When pieces of knowledge concerning the person being translated are differently assembled, attempts to balance and reverse the usual gender and national hierarchies may result in betrayal and invite vengeful acts from the translator. This section looks at the particular case of Gloria and Koyama's marital illusion and dissolution. Their case does not provide a general view of Filipina-Japanese marriages, but instead highlights some of the subtle and not-so-subtle ways in which "America" became part of the adversity Gloria and her children had to undergo.

Gloria met Koyama in Manila in the late 1970s when he visited the Philippines on vacation. Koyama was a university graduate and when they met, he had been working in the hotel-restaurant industry in San Francisco for many years. Gloria had just graduated from college and always wanted to run a business. For young Gloria, Koyama was attractive because he looked like a popular movie star in the Philippines. On the other hand, for an aspiring Gloria, Koyama's residency in the USA was also attractive and she hoped that she could perhaps join him there for her future career mobility. During the first few years, Koyama made several trips to Manila to meet Gloria. However, in the early 1980s, Koyama's business in the US failed and he returned to Yokohama where he became a cab driver. From there, he continued to commute to Manila and they eventually got married. Meanwhile, Gloria was busy running different businesses and providing for herself and later for their son and daughter. When their son reached schooling age, Gloria and Koyama decided that it was time to live together in Japan.

Gloria said that Koyama was nice while visiting the Philippines; however, upon her and their children's arrival in Yokohama in the early 1990s, he changed completely. Gloria hoped that Japan, an "advanced country," would provide her with business opportunities. As soon as she arrived in Japan, she checked the classified ads in an English newspaper. While she could barely say basic greetings in Japanese, she landed a job in a trading company and received a 25 percent raise in two weeks. Two months later, she was asked to manage the company's office on the island of Cebu, in the central Philippines. For this, she was offered a monthly salary of 300,000 yen (US$2,700), which would give her an income that was close to 90 percent of Koyama's over 4 million yen (US$36,000) annual earnings. She immediately reported this to Koyama, only to hear that she could not go because their children had just started schooling. Koyama "wanted me to be a plain housewife," Gloria bitterly told me. Gloria of course had also not expected that, unlike in the Philippines, maid services were not easily affordable in Japan, and that being a housewife in Japan usually means that she would have to perform "maid's jobs" all by herself.

It did not take much time for Gloria and Koyama to find themselves in serious quarrels over different matters. Although Koyama did not treat Gloria like a prostitute, he began disparaging Filipinas for being "all prostitutes" and called them "the worst" (*saitei*) and "stupid" (*baka*). When Gloria talked back, Koyama verbally criticized her for being "conceited" (*namaiki*) and "arrogant" (*erasō*), especially when she explained the rationale for her decisions and deeds or commented on the logical flaws of his thoughts. Eventually, such quarrels turned into domestic violence. Gloria and her children became physically attacked, verbally abused and financially controlled, and their movements were surveyed. She actually observed an early sign of such violence when, upon their arrival in Japan, the children commented on their "2DK" apartment, consisting of two bedrooms with a dining-kitchen and no living room. They said to their father that it was "smaller than the bathroom in Mother's home in the Philippines!" Noticing such "naughty behaviors" of the children, Koyama insisted that they needed "discipline" because "they are like animals." When they did not follow his instructions, he slapped and began hitting their heads against the faucet and wall. Having gone through very complex processes, the couple now lives separately, but Gloria continues to suffer from the aftermath of their marital dissolution and from her personal aspirations even to this day.

The stories I obtained of marital illusions and dissolutions, including Gloria's case, predominantly came from the women, although I did meet or briefly encounter some of the divorced or separated partners before their relationships broke up. This leaves the discussions necessarily one-sided and speculative in certain areas. Although further research is needed to provide detailed answers to the reasons why husbands like Koyama become batterers, I want to point out a few things that seem to have triggered Koyama to take recourse to violence. Here, I argue that certain traces of "America" haunted, and continue to haunt, some of these Filipina-Japanese marriages.

Aside from his sense of insecurity and the fact that his business failed in the USA, Gloria analyzes that Koyama was hungry for social recognition, but failed to achieve it even from his immediate relatives. His sense of anxiety probably started to worsen after his business collapsed in the States. America, the "land of opportunity" betrayed him, or he was not good enough for America. In her dream, Gloria hoped that their relationship would develop in the USA, but in the end, she alone was able to keep her generative and genealogical ties with "America." Although Gloria came to learn the Japanese language, when she needed to express herself to non-Tagalog speakers, she had to do so in English. Koyama does understand the language, but his level of competence is not high enough. This linguistic problem led Gloria to quarrel with him in English. In doing so, she overwhelmed Koyama with logical thinking and rationality — attributes commonly associated with the West. Her business sense supported by her linguistic skills allowed her to immediately land a job and garner promotions, which could have enabled her to make as much income as he did. Koyama, on the other hand, failed in the USA, and back in Japan, his wife was overwhelming him with the language of power and "Western" reasoning. On top of these, their children made the material remark about the size of their homes in Japan and the Philippines, where he could afford only a "bathroom-sized" apartment for the entire family.

Koyama, in his mid-40s, who suddenly became the provider for a family of four with two growing children, was trying to make ends meet as a cab driver working under the Heisei recession in the 1990s.[8] Yet, he was not able to give his family a better home, not to mention the kind of affluent material life he had himself enjoyed while visiting the Philippines. Gloria was then deemed to embody and enact excess in the gender, national and class hierarchies and the superfluity of her linguistic, cultural and material performances thus needed to be put back in order. Koyama's frequent use of "prostitutes," "worst" and "stupid" in reference to Filipinas and the Philippines is hence an attempt to intentionally retranslate and misrecognize the people — and his educated, competent and not-white, yet-alike wife in particular — and their nation-state by relocating them in their "proper" location in the backward, underdeveloped, poverty-stricken Third World, as the prevailing discourse has depicted them. In so doing, Koyama's use of violence refracted his subverted and not-white, not-quite gender, national and class identities by rejecting the "America" executed by Gloria and simultaneously expressed his irrepressible and ironic desire for an identity that would make him a man of the North and a member of the modern First World and "America."

Conclusion

The transnationalization of daily life amid the widening gap between the rich and poor, and peoples' simultaneous attempts to achieve modern lifestyles equal to those in global centers, have resulted in the worldwide growth of overseas migration and of cross-national, cross-ethnic marriages. Although professional, white-collar and skilled workers have also joined these movements, they seldom excite the interests of curious global audiences. The presence of "foreigners" has become an everyday scene, even in Japan, but their representations have been quite limited and often negative and destructive. This situation has fueled a sense of xenophobia as well as different kinds of anxiety, fear and suspicion among the local population. These responses have in turn created physical, psychological and social barriers between nation-states and peoples of diverse gender, class, racial, sexual, religious and national backgrounds.

With reference to women migrants, one common conceptualization is to see them as the sexual, material and moral other. They have thus been incarcerated within the identification of being impoverished and pitiful women of the South who are victimized by the violence and chauvinism of men in both their local societies and the powerful West and North. Such a view may be important for the sake of advocacy on behalf of victimized people, but it has failed to consider the workings of the women's and men's fantasies and translation that emerge in differential histories and shifting positionalities of immigrants and local people. As a consequence, the limited conceptualization has paradoxically redrawn boundary markers around the women and their "oppressive" partners, and as colonists and imperialists have done (and continue to do), has repositioned them within "appropriate" gendered, classed and nationalized locations.

In this chapter, I have shown that being far from static or binary-divided, their identities and acts of identification of the self and other change as they live their lives. Likewise, the intermarried women and men subtly and deliberately shape their relationships in attempts to explore, negotiate and translate a range of identities that they unconsciously and tactically imagine and conjure in their daily lives. Such acts have engendered both promising and discouraging results. In the case of Filipina-Japanese relationships, one significant context in which these negotiations take place and become very dynamic is that of their being hybrid and amphibious. The women and men described in this essay translate their differential miscegenous attributes in shifting circumstances, both moving between discrepant histories and uneven power. Most salient of all is the "America" differentially imagined in their minds. On one hand, Filipinas living under the legacies of US colonialism can transform themselves from being "poor women of the South" by wittingly and unwittingly deploying American symbols. The Japanese's relation to America is not as intimate or spontaneous. Although Japanese assert their identities as members of the North, which leads them to dominate the Philippines and

Filipinos, like the Americans, the North is not granted other privileges of the West in the global racial-national-linguistic hierarchy. This has led them to feel a sense of inferiority as "backward" Asians. When Filipinos and Japanese are found in unsettling locations between the North, South, East and West, the axis of the North-South in which their relations are normally positioned, can move to the axis of the East-West. When their power relations shift in this way, Filipinas are enabled to project their generative claim on America and the West by extension through the English language and "Western" practices as well as their genealogical filiations through being former colonials who received "American" education. Emerging as "Westerners" in this way, their Japanese husbands are pushed to somewhere in the "North-East" corner to entertain their pride in having such "modern" and "international" wives. Other husbands feel that their "too modern" wives are intimidating their national and masculine prides, leading them to take vengeance against these "out of place" women. This is an ironic working out of the women's and men's (differently) romanticized "America," which has never really existed but nevertheless haunts their lives.

If we wish to go beyond decades-old clichés, we should not look at, search for or imagine only differences between the people being studied (and between these people and researchers), but also similarities such as the act of imagining "America" and how those similarities and differences articulate in particular socio-historical, political and economic contexts. People's lives do not stop at one place or time, but are being constantly transformed as people live — even though individuals may be caught in contradictions and their actions engender unintended consequences. It is also important to recognize the empowering fantasies of America, the source of global power in the contemporary world, and the violence often thereby engendered. It is equally important not to valorize "America" and associated ideological assumptions such as freedom, democracy and equality because they have never really existed in their ideal forms and have yet to be born. If we are to produce critical, radical and subversive knowledge and give sight to a more inclusive picture of what is happening in the transnationalizing yet unequal world, it is time for us to deconstruct our own conceptual frameworks and decolonize the allegories of people and their fantastic worlds.

Notes

1. Ethnographic descriptions in this essay are derived from fieldwork conducted at various points of time from 1990 to 2007. All personal names are pseudonyms. In this essay, as I did during my fieldwork following social conventions, I call Filipinos by their first names and Japanese by their family names.
2. This "book" refers to a journal in which one of my articles was published. I described Julie in the article and gave her the whole journal.
3. Unlike many Asian countries and regions, Japan has not allowed the entry of domestic workers.
4. Some notable exceptions include Choy (2003) and Yeoh and Khoo (1998). Curiously, there has been much less discussion about foreign trainees — many of them men — and male entertainers coming to Japan who may as well be deceived and abused in the migration process and at work. Unlike women migrants, these (male) workers are as well generally excluded in the issue of human trafficking (see below).
5. The influx was slowed in March 2005 when the Japanese Ministry of Justice unprecedentedly tightened the issuance of entertainer visas due to increasing criticisms against the work many entertainers engaged in at nightclubs being a cover for human trafficking. The number of Filipino entrants with entertainer visas decreased from about 80,000 in 2004 to 5,595 in 2007 (Japanese Ministry of Justice 2007). Human trafficking and other criminal and brutal treatments of migrant workers do happen, but such arguments have tended to be sensationalized based on a small number of cases or ungrounded assertions. In this essay, to include a critical discussion of such arguments is beyond the scope.
6. Other assignments include: to welcome customers, take orders, make drinks, light cigarettes, clean the table, sing karaoke, dance with customers and perform on the stage. Sex may or may not be part of the job. After the massive curtailment of the entertainer visa (note 5), former entertainers in Japan now in their mid-30s and above have returned to the nightclubs, jokingly telling me that

there is "no age limit" and "no [body] shape limit." This suggests that youthful sex and sexuality are not always what customers expect at bars in Japan.

7. Note here that the idea of Japanese (and Chinese) men's forceful subjugation of women resonates with the discourse of the "yellow peril" in the US (Koshy 2004).
8. Although I do not at all intend to defend Koyama's and other batterers' violence, it is important to keep in mind the workings of gender ideology, especially that in Japan with its elaborate state machinery, which dictates men to be the providers for their families, as well as of the psycho-social processes in which batterers learn to justify the use of violence in their lives. Criticizing individual men alone is not productive and we need to situate the violence within various social mechanisms.

chapter 12

Refiguring Identities in an Ifugao Village: Sketches of Joint Projects from a Filipino Filmmaker, a Native Intellectual, and a Japanese Anthropologist under American Shadow(s)

Hiromu Shimizu

The Ifugao are probably the most famous and intensively studied indigenous people in the Philippines. Rice terraces in and around Banaue attract tourists from all over the world, and its scenery figures in the background design of the 1,000 pesos note. The Ifugao Rice Terraces (clusters in Banaue, Hapao, Batad and Mayoyao) were inscribed in the UNESCO World Heritage List as a living cultural heritage in 1995 "because of its great beauty that expresses conquered and conserved harmony between humankind and the environment." Anthropologically, Ifugao is well known not only for rice terraces (Conklin 1980), but also for customary laws (Barton 1919 [1969]), myths and rituals (Lambrecht 1932–1941, 1955–1957), and so forth.

In this paper, I will introduce three men who are carrying out their own project separately but in cooperation in Hapao, a small Ifugao village in Hungduan Municipality.[1] The protagonist is Reynaldo Lopez Nauyac, a native intellectual and the president of a small NGO (Ifugao Global Forest City Movement), which was organized in the middle of the 1990s and has been implementing a reforestation project and a cultural revitalization movement with support from a Japanese NGO and five funding agencies including JICA. The second character is Kidlat Tahimik, a University of the Philippines graduate film director with an MBA from the Wharton School of Finance and cultural activist. I am the third person to form this group, myself a Japanese anthropologist and participant observer of this movement. Through examining the purpose and background of each other's projects, I will discuss how they try to pursue their own identity and refigure their post-colonial subjectivity in and against the American shadow.

It is generally believed that Japan and the Philippines have totally different cultures, societies, and histories. Japan has succeeded in nation-state building and rapid economic growth since the Meiji Restoration, while the Philippines has faced difficulties in nation-building and economic development. Japan has an authentic cultural heritage, while the Philippines does not have that kind of cultural tradition. In that sense, Japan and the Philippines occupy opposite poles in Asia. My personal experience makes me feel that something is wrong with this perception. When I first visited Olongapo city in 1977 on the way to Mt. Pinatubo for preliminary research on indigenous Aetas in the mountains, I felt the atmosphere of the city somehow familiar and I was possessed by a feeling of *déjà vu*. It is probably because I was born and brought up in Yokosuka city located at the mouth of Tokyo Bay, where America has maintained a big naval base for the seventh fleet up to now.

As far as those Japanese living in Yokosuka city were concerned, the US base was called "Sinchu-gun" (進駐軍, occupational army), and it was a fact, at least until the late 1970s (several years after the end of the Vietnam War), that Japan was defeated in the Second World War and capitulated on an unconditional surrender, that the Americans were not guests nor liberators as was generally perceived (c.f. Dower 1999), but conquerors and dominators. In this paper, I will present a challenging perspective that Japanese and Filipinos are half-siblings in Asia under the shadow of American politico-military domination and cultural hegemony. The rule of American-led GHQ shaped the foundation of Japanese polity and consciousness through strict censorship for several years just after the war until the San Francisco Peace Treaty in 1951, but this fact almost sank into oblivion though it must not be forgotten. In contrast to this, Filipinos cannot and do not forget the half century of the American colonial rule, even though they might want to forget it. With this situation in mind, I would like to introduce the attempts of three men to refigure their identity and subjectivity.

Former Prime Minister Koizumi Symbolizes Japan under the US Shadow

Former Prime Minister of Japan, Junichiro Koizumi, made his sixth trip to the US to meet President Bush at the end of June 2006, three months before his retirement, and reaffirmed personal friendship with him. They flew together to Memphis, Tennessee, to visit Graceland, the sacred place for Elvis fans, including Koizumi himself. Mutual trust and comradeship of the two leaders made the US-Japan relationship its best and smoothest in the post-Second World War era. Koizumi consistently supported foreign policies of the Bush administration including wars against Afghanistan and Iraq during the five years and five months of his term in office since April 2001.

When then Prime Minister Koizumi met Bush for the first time in Camp David on June 30, 2001, he enthusiastically and vividly explained how he was fascinated by the movie *High Noon* when he was a high school student. Actually, he went to a barbershop after having seen the movie, and had his hair cut just like Gary Cooper's. He made the second trip to Washington on September 25, two weeks after the 9-11 attack, and strongly supported the US War against terrorism.[2]

And their sixth and the last meeting was featured as follows:

Memphis, June 30, 2006 — Plenty of awestruck Elvis impersonators have passed through the wrought-iron gates of Graceland. Until Friday, none had the president of the United States in tow.

"It's like a dream," Prime Minister Junichiro Koizumi of Japan said to President Bush in the Jungle Room of the Presley home here. Amid the faux leopard print chairs and green shag carpet covering both floor and ceiling, the prime minister then serenaded the president.

"Loooovve mee tenderrrrr," Mr. Koizumi crooned, as Priscilla Presley, Elvis's former wife, and Lisa Marie, his daughter, looked on. (After humming a few words from "Love Me Tender," Koizumi segued into "Can't Help Falling in Love.") When Priscilla Presley pointed out the oversized gold-rimmed sunglasses once worn by the King of Rock 'n' Roll, the prime minister eagerly donned them, thrusting his hips and arms forward in imitation of a classic Elvis move.

"I knew he loved Elvis," Mr. Bush said afterward. "I didn't realize how much he loved Elvis."

If the visit, the first time a sitting president has toured Graceland, resembled an Elvis lovefest, it was a Bush-Koizumi lovefest as well, orchestrated by the White House to spotlight the close relationship between Japan and the United States. Mr. Koizumi, who will step down in September, is among Mr. Bush's closest friends on the world stage; the trip was both a farewell gift and a thank you for Japan's support on the war on terror.

The prime minister's obsession with Elvis is well known; he shares a birthday, Jan. 8, and a hairstyle with Elvis, and worked in the 1980's to erect a bronze statue of the singer in Tokyo. At one point Friday, Mr. Koizumi happily remarked to Lisa Marie Presley that she looked like her father. He later threw his arm around her, belting out some Elvis lyrics, "Hold me close, hold me tight."

Mr. Bush, though, eventually cut off the performance, clapping the prime minister on the shoulder and firmly shaking his hand in a none-too-subtle message that the curtain was about to fall.

(*Source:* Sheryl Gay Stolberg and Shaila Dewan, "In Memphis, Two Heads of Government Visit the Home of Rock 'n' Roll Royalty," July 1, 2006, at <http://www.nytimes.com/2006/07/01/washington/01bush.html>).

The pilgrimage to Graceland was the highlight of Prime Minister Koizumi's visit to the US. More than 300 reporters showed up. Both in US and Japan, newspapers as well as TV and journals gave prominent coverage to his performance, almost ignoring their following visit to the National Civil Rights Museum, next door to the Lorraine Motel, where Rev. Martin Luther King Jr. was killed. At that time, the expected launch of long-range missiles by North Korea was an imminent issue to be dealt with by two heads. Although the joint statement against the launch was issued, it attracted far less attention from the public.

Koizumi crooned "Love me Tender" and "Can't Help Falling in Love" not only as an Elvis fan personally, but also as a representative of the Japanese in general, who willingly accepted the American Occupation together with democracy and attractive popular cultures. The Japanese attitude toward America after the unconditional surrender in August 1945 is well examined and illustrated in Dower's "Embracing the Defeat" (1999). Koizumi was born and raised in Yokosuka city where the US Navy maintained a big base for the seventh fleet. In a sense, Yokosuka is still under the shadow of US military occupation which officially ended in 1952 with the coming into effect of the San Francisco Treaty.

Koizumi's performance in Graceland is also a good example to illuminate his gifted ability to attract tremendous popularity in Japan. When he became Prime Minister in 2001 after unexpected victory in the election for the party president of LDP over Hashimoto, the leader of the biggest political faction, nobody predicted he would serve such a long period (1,980 days), the third longest term among 30 prime ministers after the Second World War, following Eisaku Sato and Sigeru Yoshida. As he did not have a solid base in the ruling LDP, he had to procure direct and strong support from the general public for the sake of stability of the government and strong leadership. The approval rate of his government continuously kept around 50%, which is the second highest next to Hosokawa within 60 years.

His popularity depends much on his style of self-representation. He played a strong leader image as a reformer, or a destroyer to abolish old systems in politics and economics in order to build a new and affluent society. He skillfully portrayed his opponents as reactionaries whose motivation was to protect their own vested rights, and fiercely attacked them with clear and crisp words. He always spoke affirmatively with little hesitation. Twice a day, in the morning and afternoon, he stood before TV cameras and reporters, and responded briefly and clearly to questions concerning current issues. His style is often described banteringly as "one-phrase politics" or "politics of theatrical performances." His aggressiveness and self-confidence, however, provided the general public with some hope for the future instead of a decade of recession in the aftereffects of the bubble economy.

He is really an exceptional prime minister in the history of Japanese politics. Besides not belonging to or being supported by the core circle of LDP powerful figures, his electoral district Yokosuka city is not a rural area like those of previous prime ministers. Unlike his predecessors, he represents the profits of urban dwellers, i.e., office workers, merchants, small entrepreneurs, contractors, etc., and moreover, he consciously or unconsciously responds to unarticulated sense, feeling, desire and ethics of urban dwellers, who are the majority of Japan today. That is probably the reason why he could successfully maintain a high level of popularity nationwide.

Koizumi is the third generation of a political family in Yokosuka city. Both his father and grandfather became cabinet members. His house is only a few kilometers away from the US Naval Base, and within walking distance from a red light district for American sailors. His father, Junya Koizumi, was an advocate for the revision of the Japan-US Security Treaty in 1960, and therefore had the nickname of "the man of Security Treaty." As a member of the committee for foreign affairs of the House of Representatives, he accompanied Prime Minister Nobusuke Kishi to the US to attend the signing ceremony.

In contrast to his father's devotion for the treaty, civil movements for anti-revision prevailed nationwide, and dominated in the trends and atmosphere of that time. Also in Yokosuka High School where Koizumi went, most teachers were members of the left-wing Teachers Union and were very active in social and labor movement. Koizumi was just split between pro-treaty in the house and anti-treaty in the school, as well as between the real America in and around the base and imaginative America in Hollywood movies and popular songs. Real America in Yokosuka was so close to residents there together with the smell of sex, violence and death due to the wars in Korea and Vietnam. Koizumi, however, seemed to keep a distance from anything "real America" and indulged instead in "fantastic America."

Totally different from present images, Koizumi was quiet and uncommunicative during his boyhood. For example, many of his classmates in junior high school do not have clear memories of him, except for one occasion in which he sang "Love Me Tender" in English in the return trip bus of an excursion tour and everybody got surprised. Probably he could not mediate two contradicting worlds of America, and secured himself in a cocoon of dreamy American cultures (Iwasaki 2006: 102–4).

Prominent political scientist Mikuriya (2006) suggests that the essence of Koizumi's political maneuvering is nihilism, while another distinguished scholar Otake (2006) also paints him as a kind of active/aggressive nihilist as was illustrated by Andre Malraux, in addition to being a Machiavelist and a populist. I believe Koizumi's inclination to nihilism was nursed in Yokosuka by a strong awareness of America's presence and Japanese incompetence. He was put under contradiction of two dissimilar Americas, an overpowering politico-military force and a seductive soft cultural power.

After Circumnavigation into the World of the Ifugao

It is not wrong to say that Kidlat Tahimik is, at least was, a super elite in the Philippine society. His mother served as President of the University of the Philippines Women's Association and beat young Ferdinand Marcos at a speech contest in 1938. She also served as Acting Mayor of Baguio city just after the Second World War, and held the ceremony for US flag-lowering and national flagraising. His maternal grandfather studied forestry at Yale University and became the first City Forester of the Philippines and was eventually honored as the "Father of Philippine Forestry." As we will see later, this might be related to his own long-time commitment to reforestation and the cultural revitalization movement in Hapao village, Hungduan Municipality, Ifugao Province.

Kidlat was born and grew up in Baguio, and remembers well the days when his family evacuated to the mountains to escape the bombings from American planes against the Japanese army. While he was a student of the University of the Philippines, he served the chairman of the student council in 1962. The position was thought to be a stepping stone into the world of the political establishment, and Kidlat himself dreamed to become a president at that time. After graduation, he got a scholarship to study at Walton School of Finance in Philadelphia, USA. With a prestigious MBA, he got a position in OECD's main office in Paris in 1968 and was in charge of fertilizer distribution for the green revolution. Up to this point, his life course was the most desirable and ideal one in the Philippines.

During his four years in Paris, he enjoyed the social world of the establishment thanks to the companionship of his French classmate from an aristocratic family, with whom Kidlat formed a close friendship during his Walton School days. At the same time, however, he felt some alienation or estrangement from this world of the establishment as well as from his own "true self." He once kindly narrated to me an unforgettable experience in which he was beaten down by riot police just after arriving in Paris in 1968. It was the time of the reverberations of the May Revolution. Kidlat stood on a sidewalk watching a demonstration march of workers and students. On the other side of the street stood an elegant condominium, and a middle-aged lady in a gown stood on the third or fourth balcony, looking down coolly at demonstrators with no sign of fear or curiosity.

Since he was shocked as well as fascinated by the contrast between two classes, one on the street and the other on the balcony, he was absorbed in taking pictures of the scene. All of sudden, he was hit by a truncheon on the shoulder-neck and collapsed to the ground. He was then taken to a police station. A policeman pulled out the film, put it around his neck like a dog collar, then insolently investigated him. He felt racial discrimination, and sensed that he was not on the side which the police would defend and that he would not be fully accepted by that society. Four years after this incident and a few months before the Olympics in Munich in 1972, he resigned from his position and joined a community of vegetarian artists there. The position in OECD was the fruit of his labor and proof of his achievements, but at the same time, this was a preparation period for his awakening and transformation.

When he made up his mind to drop out from his highly prestigious and well-paid career course, he gave away all 30 fancy suits he had tailored in *haute couture*. He also tore up the MBA certificate which would guarantee his future success, and the MBA became instead an acronym for "Mababangong Bangungot ng Amerika" (Perfumed Nightmare of America), "Mababangong Bangungot ng Aliw-Wood" (Perfumed Nightmare of Holly/Pleasure Wood), "Mackinley's Benevolent Assassination (*not assimilation)." In these expressions, the symbolism of the MBA was transformed from the proof of his achievement in the American educational system to the realization that not only Kidlat himself but also Philippine culture and society have accepted American hegemony and shaped itself willingly in accordance with American values and aesthetics.

"Mababangong Bangungot" is the title of his first movie produced in 1975–1977.[3] After joining an artist commune, he married a German stained-glass artist and began to study filmmaking by himself with a little advice and teaching from his film director friend in the commune. He produced, directed, partly shot and edited the film *Mababangong Bangungot* (about 90 minutes) with a $10,000 budget, in which he played the leading part. Thus, Kidlat calls himself a "one-man band organ (a Yamaha brand name)" player. This way of handicraft manufacturing itself is, according to him, the antithesis of the Hollywood production system, i.e., Fordism, and a critic of the American way of life as a whole. It is obvious that his limited budget forced him to minimize every manufacturing cost, and thus, Kidlat did many things with available instruments and materials as a bricoleur.

The protagonist in the movie is a jeepney driver, who makes round trips between a village and a town market passing through a bridge which separates as well as connects two worlds. He is the self-appointed president of W. von Brown (the leader of the NASA space development project) fan club in the village, most members of which are village boys and girls. One day, he meets a foreign tourist, who kindly brings him to Paris where becomes disillusioned with development and civilization. This village is his father's home village in Laguna, and almost the entire cast were played by villagers there. It is for this reason that watching the film makes us feel very at home and relaxed, while it is a story about the allurement of and disillusionment with western civilization, progress and modernity. Kidlat explains the theme of the film thus: "the sleeping Kidlat must shed his cocoon of colonized dreams to unleash his true *indio*-genius strength" (Tahimik 1997: 20).

Francis Coppola highly praised *Mababangong Bangungot* and distributed it in the United States. Susan Sontag remarked, "After many months of dreary movie-going, it is ecstatic surprise to encounter *The Perfumed Nightmare* which reminds us that spontaneous dream states, poetic meandering, even innocence are still available in cinema" (1980). Two of the most prominent German filmmakers at that time were also impressed by Kidlat's indigenous approach to filmmaking. Wim Wenders remarked: "*Perfumed Nightmare* turned out to be one of the nicest unperfumed daydreams ever saw on the screen!," and Werner Herzog commented: "Kidlat Tahimik's *Perfumed Nightmare* is one of the most original and poetic works of film made anywhere in the 70's ..." (De Guia 1997 vol. 2: 34).

Perhaps one of the most significant appreciations and reactions to the film came from Frederic Jameson, who discussed it in one whole chapter of his book, *Geopolitical Aesthetic*. The title of the chapter is "'Art Naïf' and Admixture of Worlds." As Jameson indicates, Kidlat is very much conscious of the cultural hegemony of the First World, especially in the United States. Kidlat admits that he himself had been over-educated and overdeveloped by American pedagogy, and therefore, was forced to hold down his inner self to become an obedient good boy, and at best to be a honorary white man. His life after dropping out from the elite bureaucracy in the international organization has been a struggle to refigure himself as a true Filipino.[4] He supported himself by selling Philippine-made souvenir goods on the streets and in flea markets before and after the Olympic games in Munich. According to him, it was an unconscious process of liberating the *indio*-genius *dwende* inside the over-schooled him — that amazing gnome one finds in unschooled Filipinos living the *Bathala Na* way. In order to become a true Filipino with dignity, he had to unlearn and start from scratch. In the ending scene of *Mababangong Bangungot*, Kidlat says, "When the Sleeping Typhoon blows off its cocoon ... the emancipated Butterfly shall embrace the sun ..." This "hybrid Pinoy haiku" was written in 1972 as he first recognized his cocoon of American dreams. He writes as follows:

> We Filipinos are sleeping typhoons, unaware of our indigenous power. Trapped in our cocoons of colonized aspirations, the *indio*-genius in us is kept comatose (thanks to our school system, our film/TV pedagogues, our mall "universities of consumption"). Unless we wake up and realize the nature of this cocoon, our sleeping potential will remain just that (Tahimik 1997: 44).

It should be noted that in his very first film, he appeared with mushroom-shaped hair *à la* the Beatles. I felt this was just a little bit funny when I saw the film in Tokyo at the Asian Film Festival sponsored by the Japan Foundation in 1982. Later, I noticed that it was not at all an imitation of the Beatles, the symbol of western cultural hegemony, but mimicry of traditional or authentic Ifugao men. In the beginning of his unlearning process, it was already foreseen that Ifugao culture was a model for him to follow or a paradigm to learn.[5] However, it would be no problem if the culture was not Ifugaos' but Kalingas' or Bontocs'. For him, indigenous cultures are a "collective brake system" of a people against the rushing trend of Americanization, which is reinforcing that *cocoon-ization* (chrysalis-ization) process.

Those indigenous peoples in the mountains of northern Luzon resisted the Spanish, American and Japanese invaders/colonizers, and have kept their own cultural heritage even after they were pacified and Christianized, and became members of the national community. The reason why Kidlat did not choose Kalinga or Bontoc but Ifugao is that he has an old friend from Ifugao, Reynaldo Lopez Nauyac. According to Kidlat, Nauyac is truly an *indio*-genius woodcarver, grassroots philosopher, a soul-brother, and a guru for his relearning practice. When Nauyac retired from his woodcarving business in Baguio and returned home to Hapao village in 1997 in order to fully engage himself in the a reforestation movement there, Kidlat purchased a traditional Ifugao house and frequently visited Hapao to join and film activities of Nauyac.

Planting Trees to Rehabilitate the Past for Future

Not only for Kidlat, but also for the Philippines as a post-colonial nation, Ifugao represents the supposed "autochthony" of Filipinos. Probably that is why the scenery of rice terraces in Banaue is used as a background of the 1,000 *peso* notes, and the government made efforts to have Ifugao terraces inscribed in the UNESCO World Heritage List. It was the Ramos government that established the Ifugao Terraces Commission to preserve and promote Terraces for national heritage and the tourism industry.

For Kidlat, nobody else but Nauyac embodies true and authentic Ifugao-ness. Nauyac's words and works are a source of inspiration for unlearning/relearning practices as well as filmmaking. Kidlat made several films featuring Nauyac. One is *Our Bomb Mission to Hiroshima* (1995, Color Video, 20 minutes). It is a documentary of their performances in Hiroshima where they were invited by an NGO to participate in the 50th anniversary commemoration of the atomic bomb atrocities. On this occasion, Nauyac excavated an unexploded 108kg bomb on the bank of the Asin River near his house in Baguio city. He cut off the head part, removed the contents, and made it into a bell. Nauyac and Kidlat brought the bell to Hiroshima, where they, dressed in Ifugao style, i.e., G-strings, performed an Ifugao ritual to console spirits of the dead. After coming back from Hiroshima to Baguio, Nauyac put the warhead-bell at the top of a newly built church roof in Asin Road *baranggay*, where most of the residents are Ifugaos and other indigenous peoples are from the Cordillera region.

During the Second World War, both Kidlat and Nauyac evacuated whenever American planes came to drop bombs over them respectively in Baguio and in Ifugao. Nauyac has a crescent-shaped scar on his forehead, from a wound by a broken peace of a rock hit by a bomb during evacuation. So the bomb-bell first reminds us the same fate of war victims in Baguio, Ifugao and Hiroshima, and then rang to console the 150,000 dead in Hiroshima, and finally came back home and was transformed into a peace-praying bell in a community of indigenous peoples. Thanks to Nauyac's activities and signifying practice and Kidlat's participant documentation, we can understand that the bomb-bell symbolizes "coevalness" of time in Fabian's sense (1983), or the synchronicity/simultaneousness of our lives. The bell in itself connects different places and peoples (Baguio/Ifugao/Hiroshima, America/Philippines/Japan) as well as different layers of time (past, present, future), and symbolizes the relatedness among them. It symbolizes as well the transformation of the bomb from something evil into something good and benevolent.

After one year, Kidlat arranged and again accompanied Nauyac on a journey to Take-dera (Bamboo temple) in Saitama prefecture, Japan, and made the film, *Bahag Ko, Mahal Ko* (*My G-String, My Love*, 1984–1896, Color Video, 60 minutes). In August 1996, Nauyac led five Ifugao carvers together with Kidlat to Take-dera and stayed for a few weeks to carve a big old Sugi (Japanese cedar) tree beside the Cow Shrine, which was struck by lightning and withered in 1994. They made a beautiful totem pole from the tree with a Cow God and other Ifugao sacred figures on it. The film focused upon Nauyac's works, his interaction with fellow carvers and Japanese.

His latest film, *Banal Kahoy* (*Holy Wood*, digital video and 16mm film, 68 minutes), is a compiled and revised version of his previous films with many glimpses of the Ifugao world incorporated. It is a documentation of Nauyac's activities in Take-dera (woodcarving) and Hapao (tree-planting, cultural and ritual performance), Ifugao way of living, rice terraces, *pinugo* (private forest owned and managed by a family or a clan), and the companionship and participant activities of Kidlat with his three boys. As the title *Banal Kahoy* (*Holy Wood*) suggests, it shows an alternative world of Hollywood movies, i.e., a tranquil, humble, spiritual world of Ifugao with reverence to nature.

As shown in this movie, Nauyac has devoted himself to tree-planting in and around his home village, Hapao, in the Municipality of Hungduan for nearly a decade. He was born in 1938 and grew up there until he went to a high school in Banaue. After graduating from high school in 1958 at the age of 16, he went to Baguio to become a working student at a college. He attended four semesters before he stopped and concentrated on handicraft works in a shop run by a relative. He later became an independent carver, got married, and ran a wholesale shop beside his carving works. He served Asin Road *baranggay* community as a councilman (1978–1982) and then a *baranggay* captain for three terms (1982–1997). In 1993, he went to New York with several other natives from Luzon and Mindanao to participate in the Indigenous People at the World Convention organized by UNESCO. He was awarded the Most Outstanding Baranggay Captain in the Philippines in 1995, and the plaque was presented by then president Ramos at Malacanang Palace.

Soon after quitting the political world in 1997, he went back to Hapao to settle down with his wife and three married children left in Baguio. He purchased a piece of land along the main road and an old Ifugao-style house, which he dismantled and reconstructed on the purchased land. It became the base of his life in Hapao as well as the office of the Ifugao Global Forest City Movement (IGFCM), which he had established with some 100 villagers and registered at the National Securities and Exchange Commission in 1998. At Nauyac's own house lot near the rice terraces in *sitio* Patpat, Kidlat transferred an old Ifugao house in 1998. He built a new house with a perfectly authentic Ifugao-style house beside the old house in 2005.

With almost 340 households and a base population of 1,750, as of 2006, Hapao is the biggest *baranggay* in Hungduan Municipality. Basic subsistence is rice cultivation in terraces, swidden agriculture of sweet potatoes, beans and vegetables, with woodcarving as a sideline for cash income. More than 100 men are actively engaged in carving. As big hard trees suitable for carvings have been decreasing in number, some go to other provinces like Nueva Viscaya, Quirino and Aurora in a group to camp and work in a forest. Those who work in the village produce only small carvings which do not make much money. Nauyac has been very much worried about disappearance of big trees in the surrounding mountains of Hapao, as well as the deforestation of some slopes in the mountains, especially those above irrigation channels for terraces. With the disappearance of forest cover which is caused by swidden fire and rampant logging, those slopes are vulnerable to landslides which fill up channels and damage irrigation systems, sometimes burying terraces. Without trees and forests, two components of subsistence economy, agriculture and woodcarving in Hapao cannot be maintained. That is the reason why Nauyac made up his mind to go back home to rehabilitate forests and the damaged terrace-system.

Nauyac said that trees and forests have provided him and many other Ifugaos with a means of livelihood to support a family. For many generations, their forefathers cut down but immediately replanted trees. Regrettably, however, people recently have only deprived the nature of its richness without offering any gratitude in return to maintain a human-nature cordial relationship. Therefore, hard trees for carvings have disappeared, and so many Ifugaos are forced to work in forest camps in other provinces, or migrate to work in Baguio and Manila. In order to make a living in Hapao with a proper harvest and cash income, people have to rehabilitate and recycle forests by continuously planting indigenous trees.

In early 1990, Nauyac organized a woodcarvers association in Asin Road *baranggay* for micro credit and mutual assistance, and among members, promoted tree-planting activities in Baguio and Hapao. He collected seeds from indigenous trees, germinated them in a nursery at the backyard of his house in Asin Road, and distributed them among member carvers. Sometimes, he loaded pots of seedlings in a jeepney which carried carved products to Baguio, and accompanied them on a return trip to Hapao in order to plant them there together with volunteer villagers.

What is interesting and important is the way he explains the necessity of reforestation in Hapao as well as the priority of Hapao to receive funds from governments and NGOs in and outside of the Philippines. Hapao is located near the place where General Yamashita, the commander-in-chief of the Japanese Imperial Army in the Philippines, evacuated and built the final position of his main force in June 1945. Yamashita, however, gave up in the final battle, and went down along Asin Valley to Kiangan to surrender. Nauyac said, "At the last moment of World War II, peace for the world finally descended here in Hapao, Hungduan, thanks to the spiritual atmosphere of forests which appeased General Yamashita's combative samurai spirit."

When Japanese soldiers retreated to the area, Hapao villagers evacuated deep into the mountains or other places. American planes dropped bombs on camps of Japanese troops and napalm bombs on forests, which destroyed terraces and irrigation channels. Population figures decreased in Hungduan from 12,000 to 4,000 after the war. The lack of manpower did not allow Ifugaos to repair and rehabilitate damaged portions in terraces and channels. The scars of this destruction are still inscribed in the scenery of village surroundings to remind the people of the sufferings of war just like Nauyac's scar on his forehead. Nauyac himself lost his mother, younger brother and sister due to malnutrition and diseases during the evacuation. According to him, he was saved and could live until today because he was given a mission by God. That is, to plant trees, recover forests, and to rehabilitate terraces and the living environment so that his fellow villagers could survive in this world as Ifugaos with pride and prestige.

He cannot forget the days of suffering and difficulty during the war, but never accused me or Japanese soldiers when he narrated memories of the incidences in the war, usually over a cup of *tapoy* (native rice wine). He said that the tragedy occurred because of the war, which was already over more than a half a century ago. He commented, however, that neither the Japanese government nor the American government had compensated the damages which they caused on Ifugaos. What he sincerely hoped for was that both Japanese and American people would feel sorry and responsible for the loss of lives, damage to Ifugaos' properties, and realize that they obtained eternal peace (hopefully) at the cost of the Ifugao people. Then, he demanded that Japanese and American people should help his movement/project of reforestation and rehabilitation of terraces for the sake of the future of younger Ifugao generation.

His project is therefore to reject Japanese's and Americans' amnesia of history thus far and no further, but to remind them of it and to make them responsible to return the place to its original state. It is not to accuse them of evil deeds, but to reconnect a relationship which was already established by the war among Ifugaos, Japanese, and Americans. That is why he named the People's Organization "Ifugao Global Forest City Movement." It is global because the project site itself is just the same as the place where a final battle of the Second World War was supposed to be fought but world peace was born instead. Moreover, until the present, rice terraces have attracted tourists from all over the world. As terraces in Hapao are much more magnificent than those in Banaue, which is the most popular destination for sightseeing, tourists would be more satisfied to come and see Hapao terraces and forests. Besides, foreigners spend money which would contribute to economic development, and they would praise and admire forests, terraces, and the Ifugao way of life. Their appreciation and esteem of the Hapao world would promote an awakening and revaluation of Ifugao cultural heritage among Hapao youth. According to him, both the past which was shaped by the war and the future which could be opened by tourism are connected directly to the outside world, and that is why his project is "global." He has a plan to reforest the area near Hapao where General Yamashita encamped and wants to build a World Peace Forest Park.

The name "Forest City" reveals Nauyac's desire and intension to change the remote and stagnant image of Hapao into an attractive and future-oriented one. Just like cities are filled up by tall buildings as well as many different peoples, Hapao and its surrounding areas could be covered by big tall trees and be open to visitors from different places and countries. The image of buildings for trees and the metaphor of a city for Hapao provide villagers and concerned peoples (government staff, NGO workers) with a refreshing and eye-opening effect. Nauyac also explains that rehabilitation of the *pinugo* forests is indispensable for maintaining rice terraces, which have been inherited from many generations back and are the fruits of their ancestors' hard labor for descendants and the proof of bonds of each generation which cultivated and will cultivate them in succession from the past to the future. That is the reason why a present cultivator refers to the names of ancestors when he chants prayers in rituals in the terraces.

For Nauyac, IGFCM is a multi-purpose project. It is: 1) to realize his longtime dream to come back home to spend a retired life in a familiar and comfortable environment; 2) to atone for his own and fellow villagers' cutting down of so many trees for carving and to reconcile with Mother Nature; 3) to rehabilitate the foundation for villagers' subsistence to be continued for future; and 4) not merely to restore the past but to build a better future, by opening the village to outsiders and building up closer connections with artists, concerned peoples, government officials and NGOs in Baguio, Manila, and in Japan together with Kidlat.

In short, restoration of terraces and forests and remembering hard times during the war are interrelated projects for him so that Ifugaos can survive as indigenous people with cultural heritage, self-esteem and stable incomes in order to establish a special position in the Philippine society with honor and dignity. In signifying practices for these activities, he connects local and global, and the past and the future. His strong intention to live as a member of this contemporary world makes him refigure his own identity, not from a backward primitive to a modernized citizen, but from an isolated minority to a contemporary citizen who has shared the same experiences of the World War, survived its aftereffects, and now tries to live in networks beyond national boundaries.

Committed Anthropologist from Yokosuka

I first met Nauyac in Baguio in May 1997, and accompanied him on his trip by a hired jeepney from his house in Baguio to Hapao via Bontoc to finally settle down there in March 1998. Then, I conducted a two-week period of preliminary research in Hapao, staying with him in his Ifugao-style house/office. One night during the first fieldwork trip, Nauyac narrated to me his experiences and memories of the war and his plans for reforestation, and then appointed me as a liaison officer in

Japan for his movement. He told me not to be a non-committed researcher but to find a partner NGO in Japan for IGFCM and to get funds for his project. Although IGFCM already received 400,000 pesos from the Ifugao Terraces Commission, it was not enough for his project. Coming back to Manila, I got in contact with my friend, Kazuya Tomita, and asked him to help me and Nauyac in Hapao.

Tomita came to the Philippines in 1992 just after the Mt. Pinatubo eruption as a Japanese Oversees Cooperation Volunteer to work in a rehabilitation project for the Aeta (Negrito-type people in Pinatubo area) victims/refuges, which was implemented by an NGO (Aeta Development Association). After completing a three-year term there, he voluntarily remained in Casterijos, Zambales and became a field representative of a small Japanese NGO (IKGS) in Hyogo prefecture to start a new project of reforestation in areas damaged by ash. When I asked his help, he got very much interested in Hapao and Nauyac's project, went to Hapao to see Nauyac and project sites. He gradually shifted the focus of activities from Pinatubo to Hapao, and since 2000, he has been on fully committed reforestation projects there receiving funds from six different agencies in Japan including JICA (Partnership Program). The eight years' total budget amounted to about 80 million yen (as of December 2008, equivalent to $900,000), and I have also committed myself in these projects as an advisor for Tomita.

When I first visited Hapao, I felt very much at home, because a good friend of mine, Dr. Sylvano Mahiwo, with whom I have been friends for 25 years, is from this village. He received his PhD in International Relations from the University of Tokyo and is now a Professor at the University of the Philippines' Asian Center. Owning property in Hapao, he never fails to return there at least once a year for the clan-reunion during the Holy Week vacation, and his brother, Joseph, who also lives in Hapao, takes care of the property. When I first came to the Philippines in 1976, my original plan was to conduct research in the Cordillera region. In April and

May 1977, I made several trips in Ifugao and Kalinga to find a village for my fieldwork. Because of an untoward situation, I changed my mind and conducted fieldwork at an Aeta village in Mt. Pinatubo, Zambales. Thus, when I spent the first night in Hapao together with Nauyac in 1998, I felt that I had finally come full circle to the original plan after 30 years and that a longtime dream had finally been realized.

Here, my personal background makes itself felt in that I came to be interested in and then deeply involved in the projects of Kidlat and Nauyac in Hapao. When I was a university student, I studied anthropology and the Chinese language because I was interested in Chinese culture and society, and was specially fascinated by Mao Ze Tong's ideas and the Cultural Revolution. Yet, I wrote a graduation thesis and an MA thesis on rituals and religious practices in Taiwan, just because much more anthropological materials were available on topics about Taiwan than about mainland China. Studying culture and religion in Taiwan was to be a kind of preliminary preparation work for me to conduct fieldwork in mainland China. Unfortunately, however, China was still in a state of confusion due to the aftermath of the Cultural Revolution when I planned to go there for fieldwork in the middle of 1970s. To add to this, it was also difficult to obtain a scholarship which enabled me to go to Taiwan, because the Japanese government broke off diplomatic relations with Taiwan when it recognized mainland China as the legitimate government of Chinese people.

Why was I interested in China? As mentioned, I came to be interested in and attracted to Mao Ze Tong's ideas and the Cultural Revolution because the ongoing spectacular experiment seemed to be an attempt to construct a new society which was the antithesis of "US Imperialism" or an alternative to a society built and dominated by Western ideology. For me, the Philippines was just second best at that time, and a place for an emergency evacuation; a place to wait until the doors of mainland China opened. Frankly speaking, I was not so excited when I luckily received a Monbusho Scholarship (Ministry of Education) to go to the Philippines. My prejudice was that the

Philippines had been too Americanized and that lowlander Filipinos had lost any authentic cultural heritage they might have had. Moreover, I was worried about their feelings and attitude toward Japanese, as Japan had invaded the Philippines, imposed a military rule and caused atrocities among ordinary people. Such slight reluctance and half-heartedness of mine about going to the Philippines was surely based on my personal background, probably on a kind of "avoidance of the same kind."

I was born in Yokosuka city which is located in the Miura Peninsula embracing Tokyo Bay. There used to be a mother port for the Japanese Imperial Navy before the war, which was turned into one for the US seventh fleet after the war. I was born and raised in a shabby housing complex for those repatriated from China, Korea and Southeast Asia, which had been used before and during the war as dormitories for workers in the naval base, newly recruited sailors and their relatives. Each dorm was a two-storied wood building with corridors in the center and some ten rooms on both sides. One family occupied one room, and shared a common kitchen with several stoves at the end of the corridor and a common toilet outside. Those repatriated who had relatives to rely on in the countryside proceeded to their respective destinations, but those with no place to go for help just stayed behind in a dorm.

Some residents worked inside the US base as casual laborers, some as manual laborers in relief programs for the unemployed, some others in informal sectors. When I was a boy, I thought that Japanese were poor except for a few who had a special relationship in the base or with American sailors. Interpreters inside the base and bar girls (especially "only-san" who entertained only one person as a lover or a mistress) outside the base were those few who benefited a lot from the base. They enjoyed fairly good income in addition to imported whiskey, cigarettes and chocolate, only because they could speak English. I very much had an ambivalent perception and attitude toward them with mixed feelings of envy and contempt, which must have been influenced by and reflected in the general attitude of adults around me, of course including my parents. It was an undeniable fact that the nearer a Japanese was to the American world, the richer and more comfortable his/her life seemed to be. As their way of life was very attractive but difficult to obtain for ordinary Japanese, many told themselves that decent Japanese should not abandon their pride, integrity, and principles by taking a servile attitude toward Americans.

I remember the first day of an English class in junior high school when an American middle-aged woman, the wife of an officer in the base, came to teach in direct method. I murmured in a small voice, "Yankee go home," which was the only English I knew at that time. Although my memory is not so clear and it is hard to explain the reason or the intention of my murmuring, it was not at all out of hostility but a kind of a conditioned response. Of course, I was called to the teachers' room and was scolded by a class teacher. I thought at that time ordinary Japanese should keep distance from the Base and Americans there. I, however, studied English hard as a good student, because English is an important subject in the entrance examinations of any University. Moreover, many of my favorite TV programs at the time (the 1960s) were American home dramas/comedies and cowboy movies, and my favorite music was American folk songs and folk rock. I loved American new cinemas in the 1970s. I was split in two different directions — one to avoid the real American world in Yokosuka, and the other to be fascinated by the fantastic American world on the TV, movie screen and records. I could somehow maintain my integrity in a mixture of a love-hate attitude toward America. My compromise over the conflict was to study English in preparation for an entrance examination, only in reading and grammar but never in speaking or conversation with a flesh-and-blood American.

I have narrated such a very personal story because I am sure that I share with Kidlat and Nauyac similar feelings, a love-hate relationship with America. My project in Hapao was originally to conduct research for an ethnographic monograph on Nauyac-initiated movement for reforestation, rice terrace rehabilitation, biodiversity conservation, cultural revitalization, socioeconomic development, and grassroots empowerment. Through my close association and conversations with Nauyac and Kidlat, I was gradually initiated retrospectively to rethink the process of my own identity formation. Refiguring my own subjectivity has just begun and has a long way to go from now on.

By Way of Conclusion

Thus far, four figures I introduced bear the marks of vestiges, damages and influences of American colonization/occupation and continuous domination. On Nauyac's forehead was a crescent-shaped scar caused by US bombing just like broken terraces on the mountain slopes in Hapao. The colonial legacy of education, with English as the medium of instruction (and even brainwashing), deeply inscribed Kidlat's psychology, and his life after dropping out of OECF was dedicated to liberate himself and reconstruct his new and true self. A dichotomous love-hate attitude toward the real and the imaginative America was induced in me by the direct and indirect influence of the US naval base in Yokosuka. Probably former Prime Minister Koizumi shared an ambivalent attitude similar to mine.

Kidlat, Nauyac, and I have different careers and backgrounds, but recognize one another as comrades fighting for the same cause or for a similar reason. We were once and are still under the shadow of US, and are trying to get rid of, or tame it for the better future and enhanced self.

Notes

1. I went to Hapao in 1998 for the first time, and since then, have conducted two to three weeks' fieldwork every summer, winter or spring vacation for ten years.
2. The third meeting was held in New York on September 12, 2002, the day Bush addressed the UN, and Koizumi persuaded Bush to pursue the foreign policy of international cooperation toward the Iraq issue. Immediately after Bush delivered an ultimatum of a 48 hour-

moratorium to Iraq on March 18, however, Koizumi said he could understand Bush's anguish and would fully support Bush's decision. At the fourth meeting with Bush in Texas, Koizumi expressed his intention to send the Japanese Self Defence Force to Iraq to assist post-war rehabilitation, the first dispatch of the force abroad in history.

3. His movies always go through several revisions after the tentative completion of a first version.
4. His wife and fellow cultural activist Katrin writes even today that "Life alongside Kidlat Tahimik means deconstruction of anything mainstream society wants one to believe in, including clothing habits, time schedule, creative techniques, home arrangement or management style. Thus, no colonial holidays remained sacred for our children. Christmas gifts were held back until December 30 when "Happy Rizal Day" presents moored their attention to another, more Pinoy, cause celebration. Birthdays morphed into "Orbit Days" to highlight the completion of the annual 365-day orbit around the sun. Hence, the greeting "Happy Orbit to you!" This need to make sense of such daily epistemological chaos ultimately led to my study of Sikolohiyang Pilipino and the writing of this book (De Guia 2005: 92).
5. The archetypal quality of Kidlat Tahimik's stubborn clinging to anything he recognized as natively Filipino was immediately realized by German filmmaker Werner Herzog. Spontaneously, Herzog wrote a bit role for the artist in his prizewinning film "Kaspar Hauser" (1974). In the film, Kidlat played a chieftain who never stopped playing his flute, lest his tribe in the mountains died (De Guia 2005: 91).

Bibliography

Books, Articles and Theses

Abaya, Hernando J. *Betrayal in the Philippines*. New York/Quezon City: A.A. Wyn and Malaya Books, 1946, 1970.

Afable, Patricia O. "Language, Culture, and Society in a Kallahan Community, Northern Luzon Philippines." PhD thesis, Yale University, 1989.

———. "A Brief Linguistic and Historical Note about '*Kanyaw*'." *The Igorot Quarterly* 7, 4 (1998a): 55–6.

———. "Eduardo Masferré's Subjects: A Century of Self-Representation in the Philippines." In *Anales del Museo Nacional de Antropología*, V. Madrid, 1998b.

———. ed. *Japanese Pioneers in the Northern Philippine Highlands: A Centennial Tribute, 1903–2003*. Baguio City: Filipino-Japanese Foundation of Northern Luzon, 2004.

Agoncillo, Felipe ["Semper Vigilans"]. "Aguinaldo's Case Against the United States." *North American Review* 169 (September 1899a): 425–32.

———. *Memorials from Senor Felipe Agoncillo and Constitution of the Provisional Philippine Government*. Boston: Anti-Imperialist League, 1899b.

———. *To The American People*. Paris: Imprimerie Chaix, 1900.

Agoncillo, Teodoro A. *Malolos: The Crisis of a Republic*. Quezon City: University of the Philippines Press, 1960.

———. *The Fateful Years: Japan's Adventure in the Philippines, 1941–45*, 2 vols. Quezon City: R.P. Garcia Publishing Co., 1965.

———. *The Burden of Proof: The Vargas-Laurel Collaboration Case*. Quezon City: University of the Philippines Press, 1984.

Agoncillo, Teodoro A., and Milagros C. Guerrero. *History of the Filipino People*. Quezon City: R.P. Garcia Publishing Co., 1973.

Agpalo, Remigio E. *Jose P. Laurel: National Leader and Political Philosopher*. Quezon City: J.P. Laurel Memorial Corp., 1992.

Allen, James S. *The Radical Left on the Eve of War: A Political Memoir*. Quezon City: Foundation for Nationalist Studies, 1985.

Alzona, Encarnación. *Galicano Apacible: Profile of a Filipino Patriot*. N.p.: The Heirs of Galicano Apacible, 1971.

Amino, Yoshihiko. *Mouko Shurai: Tenkan suru Shakai* [*The Mongolian Invasions: The Transforming Society*]. Tokyo: Shogakukan Bunko, 1974 [2001].

———. *Muen, Kugai and Raku: Nihon Chusei no Jiyu to Heiwa* [*Muen, Kugai and Raku: Freedom and Peace in the Medieval Japan*]. Tokyo: Heibonsha, 1978 [1996].

———. *Ikei no Oken* [*Kingdom of Anomaly*]. Tokyo: Heibonsha, 1986 [1993].

———. *Nihon no Rekishi o Yominaosu* [*Re-Reading Japanese History*], vols. 1 and 2. Tokyo: Chikuma Gakugei Bunko, 1991, 1996 [2005].

Anderson, Benedict. *Imagined Communities: Reflections on the Origin and Spread of Nationalism*. London: Verso, 1983.

———. "Hard to Imagine: A Puzzle in the History of Philippine Nationalism." In *Cultures and Texts, Representations of Philippine Society*, eds. R. Pertierra and E. Ugarte. Quezon City: University of the Philippines Press, 1994.

———. *Under Three Flags: Anarchism and the Anti-Colonial Imagination*. New York: Verso, 2005.

Appadurai, Arjun. *Modernity at Large: Cultural Dimensions of Globalization*. Minneapolis: University of Minnesota Press, 1996.

Arcellana, Emerenciana. *The Life and Times of Claro M. Recto*. Pasay City: Recto Foundation, 1990.

Arnold, J.R. *The Philippines, the Land of Palm and Pine: An Official Guide and Handbook*. Manila: Department of Commerce and Police, 1912.

Austin, Eulalio Amoyen. "The Bago: Its Origin and Culture." Unpublished manuscript, 2001.

Azuma, Eiichiro. *Between Two Empires: Race, History, and Transnationalism in Japanese America*. New York: Oxford University Press, 2005.

Azurin, Arnold M. *Beddeng: Exploring the Ilokano-Igorot Confluence.* N.p.: Museo ng Kalinangan Pilipino, 1991.

Bankoff, Greg. "Response: A Tale of Two Wars." *Foreign Affairs* 81 (2002): 179–81.

Barclay, Paul. "'They Have for the Coast Dwellers a Traditional Hatred': Governing Igorots in Northern Luzon and Central Taiwan, 1895–1915." In *The American Colonial State in the Philippines: Global Perspectives*, eds. Julian Go and Anne L. Foster. Durham: Duke University Press, 2003.

———. "Cultural Brokerage and Interethnic Marriage in Colonial Taiwan: Japanese Subalterns and their Aborigine Wives, 1895–1930." *The Journal of Asian Studies* 64, 2 (2005): 323–60.

Barlow, Tani E., ed. *Formations of Colonial Modernity in East Asia.* Durham: Duke University Press, 1997.

Barrows, David P. *A History of the Philippines.* Manila: Amer. Bk. Co., 1905 [2nd ed., 1907].

Barton, Roy Franklin. *The Kalingas, their Institutions and Custom Law.* Chicago: University of Chicago Press, 1949.

———. *The Religion of the Ifugaos.* New York: Kraus Reprint, 1962 [1946].

———. *Ifugao Law.* Berkeley: University of California Press, 1919 [1969].

Beale, Howard. *Theodore Roosevelt and the Rise of America to World Power.* Baltimore, MD: Johns Hopkins University Press, 1956.

Beisner, Robert L. *Twelve Against Empire: The Anti-Imperialists, 1898–1900.* Chicago: University of Chicago Press, 1985.

Bhabha, Homi. "Of Mimicry and Man: The Ambivalence of Colonial Discourse." In *The Location of Culture.* London: Routledge, 1994.

Billiet, Fancisco, and Francis Lambrecht. *The Kalinga Ullalim/Ifugaw Orthography.* Baguio City: Immaculate Heart Printhall, 1970 [2001].

Bix, Herbert. *Hirohito and the Making of Modern Japan.* New York: Harper Collins Publishers, 2000.

Boot, Max. *The Savage Wars of Peace: Small Wars and the Rise of American Power.* New York: Basic Books, 2002.

———. "Neither New nor Nefarious: The Liberal Empire Strikes Back." *Current History* 102 (2003): 361–6.

Brainard, Cecilia Manguerra. *When the Rainbow Goddess Wept.* Ann Arbor: University of Michigan Press. 1999 [first published as *Song of Yvonne* by New Day Publishers, 1991].

Brands, H.W. *Bound to Empire: The United States and the Philippines.* New York: Oxford University Press, 1992.

Buaken, Manuel. *I Have Lived with the American People.* Caldwell, ID: Caxton Printers, 1948.

Buenafe, Manuel E. *Wartime Philippines.* Manila: Philippine Educational Foundation, 1950.

Buenaventura, Antonio, Jose M. Hernandez, and Jose Villa Panganiban, eds. *Sing and be Happy: For Grade V and VI.* Manila: Macaraig Publisher, 1966.

Buenconsejo, Jose S. "On the Poetics of a Particular Recorded Musical Medium: An Analysis of Joey Ayala's Pinoy 'Altered Native' Music." Unpublished manuscript, 2005.

Cámara de Comercio de las Islas Filipinas. *Yearbook of the Philippine Islands, 1920.* Manila: Bureau of Printing, 1920.

Canclini, Nestor Garcia. *Hybrid Culture: Strategies for Entering and Leaving Modernity.* Minneapolis: University of Minnesota Press, 1995.

Cannell, Fenella. *Power and Intimacy in the Christian Philippines.* Quezon City: Ateneo de Manila University Press, 1999.

Cano, Gloria. "The 'Spanish Colonial Past' in the Construction of Modern Philippine History: A Critical Inquiry into the (Mis)use of Spanish Sources." PhD thesis, National University of Singapore, 2006.

Carruthers, Susan. "The Imperial Interrogative: Questioning American Empire." Paper presented at the Third Drew Colloquium in Transdisciplinary Theological Studies, "An American Empire? Globalization, War, and Religion," September 25–27, 2003.

Casas, Bartolomé de las. *Apologia: In Defense of the Indians. The Defense of the Most Reverend Lord, Don Fray Bartolomé de Las Casas, of the Order of Preachers, Late Bishop of Chiapa, against the Persecutors and Slanderers of the Peoples of the New World Discovered Across the Seas,* trans., ed., and annotated by C.M. Stafford Poole. DeKalb, IL: Northern Illinois University Press, 1974.

Census of the Philippines, 1939, vol. 1, part 3. Reports by Provinces. Manila, 1940.

Chakrabarty, Dipesh. *Provincializing Europe: Postcolonial Thought and Historical Difference.* Princeton, NJ: Princeton University Press, 2000.

Challener, Richard. *Admirals, Generals, and American Foreign Policy.* Princeton, NJ: Princeton University Press, 1973.

Chan, Sucheng. *Asian Americans: An Interpretive History*. Philadelphia: Temple University Press, 1990.

Chang, Iris. *The Rape of Nanking: The Forgotten Holocaust of World War II*. New York: Basic Books, 1997.

Ching, Leo. Becoming *"Japanese": Colonial Taiwan and the Politics of Identity Formation*. Berkeley: University of California Press, 2001a.

———. "'Give Me Japan and Nothing Else!': Postcoloniality, Identity, and the Traces of Colonialism." *South Atlantic Quarterly* 99, 4 (2001b): 763–88.

Choy, Catherine Ceniza. *Empire of Care: Nursing and Migration in Filipino American History*. Durham: Duke University Press, 2003.

Clemente Laoyan I Foundation. *Clemente Laoyan I: His Life, His Family*. La Trinidad: Benguet, 2002.

Clewell, Tammy. "Mourning Beyond Melancholia: Freud's Psychoanalysis of Loss." *Journal of American Psychoanalytical Association* 52, 1 (Spring 2004): 43–67.

Cohen, Theodore. *Remaking Japan: The American Occupation as New Deal*. New York: Free Press, 1987.

Collas, Juan, comp. *The Quirino Way*. Manila, 1955.

Cole, Faye-Cooper. "A Few Field Notes on the Balbalasang Area." Unpublished manuscript, 1907–1908.

———. "The Tinguian: Social, Religious, and Economic Life of a Philippine Tribe." In *Anthropological Series* vol. 14, no. 2. Chicago: Field Museum of National History, 1922.

Commission on Elections (Philippines). *Report of the Commission on Elections to the President of the Philippines and the Congress*. Manila: Bureau of Printing, 1958.

Conklin, Harold. *Ethnographic Atlas of Ifugao: A Study of Environment, Culture, and Society in Northern Luzon*. New Haven: Yale University Press, 1980.

Constable, Nicole, ed. *Cross-Border Marriages: Gender and Mobility in Transnational Asia*. Philadelphia: University of Pennsylvania Press, 2005.

Constantino, Renato., ed. *Thinking for Ourselves: A Representative Collection of Filipino Essays*. Manila: Cacho Hermanos, 1985 [first published in Manila by the Oriental Commercial Co., 1928].

Constantino, Renato, and Letizia R. Constantino. *The Philippines: The Continuing Past*. Quezon City: Foundation for Nationalist Studies, 1978.

Croghan, Richard, ed. *The Development of Philippine Literature in English (Since 1900)*. Quezon City: Alemar-Phoenix, 1975.

Cullinane, Michael. "Implementing the "New Order": The Structure and Supervision of Local Government During the Taft Era." In *Compadre Colonialism: Studies on the Philippines Under American Rule*, ed. Norman Owen. Ann Arbor: University of Michigan Center for South and Southeast Asian Studies, Michigan Papers on South and Southeast Asian Studies no. 3, 1971.

———. "The Master and Juan de la Cruz: Hilario C. Moncado, Politiko and Man of Mystery." In *Lives at the Margin: Biography of Filipinos Obscure, Ordinary, and Heroic*. ed. Alfred W. McCoy. Quezon City: Ateneo de Manila University Press, 2000.

Dahm, Bernhard. "Sukarno and History." In *Man, State, and Society in Southeast Asia*, ed. R.O. Tilman. New York: Praeger Publishers, 1969.

Daniels, Roger. *The Politics of Prejudice: The Anti-Japanese Movement in California and the Struggle for Japanese Exclusion*. New York: Atheneum, 1969.

De Guia, Katrin Luis. *Filipino Artists as Culture Bearers: Lifestyles and Worldviews of Some Contemporary Filipino Artists*, vols. 1 and 2. PhD thesis, University of the Philippines, 1997.

———. Kapwa: *The Self in the Other*. Pasig City: Anvil Publishing, 2005.

De Vera, Arleen. "Constituting Community: A Study of Nationalism, Colonialism, Gender, and Identity among Filipinos in California, 1919–1946." PhD thesis, University of California, Los Angeles, 2002.

De Viana, Augusto V. *Kulaboretor! The Issue of Political Collaboration during World War II*. Manila: University of Santo Tomas Pub. House, 2003.

Desjarlais, Robert R. *Body and Emotion: The Aesthetics of Illness and Healing in the Nepal Himalayas*. Philadelphia: University of Pennsylvania Press, 1992.

Diowan, Dinnah (approximately be translated). "Intabyu: Watashi no Japayuki Taiken [Interview: My Experience being a Japanese-bound Entertainer." Interviewed by Hinago Akira. In *Bessatsu Takarajima no. 54, Japayuki-san Monogatari*. Tokyo: JICC Shuppansha, 1986.

Doronila, Maria Luisa. "The Nature, Organization and Sources of Students' National Identity." In *Towards Relevant Education*, ed.

Education Forum. Quezon City: Association of Major Religious Superiors in the Philippines, 1986.

Dower, John W. *Empire and Aftermath: Yoshida Shigeru and the Japanese Experience, 1878–1954.* Cambridge, Mass.: Harvard University Press, 1988.

________. *Embracing Defeat: Japan in the Wake of World War II.* New York: W.W. Norton & Co., 1999.

Dozier, Edward P. *Mountain Arbiters: The Changing Life of a Philippine Hill People.* Tucson, AZ: University of Arizona Press, 1966.

Dulles, Foster Rhea, and Gerald E. Ridinger. "The Anti-Colonial Policies of Franklin D. Roosevelt." *Political Science Quarterly* 70 (1955): 1–18.

Duus, Peter. *The Abacus and the Sword: The Japanese Penetration of Korea, 1895–1910.* Berkeley: University of California Press, 1995.

Duus, Peter, Ramon H. Myers, and Mark R. Peattie, eds. *The Japanese Informal Empire in China, 1895–1937.* Princeton, NJ: Princeton University Press, 1989

———, eds. *The Japanese Wartime Empire, 1931–1945.* Princeton, NJ: Princeton University Press, 1996.

Eco, Umberto. *A Theory of Semiotics.* Indianapolis: Indiana University Press, 1979.

Ellis, George R. "Arts and Peoples of the Northern Philippines." In *The People and the Art of the Philippines*, eds. G. Casal, R.T. Jose Jr., *et al.* Los Angeles: Museum of Cultural History, University of California, 1981.

Eng, David L., and David Kazanjian, eds. *Loss: The Politics of Mourning.* Berkeley: University of California Press, 2003.

Engels, Dagmar, and Shula Marks. *Contesting Colonial Hegemony: State and Society in Africa and India.* London and New York: I.B. Tauris, 1994.

Enriquez, Salud R., and Aljandro Del Rosario. *Music to Remember for Secondary Schools Part II, Book Two.* N.p.: Philippine Book Company, 1968.

Espiritu, Augusto. *Five Faces of Exile: The Nation and Filipino American Intellectuals.* Stanford: Stanford University Press, 2005.

Fabian, Johannes. *Time and the Other: How Anthropology Makes its Object.* New York: Columbia University Press, 1983.

Fall, Brian. "Ho Chi Minh, Like it or Not." In *Man, State, and Society in Southeast Asia*, ed. R.O. Tilman. New York: Praeger Publishers, 1969.

Fallows, James. "A Damaged Culture." *The Atlantic Monthly* (November 1987): 49–58.

Fegan, Brian. "Light in the East: Continuities in Central Luzon Peasant Movements." Unpublished draft, 1979.

Fenby, Jonathan. *Generalissimo: Chiang Kai-Shek and the China He Lost.* London: Free Press, 2003.

Ferguson, Niall. *Colossus: The Price of America's Empire.* New York: Penguin Press, 2004.

Finin, Gerard A. *The Making of the Igorot: Ramut ti Panagkaykaysa Dagiti Taga Cordillera before Contours of Cordillera Consciousness.* Quezon City: Ateneo de Manila University Press, 2005.

Flores, Patrick. "Makulay na Daigdig: Nora Aunor and the Aesthetics of Sufferance." PhD thesis, University of the Philippines, 2000.

Fonacier, Consuelo V., comp. *At the Helm of the Nation: Inaugural Addresses of the Presidents of the Philippine Republic and the Commonwealth.* Manila: National Media Production Center, 1973.

Forbes, W. Cameron. "Journal of W. Cameron Forbes" (First Series: February 1904 to November 1913), 5 vols. Washington: Library of Congress, 1904–1913.

———. *The Philippine Islands.* Boston: Houghton Mifflin Company, 1928.

Francisco, Luzviminda. "The First Vietnam: The U.S.-Philippine War of 1899." *Bulletin of Concerned Asian Scholars* 5, 4 (December 1973): 2–16.

Freud, Sigmund. "Mourning and Melancholia (1917 [1915])." In *The Standard Edition of the Complete Psychological Works of Sigmund Freud. Volume XIV (1914–16): On the History of the Psycho-Analytic Movement, Papers on Metapsychology and Other Works.* London: Hogarth Press, 1953.

Friend, Theodore. *Between Two Empires: The Ordeal of the Philippines, 1929–1945.* New Haven: Yale University Press, 1965.

———. *Lordship and Bondage: The Philippines, Indonesia and Japanese Impact, 1942–1945.* Washington: Asia Program, Wilson Center, Occasional Paper no. 19, 1984.

———. *The Blue-Eyed Enemy. Japan Against the West in Java and Luzon, 1942–1945.* Princeton, NJ: Princeton University Press, 1988.

Fry, Howard T. *A History of the Mountain Province.* Quezon City: New Day Publishers, 1983.

Fujikane, Candace. "Sweeping Racism under the Rug of 'Censorship': The Controversy over Lois-Ann Yamanaka's *Blu's Hanging.*" *Amerasia Journal* 26 (2000): 158–94.

Fujitani, Takashi. "Reischauer moto Beikokutaishi no Kairaiseiken Koso [Former US Ambassador Reischauer's Idea on the Puppet Emperor System]." *Sekai* 672 (March 2000): 137–46.

———. "Shocho Tenno-sei no Mirai ni tsuite [On the Future of Symbolized Emperor System." In *Nihon wa Dokoe Ikunoka* [*Where Will Japan Go?*], *Nihon no Rekishi* [*History of Japan*], vol. 25. Tokyo: Kodansha, 2003.

Gates, John. "War-related Deaths in the Philippines, 1898–1902." *Pacific Historical Review* 53 (1984): 367–78.

Gleeck, Lewis E., Jr. 1976. *American Institutions in the Philippines (1989–1941)*. Manila: Historical Conservation Society.

Go, Julian. "The Provinciality of American Empire: 'Liberal Exceptionalism' and US Colonial Rule." *Comparative Studies in Society and History* 49 (2007): 74–108.

———. *American Empire and the Politics of Meaning: Elite Political Cultures in the Philippines and Puerto Rico during U.S. Colonialism*. Durham: Duke University Press, 2008.

Go, Liza, and Yeong-hae Jung. *Watashi to Iu Tabi: Gender to Raicism o Koete* [*The Journey Called Me: Beyond Gender and Racism*]. Tokyo: Seidosha, 1999.

Golay, Frank Hindman. *Face of Empire: United States-Philippine Relations, 1898–1946*. Quezon City: Ateneo de Manila University Press, 1997.

Gonzalez, Andrew B. *Language and Nationalism: The Philippine Experience Thus Far*. Quezon City: Ateneo de Manila University Press, 1980.

Gonzalez, N.V.M. *Look, Stranger, on This Island Now*. Manila: Benipayo Press, 1963.

———. *Mindoro and Beyond: Twenty-One Stories*. Quezon City: University of the Philippines Press, 1979.

———. *The Bamboo Dancers*. Metro Manila: Bookmark, Inc., 1993a [first published 1959].

———. *The Bread of Salt and Other Stories*. Seattle: University of Washington Press, 1993b.

Gonzalez, Narita. *Writer's Wives*. Pasig City: Anvil Publishing, 2000.

Goodman, Grant K. "General Artemio Ricarte and Japan." *Journal of Southeast Asian History* 7, 2 (September 1966): 48–60.

———. *Davao: A Case Study in Japanese-Philippine Relations*. Lawrence: University of Kansas Center for East Asian Studies, Research Publication no. 1, 1967a.

———. *Four Aspects of Philippine-Japanese Relations, 1930–1940*. New Haven: Yale University Southeast Asia Studies, Monograph Series no. 9, 1967b.

Goto, Hisao, Kazuko Sinoto, and Alexander Spoehr. "Craft History and the Merging of Tool Traditions: Carpenters of Japanese Ancestry in Hawaii." *The Hawaiian Journal of History* 17 (1983): 156–84.

Gottschewski, Herman. "Nihon ni okeru Yogaku-juyo Kenkyu [A Study of Reception of Western Music in Japan]." *Toyo Ongaku Kenkyu*. 63 (1998): 131–141.

Gould, Lewis L. *The Spanish-American War & President McKinley*. Lawrence: University Press of Kansas, 1982.

Guerrero, Milagros, and Ramon Villegas. "The Historian as Inventor." *Public Policy* 1, 1 (October–December 1997): 137–42.

Guha, Ranajit. *Dominance without Hegemony: History and Power in Colonial India*. Cambridge, Mass.: Harvard University Press, 1997.

Gulick, Sidney L. *The White Peril in the Far East: An Interpretation of the Significance of the Russo-Japanese War*. New York: F.H. Revell Company, 1905.

Halsema, James J. "Hubert Phelps Whitmarsh: Adventurer, Writer, and First Governor of Benguet," Parts 1 and 2. *Bulletin of the American Historical Collection* 9, 2 (35): 51–71 and 9, 3 (36) (1981): 65–82.

———. *E.J. Halsema: Colonial Engineer, A Biography*. Quezon City: New Day Publishers, 1991.

Hartendorp, A.V.H. "Ifugao Small Wood Carving." *Philippines Quarterly* 1, 2 (1951): 17–28.

———. *The Santo Tomas Story*. New York: McGraw-Hill Book Co., 1964.

Hayase, Shinzo. "Tribes, Settlers and Administrators on a Frontier: Economic Development and Social Change in Davao, Mindanao, the Philippines 1899–1941." PhD thesis, Murdoch University, 1984.

———. *Bengetto imin no Kyozo to Jitsuzo — Kindai Nihon Tonan Ajia Kankeishi [Japanese Migrants to Benguet: Myth and Reality — A Study in the History of Relations between Modern Japan and Southeast Asia]*. Tokyo: Dobunkan, 1989a.

———. "Diplomats of Meiji Japan in the Philippines." *Philippine Quarterly of Culture and Society* 17 (1989b): 290–308.

Hayden, Joseph Ralston. "Principal Matters Discussed with Quezon" (1944). Cited in Frank Hindman Golay, *Face of Empire: United States-*

Philippine Relations, 1898–1946. Quezon City: Ateneo de Manila University Press, 1997.

Henson, Maria Rosa. *Comfort Woman: A Filipina's Story of Prostitution and Slavery under the Japanese Military*. Lanham, MD: Rowman & Littlefield Publishers, 1999.

Hito Senbotsu Ikotsu Shushu Narabini Ireihi Konryu Kisei Kai [Association for the Promotion of the Bone Gathering of the War Dead in the Philippines as well as Erecting Memorial]. *Hito Senbotsusha wo Tomurau Houkokusho* [*Report of Memorializing the War Dead in the Philippines*], 1968.

Hito Senbotsusha Irei Kensho Kai [The Philippine Islands War Dead Memorial Association]. "Dai 38 Kai Hito Senbotsusha Ireisai [The Program of the 38th Memorial Service for the Philippine Islands War Dead," March 27, 2004.

Holborn, Louise W. *War and Peace Aims of the United Nations*, vol I. Boston: World Peace Foundation, 1943.

Holthe, Tess Uriza. *When the Elephants Dance*. New York: Penguin Books, 2003.

Hoyt, Frederick. "Agoncillo's Mission to America: Reality Confronts Mythology." *Bulletin of the American Historical Collection* 7, 1 (January 1979), 32–50.

Ichioka, Yuji. *Issei: The World of the First-Generation Japanese Americans*. New York: Free Press, 1988.

———. "Japanese Immigrant Nationalism: The Issei and the Sino-Japanese War, 1937–1941." *California History* 59 (1990): 260–75.

Ikehata, Setsuho, and Ricardo Trota-Jose, eds. *The Philippines under Japan*. Quezon City: Ateneo de Manila University Press, 1999.

Ikenberry, G. John. "America's Imperial Ambition." *Foreign Affairs* 81 (2002): 44–60.

Ileto, Reynaldo C. *Pasyon and Revolution: Popular Movements in the Philippines, 1840–1910*. Quezon City: Ateneo de Manila University, 1979.

———. "Orators and the Crowd." In *Reapprassing an Empire: New Perspectives on Philippine American History*, ed. Peter W. Stanley. Cambridge, Mass.: Harvard University Press, 1984.

———. "Cholera and the Origins of the American Sanitary Order in the Philippines." In *Imperial Medicine and Indigeneous Societies*, ed. David Arnold. Manchester: Manchester University Press, 1988.

———. *Filipinos and their Revolution: Event, Discourse, and Historiography*. Quezon City: Ateneo de Manila University Press, 1998.

———. "Colonial Wars in Southern Luzon: Remembering and Forgetting." *Hitotsubashi Journal of Social Studies* 33, 1 (July 2001): 103–18.

———. "Philippine Wars and the Politics of Memory." *Positions: East Asia Cultures Critique* 13, 1 (2005a): 215–35.

———. *Kirisuto Junanshi to Kakumei: 1840–1910-nen no Firipin Minshu Undo* [*Pasyon and Revolution: Popular Movements in the Philippines, 1840–1910*], trans. and eds. Hiromu Shimizu and Yoshiko Nagano. Tokyo: Hosei Daigaku Shuppankyoku, 2005b.

Iwasaki, Daisuke. *Darkside of Koizumi Junichiro: "Igyo no Saisho" no Satetsu [Darkside of Koizumi Junichiro: Misstep of "Anomalous Prime Minister"]*. Tokyo: Yosen-sha, 2006.

Jameson, Fredric. *The Geopolitical Aesthetic: Cinema and Space in the World System*. Bloomington: Indiana University Press, 1992.

Javellana, Stevan. *Without Seeing the Dawn*. Boston: Little, Brown and Company, 1947.

Jenista, Frank. *The White Apos: American Governors on the Cordillera Central*. Quezon City: New Day Publishers, 1987.

Jenks, Albert Ernest. *The Bontoc Igorot*. Manila: Bureau of Public Printing, 1905.

Jernegan, Prescott F. *The Philippine Citizen. A Text-Book of Civics, Describing the Nature of Government, the Philippine Government, and the Rights and Duties of Citizens of the Philippines*. Manila: Philippine Education Publishing Co., 1910.

Joaquin, Nick. *The Aquinos of Tarlac: An Essay on History as Three Generations*. Metro Manila: Solar Publishing Corp., 1983.

Joaquin, Nick (Quijano de Manila). "The Law and the Prophet: A Look into the Current Status of the Image of Jose P. Laurel," 1967. Reprinted in *The Laurel Legacy*, Memorial Series vol. 2. Manila: Lyceum, 1986.

Jung, Moon-Kie. *Reworking Race: The Making of Hawaii's Interracial Labor Movement*. New York: Columbia University Press, 2006.

Kaimon-cho Kyoudo-shi Hensan I'inkai [Kaimon Municipality Commission of Local History]. *Kaimon-Cho Kyoudo-Shi* [*Kaimon Town's Local History*], rev. ed. Kagoshima: Kaimon Municipality Government, 1994.

Karl, Rebecca. *Staging the World: Chinese Nationalism at the Turn of the Twentieth Century*. Durham: Duke University Press, 2002.

Karnow, Stanley. *In Our Image: America's Empire in the Philippines*. New York: Random House, 1989.

Kastenbaum, Robert. *Macmillan Encyclopedia of Death and Dying*, vol. 2. New York: Macmillan Reference USA, 2002.

Kato, Masuo. *The Lost War: A Japanese Reporter's Inside Story*. New York: A.A. Knopf, 1946.

Keen, Benjamin. "The Legacy of Bartolome de las Casas." *Ibero-Americana Pragensia* 11 (1977): 56–67.

Keesing, Felix M. *The Ethnohistory of Noethern Luzon*. Stanford: Stanford University Press, 1962.

Kennon, Lyman W.V. "Report of the Construction of the Benguet Road." In *Sixth Annual Report of the Philippine Commission, 1905*. Washington: Government Printing Office, 1906, Part 3, Appendix H.

Kerkvliet, Melinda Tria. *Unbending Cane: Pablo Manlapit: A Filipino Labor Leader in Hawaii*. Honolulu: Office of Multicultural Student Services, University of Hawaii, 2002.

Kirk, John M. *Jose Marti, Mentor of the Cuban Nation*. Tampa, FL: University Press of Florida, 1983.

Komori, Yoichi. *Posutokoronial* [*Postcolonial*]. Tokyo: Iwanami Shoten, 2001.

Koseisho Shakai Engo Kyoku [Ministry of Health and Welfare, Bureau of Social Welfare and War Victim's Relief Bureau]. *Engo 50 Nenshi* [*Fifty Years of the War Victim's Relief*]. Tokyo: Gyosei, 1997.

Koshy, Susan. *Sexual Naturalization: Asian Americans and Miscegenation*. Stanford: Stanford University Press, 2004.

Kristeva, Julia. *Language: The Unknown (An Initiation into Linguistics)*, trans. Anne Menke. New York: Columbia University Press, 1989.

Kundera, Milan. *The Book of Laughter and Forgetting*. London: Penguin Books, 1983.

Kyo, Nobuko [Kan, Shinja]. *Nikkan Ongaku Noto: Ekkyo-suru Tabibito no Uta o Otte* [*Notes on Music of Japan and Korea: Chasing the Songs of "Crossing-bordering" Travelers*]. Tokyo: Iwanami Shoten, 1998.

———. *Anju-shinai Watashitachi no Bunka: Higashi Ajia Ruro* [Our Culture Unsettled: Wandering in East Asia]. Tokyo: Shobunsha, 2002.

LaFeber, Walter. *The American Age: United States Foreign Policy at Home and Abroad since 1750*, 2nd ed. New York: Norton, 1994.

Lambrecht, Francis. "The Mayawyaw Ritual, 1–5." *Publications of the Catholic Anthropological Conference*, vol. 4, no. 1–5 (1932–1941).

———. "The Mayawyaw Ritual, 6–7." *University of Manila Journal of East Asiatic Studies*, vols. 4 and 6 (1955–1957).

Laurel, Celia Diaz, and Gloria Angeles Carandang, comp. *Laurel Family Tree*. Privately published, Tanauan, c.1991.

Laurel, Jose P. *Forces that Make a Nation Great (1943)*. Manila: Bureau of Printing, 1944.

Lava, Jesus B. *Memoirs of a Communist*. Pasig City: Anvil Publishing, 2002.

Legarda, Benito, Jr. "The Most Vicious Crime in Philippine History." In *Remembering World War II in the Philippines: Proceedings of the Oral History Conference Marking the 60th Anniversary of the Battle for Manila*. Manila: National Historical Institute, 2007.

Limqueco, Peter. "From Co-Prosperity to Pax Nipponica." In *Southeast Asian Perceptions of Japan*, ed. Renato Constantino. Tokyo/Quezon City: Zensei Publishing Co. and Karrel, Inc., 1991.

Lopez, S.P. "The Colonial Relationship." In *The United States and the Philippines*, ed. Frank H. Golay. Englewood Cliffs, NJ: Prentice-Hall, 1966.

Maceda, Teresita G. "Protest Song." In *CCP Encyclopedia of Philippine Art*, vol. 6. Manila: Cultural Center of the Philippines Special Publication Office, 1994.

———. *Mga Tinig Mula sa Ibaba: Kasaysayan ng Partido Komunista ng Pilipinas at Partido Sosialista ng Pilipinas sa Awit, 1930–1955* [*Sounds from Below: A History of the Communist Party of the Philippines and the Socialist Party of the Philippines through Songs*]. Quezon City: University of the Philippines Press, 1996.

Manalansan, Martin. *Global Divas: Filipino Gay Men in the Diaspora*. Durham: Duke University Press, 2003.

Maram, Linda. *Creating Masculinity in Los Angeles' Little Manila: Working-Class Filipinos and Popular Culture, 1920s–1950s*. New York: Columbia University Press, 2006.

Margold, Jane A. "Egalitarian Ideals and Exclusionary Practices: U.S. Pedagogy in the Colonial Philippines." *Journal of Historical Sociology* 8 (1995): 374–94.

Martin, Dalmacio. "Education and Propaganda in the Philippines during the Japanese Occupation." Manila, June 1952 (Typescript in the Garcia Collection, Sophia University).

Matsushita, Hiroshi, and Shun'ichi Teshirogi, eds. *Yogakushi-saiko: Kirisuto-kyo Ongaku to Nihonjin* [*Rethinking Western Music in Japan: Christian Music and Japanese*]. Tokyo: Kunitachi Ongaku Daigaku, 1993.

May, Ernest R. *Imperial Democracy: The Emergence of America as a Great Power.* New York: Harcourt, Brace & World, 1961.

May, Glenn A. *Social Engineering in the Philippines: The Aims, Execution, and Impact of American Colonial Policy, 1900–1913.* Westport, CT: Greenwood Press, 1980.

———. *Battle for Batangas: A Philippine Province at War.* New Haven: Yale University Press, 1993.

———. *Inventing a Hero: the Posthumous Re-creation of Andres Bonifacio.* Madison, WI: University of Wisconsin-Madison Center for Southeast Asian Studies, 1996.

McCoy, Alfred W. "'Politics by Other Means': World War II in the Western Visayas." In *Southeast Asia under Japanese Occupation,* ed. Alfred W. McCoy. New Haven: Yale University Southeast Asia Studies, Monograph Series no. 22, 1980.

———. "The Philippines: Independence without Decolonization." In *Asia: The Winning of Independence,* ed. Robin Jeffrey. London: Macmillan, 1981.

———. "Quezon's Commonwealth: The Emergence of Philippine Authoritarianism." In *Philippine Colonial Democracy,* ed. Ruby R. Paredes. New Haven: Yale University Southeast Asia Studies, Monograph Series no. 32, 1988.

McCoy, Alfred W., ed. *Southeast Asia under Japanese Occupation.* New Haven: Yale University Southeast Asian Studies, Monograph Series no. 22, 1985 [first published 1980].

Meyer, Hans. "Travels in Northern Luzon (Philippines); Extracts from his Diary as Manuscripts. *Globus,* XVIII, II (1882): 169–72." In W.H. Scott's unpublished manuscript [English translation by W.H. Scott] (Photocopy from the Saboy Collection).

Meyer, Milton H. *A Diplomatic History of the Philippine Republic.* Honolulu: University of Hawaii Press, 1965.

Mikuriya, Takashi. *Nihirizumu no Saisho* [*Prime Minister of Nihilism*]. Tokyo: PHP-Sensho, 2006.

Miller, Rebecca S. "Performing Ambivalence: The Case of Quadrille Music and Dance in Carriacou, Grenada." *Ethnomusicology* 49, 3 (2005): 403–40.

Miller, Stuart Creighton. *'Benevolent Assimilation': The American Conquest of the Philippines, 1899–1903.* New Haven: Yale University Press, 1982.

Mitscherlich, Alexander, and Margarete Mitscherlich. *The Inability to Mourn: Principles of Collective Behavior.* New York: Grove Press, distributed by Random House, 1975.

Moncado, Hilario Camino. *America, the Philippines, and the Orient*. New York: Fleming H. Revell Co., 1932.

Moore, Lina Espina, ed. *The Stories of Estrella D. Alfon*. Quezon City: Giraffe Books, 1994.

Morgan, H. Wayne. *William McKinley & His America*. Syracuse, NY: Syracuse University Press, 1963.

Moses, Bernard. "Control of Dependencies Inhabited by the Less Developed Races." *University of California Chronicle* 7 (1905): 3–18.

Moss, Claude Russell. "Kankanay Ceremonies." *University of California Publication in American Archaeology and Ethnology*, 15, 4 (1920a): 343-84.

———. "Nabaloi Law and Ritual." *University of California Publication in American Archaeology and Ethnology*, 15, 3 (1920b): 207–342.

Moss, Claude Russel, and A.K. Kroeber. "Nabaloi Songs." *University of California Publication in American Archaeology and Ethnology*, 15, 2 (1919): 187–206.

Myers, Ramon H., and Mark R. Peattie, eds. *The Japanese Colonial Empire, 1895–1945*. Princeton, NJ: Princeton University Press, 1983.

Nagano, Yoshiko, "Introduction," In *Firipin Rekishi Kenkyu to Shokuminchi Gensetsu* [*Philippine Historiography and Colonial Discourse*]. Eight essays by Reynaldo C. Ileto, Vicente L. Rafael and Floro C. Quibuyen, comp. and trans. Yoshiko Nagano. Tokyo: Mekong Publishing Co., 2004.

Nakamura, Masanori. *Shocho Tenno-sei eno Michi* [*A Path to the Emperor as National Symbol*]. Tokyo: Iwanami Shoten, 1989.

———. *Sengoshi to Shocho Tenno* [*The Postwar History and Emperor as National Symbol*]. Tokyo: Iwanami Shoten, 1992.

Nakamura, Rihei. *Yogaku-donyusha no Kiseki: Nihon-kindai Yogakushi-josetsu* [*A Path of Japanese Pioneer who Introduced Western Music: An Introductory History of Western Music in Modern Japan*]. Tokyo: Tosui-shobo, 1993.

Nakano, Fe Ceriaquita. *Nihon ni Totsuide 11-nen* [*Eleven Years in Japan after Marriage*]. Tokyo: Bungeisha, 1999.

Nakano, Satoshi. "Politics of Mourning." In *The Philippines-Japan Relations*, eds. Ikehata Setsuho and Lydia N. Yu-Jose. Quezon City: Ateneo de Manila University Press, 2003.

———. "Lost in Memorialization? Unmaking Of 'History Issues' in Postwar Philippines-Japan Relations." In *Proceedings of the Symposium: The Philippines-Japan Relationship in an Evolving Paradigm*. Manila: Yuchengco Center, 2006.

Nakpil, Carmen Guerrero. "Consensus of One," *Manila Sunday Times Magazine*, April 23, 1967, cited in H.W. Brands, *Bound to Empire: The United States and the Philippines*. New York: Oxford University Press, 1992.

Nettl, Bruno. *The Western Impact on World Music: Change, Adaptation, and Survival*. New York: Schirmer Books, 1985.

Nomura, Gail. "Within the Law: The Establishment of Filipino Leasing Rights on the Yakima Indian Reservation." *Amerasia Journal* 13 (1986–1987): 99–117.

Oba, Junko. "To Fight the Losing War, To Remember the Lost War: The Changing Role of Gunka, Japanese War Songs." In *Global Goes Local: Popular Culture in Asia*, eds. Timothy J. Craig and Richard King. Vancouver: UBC Press, 2002.

Orr, James J. *The Victim as Hero: Ideologies of Peace and National Identity in Postwar Japan*. Honolulu: University of Hawaii Press, 2001.

Otake, Hideo. *Koizumi Junichiro: Popurizumu no Kenkyu* [*Koizumi Junichiro: A Study of Populism*]. Tokyo: Toyo Keizai Shinnpo-sha, 2006.

Panabang, Barcelon P. "Banao Legends and History." Unpublished manuscript, 2006.

Paredes, Ruby R., ed. *Philippine Colonial Democracy*. New Haven: Yale University Southeast Asia Studies, Monograph Series no. 32, 1988.

Philippine Constabulary. *Confidential Reports*. Ms., Bandholtz Collection, Bentley Library, University of Michigan (available on microfilm).

Philippine Music Horizons. New York: Silver Burdett Company, 1953.

Pierce, Charles Sanders. *Collected Papers*, 2 vols., eds. Charles Hartshone and Paul Weiss. Cambridge, Mass.: Harvard University Press, 1931.

Ponce, Mariano. *Cartas Sobre la Revolución*. Manila: Bureau of Printing, 1932.

Posadas, Barbara. *The Filipino Americans*. Westport, CT: Greenwood Press, 1999.

Pratt, Julius William. "The Collapse of American Imperialism." *American Mercury* 31 (1934): 269–78.

Preston, Peter W. *Rethinking Development, Essays on Development and Southeast Asia*. London: Routledge & Kegan Paul, 1987.

The Progressive Music Series. New York: Silver Burdett and Company, 1919, 1932, 1948, n.d.

Prudente, Felicidad A. *et al.*, eds. *Philippine Folk Songs.* Manila: Goodwill Bookstore, 1998.

Quibuyen, Floro C. *A Nation Aborted: Rizal, American Hegemony, and Philippine Nationalism.* Quezon City: Ateneo de Manila University Press, 1999 [revised 2nd ed., 2009].

———. "Rizal and Filipino Nationalism: Critical Issues." *Philippine Studies* 50, 2 (2002): 193–229.

Quinsaat, Jesse, ed. *Letters in Exile: An Introductory Reader in Pilipino American History.* Los Angeles: UCLA Asian American Studies, 1976.

Rabinbach, Anson. "Response to Karen Brecht, 'in the Aftermath of Nazi Germany: Alexander Mitscherlich and Psychoanalysis — Legend and Legacy'." *American Imago* 52, 3 (1995): 313–28.

Rafael, Vicente L. *Contracting Colonialism: Translation and Christian Conversion in Tagalog Society under Early Spanish Rule.* Ithaca, NY: Cornell University Press, 1988.

———. "White Love: Surveillance and Nationalist Resistance in the U.S. Colonization of the Philippines." In *Cultures of United States Imperialism*, eds. Amy Kaplan and Donald Pease. Durham: Duke University Press, 1993.

———. "'Your Grief Is Our Gossip': Overseas Filipinos and Other Spectral Presences." *Public Culture* 9 (1997): 267–91.

———. *White Love and Other Events in Filipino History.* Durham: Duke University Press, 2000.

———. *The Promise of the Foreign: Nationalism and the Technics of Translation in the Spanish Philippines.* Durham: Duke University Press, 2005.

Recto, Claro M. *Asiatic Monroeism: Articles of Debate.* Manila: General Printing Press, 1930.

Reed, Robert R. *City of Pines: The Origins of Baguio as a Colonial Hill Station and Regional Capital*, 2nd ed. Baguio: A-Seven Publishing, 1999 [1st ed., 1976].

Reid, Anthony. "Indonesia: Revolution without Socialism." In *Asia: The Winning of Independence*, ed. R. Jeffrey. London: Macmillan, 1981.

Reid, Whitelaw. *Making Peace with Spain: The Diary of Whitelaw Reid*, ed. H. Wayne Morgan. Austin: University of Texas Press, 1965 [1901].

Reyes-Tolentino, Francisca. *Philippine National Dances.* Quezon City: Kayumanggi Press, 1946 [1990].

Ricarte, Artemio. *Sa Mga Kabataang Filipino*. Manila, 1942. (in Tagalog and Spanish) (Copy in the Garcia Collection, Sophia University).

________. *Memoirs of General Artemio Rizarte*. Manila: National Historical Institute, 1963.

Rivadelo, Rosita F. *Filipino Folk Songs*. Metro Manila: National Book Store, 1992.

Rivera, Temario C. "Transition Pathways and Democratic Consolidation in Post-Marcos Philippines." *Contemporary Southeast Asia* 24, 3 (December 2002): 466–83.

Rizal, Jose. *Rizal's Correspondence with Fellow Reformists (1882–1896)*, Manila: Jose Rizal National Centennial Commission, 1961a (cited as "Rizal-Fellow Reformists").

———. *Reminiscences and Travels of Jose Rizal*. Manila: Jose Rizal National Centennial Commission, 1961b (cited as "Reminiscences").

———. *The Rizal-Blumentritt Correspondence*. Part 1, 1886–1889. Manila: Jose Rizal National Centennial Commission, 1961c (cited as "Rizal-Blumentritt").

———. "The Philippines a Century Hence." In *Political and Historical Writings of Rizal*. Manila: Jose Rizal National Centennial Commission, 1961d.

Roces, Alfredo. *Looking for Liling: A Family History of World War II Martyr Rafael R. Roces, Jr.* Pasig City: Anvil Publishing, 2000.

Romualdez, Noberto. *Filipino Musical Instruments and Airs of Long Ago: Lecture Delivered at the Conservatory of Music, University of the Philippines in November 25th, 1931*. N.p.: National Media Production, 1932 [1973].

Romulo, Carlos P. *Mother America: A Living Story of Democracy*. Westport, CT: Greenwood Press, 1943.

Rummel, Rudolph J. *Statistics of Democide: Genocide and Mass Murder Since 1900*. Charlottesville, VA: Center for National Security Law, School of Law, University of Virginia, 1997.

Saboy, Anatalia M. "The Songs of the Banaos of Western Kalinga." MA thesis, Baguio Colleges Foundation, 1990.

Said, Edward. "Representing the Colonized: Anthropology's Interlocutors." *Critical Inquiry* 15, 2 (1989): 205–25.

Sakai, Naoki. *Nihon Shiso to Iu Mondai: Honyaku to Shutai* [*Story Called Japanese Thought: Translation and Subjectivity*]. Tokyo: Iwanami Shoten, 1997a.

———. *Translation and Subjectivity: On Japan and Cultural Nationalism*. Minneapolis: University of Minnesota Press, 1997b.

Salamanca, Bonficacio. *Filipino Reaction to American Rule, 1901–1913*. New Haven: Shoe String Press, 1968.

Salman, Michael. "In Our Orientalist Imagination: Historiography and the Culture of Colonialism in the United States." *Radical History Review* 50 (1991): 221–32.

San Buenaventura, Steffi. "Nativism and Ethnicity in a Filipino-American Experience." PhD thesis, University of Hawaii, Manoa, 1990.

———. "The Master and the Federation: A Filipino-American Social Movement in California and Hawaii." *Social Process in Hawaii* 33 (1991): 169–93.

Saniel, Josefa M. *Japan and the Philippines, 1868–1898*. Quezon City: University of the Philippines, 1962; New York: Russel and Russell, 1973.

———. "Okuma Shigenobu and the 1898 Philippine Problem." *Philippine Historical Review* 1 (1965): 298–319.

Santiago, Francisco. *The Development of the Music in the Philippine Island*. Quezon City: University of the Philippines, 1931 [1957].

Santos, Bienvenido N. *Villa Magdalena*. Quezon City: New Day Publishers, 1986a [first published 1965].

———. *The Volcano*. Quezon City: New Day Publishers, 1986b [first published 1965].

Schadenberg, Alexander. "Contributions to the Knowledge of the Banao People and of the Guinanes, Gran Cordillera Central, Island of Luzon, Phillipines." In "From the Transactions of the Berlin Anthropological Society, Session of 19 February, 1887," trans. W.H. Scott. Unpublished manuscript, St. Andrew's Theological Seminary, 1887.

Scheidnagel, Manuel. *Distrito de Benguet, Memoria Descriptiva y Económica*. Madrid: Imprenta de la Dirección General de Infantería, 1878.

Scheper-Hughes, Nancy, and Margaret M. Lock. "The Mindful Body: A Prolegomenon to Future Works in Medical Anthropology." In *The Art of Medical Anthropology Readings*, eds. Sjaak van der Geest and Adri Rienks. Amsterdam: Het Spinhuis Publishers, 1998.

Schumacher, John N. *The Propaganda Movement, 1890–1895: The Creators of a Filpino Consciousness, The Makers of Revolution*. Manila: Solidaridad Publishing House, 1973.

Schurman, Jacob G. *Philippine Affairs: A Retrospect and Outlook*. New York: Scribner's and Sons, 1902.

Scott, David. "Colonial Governmentality." *Social Text* 43 (1995): 191–220.

Scott, William Henry. "The Word Igorot." *Philippine Studies* 10, 2 (1962): 234–48.

———. *On the Cordillera: A Look at the people and Cultures of the Mountain Province*. Manila: MCS Enterprises, 1969.

———. *The Discovery of the Igorots: Spanish Contact with the Pagans of Northern Luzon*. Quezon City: New Day Publishers, 1974 [1977].

———. *Cracks in the Parchment Curtain: And Other Essays in Philippine History*. Quezon City: New Day Publishers, 1982.

———. *Of Igorots and Independence*. Baguio City: ERA, 1993.

Scruggs, T.M. "Let's Enjoy as Nicaraguans: The Use of Music in the Construction of a Nicaraguan National Consciousness." *Ethnomusicology* 43, 2 (1999): 297–321.

Seeley, John Robert. *The Expansion of England: Two Courses of Lectures*. London: Macmillan, 1885.

Shaw, Angel Velasco, and Luis H. Francia eds. *Vestiges of War: The Philippine-American War and the Aftermath of an Imperial Dream, 1899–1999*. New York: New York University Press, 2002.

Shin, Gi-Wook and Michael Robinson, eds. *Colonial Modernity in Korea*. Cambridge, Mass.: Harvard University Press, 1999.

Silverstein, Josef, ed. "Introduction." In *The Political Legacy of Aung San*. Ithaca, NY: Cornell University Southeast Asia Program, Data Paper no. 86, 1972.

Sims, Richard. *Japanese Political History since the Meiji Renovation: 1868–2000*. New York: Palgrave, 2001.

Smith, Tony. *America's Mission. The United States and the Worldwide Struggle for Democracy in the Twentieth Century*. Princeton, NJ: Princeton University Press, 1994.

Souvenir Pictorial of the Birth of the Philippine Republic. October 14, 1943 (Copy in the Garcia Collection, Sophia University).

Spivak, Gayatri. *Post-Colonial Critic*. London: Routledge, 1990.

Stanley, Peter W. *A Nation in the Making: The Philippines and the United States, 1899–1921*. Cambridge, Mass.: Harvard University Press, 1974.

Steinberg, David Joel. *Philippine Collaboration in World War II*. Ann Arbor: University of Michigan Press, 1967.

Stephanson, Anders. *Manifest Destiny: American Expansion and the Empire of Right*. New York: Hill and Wang, 1996.

Sturtevant, David R. *Agrarian Unrest in the Philippines: Guardia De Honor — Revitalization within the Revolution, and Rizalistas — Contemporary Revitalization Movements in the Philippines*. Athens, OH: Ohio University Center for International Studies, Southeast Asian Series no. 8, 1969.

———. *Popular Uprisings in the Philippines, 1840–1940*. Ithaca, NY: Cornell University Press, 1976.

Sullivan, Rodney J. *Exemplar of Americanism: The Philippine Career of Dean C. Worcester*. Ann Arbor: University of Michigan Center for South and Southeast Asian Studies, Michigan Papers on South and Southeast Asian Studies no. 36, 1991.

Suzuki, Ko. "Kanko Kaihatsu to Chi'iki no Hen'yo: Ibusuki-Shi [Tourism Development and the Transformation of a Local Community: In Case of Ibusuki]." *Chiri* 18, 3 (March 1973): 23–32.

Suzuki, Nobue. "Women Imagined, Women Imaging: Re/presentations of Filipinas in Japan since the 1980s." In *Filipinos in Global Migrations: At Home in the World?*, ed. Filomeno V. Aguilar. Quezon City: Philippine Migration Research Network and Philippine Social Science Council, 2002a.

———. "Gendered Surveillance and Sexual Violence in Filipina Pre-Departure Experiences to Japan." In *Gender Politics in the Asia Pacific Region*, eds. Brenda Yeoh, Peggy Teo and Shirlena Huang. London: Routledge, 2002b.

Taft, William H. *Special Report of Wm. H. Taft Secretary of War to the President on the Philippines*. Washington: Government Printing Office, 1908.

Tahimik, Kidlat. "Midlife Choice: Filmmaking vs. Fillmaking." In *Primed for Life: Writings on Midlife by 18 Men*, ed. Lorna Kalaw-Tirol. Pasig City: Anvil Publishing, 1997.

Takaki, Ronald. *Strangers from a Different Shore*. New York: Methuen, 1989.

Takemae, Eiji. *The Allied Occupation of Japan*. New York and London: Continuum, 2003.

Tapang, B.P. *The Ibaloi Cattle Enterprise in Benguet*. Baguio City: U.P. Cordillera Studies Center, 1985.

Taruc, Luis. *Born of the People* (1949). New York: International Publishers, 1953.

Taylor, J.R.M. *The Philippine Insurrection against the United States*, 5 vols. Pasay City: Eugenio Lopez Foundation, 1971 [1901–1905].

Terami-Wada, Motoe. "The Japanese Propaganda Corps in the Philippines: Laying the Foundation." In *Japanese Cultural Policies in Southeast Asia during World War 2*. ed. Grand K. Goodman. New York: St. Martin's Press, 1991.

———. "The Filipino Volunteer Armies." In *The Philippines under Japan: Occupation Policy and Reaction*, eds. Ikehata Setsuho and

Ricardo Trota Jose. Quezon City: Ateneo de Manila University Press, 1999.

Teshirogi, Shun'ichi. "Joji Oruchin-shi to L.W. Meson: Oruchin Shokan o tooshite [Rev. George Allchin and L. W. Mason: As Seen from Allchin's Letters]." In *Ongaku no Uchu: Minagawa Tatsuo Sensei Koki Kinen Ronbunshu* [*Cosmos of Music: Essays in Commemorating Seventy Years of Age of Prof. Tatsuo Minagawa*]. Tokyo: Ongaku no Tomo-sha, 1998.

———. *Sambika/Seika to Nihon no Kindai* [*Hymns/Sacred Songs and Japan's Modernity*]. Tokyo: Ongaku no Tomo-sha, 1999.

Thomas, J.B. "Annual Report, Civil Sanitarium, Benguet." In *Sixth Annual Report of the Philippine Commission, 1905*. Washington: Government Printing Office, 1906. Part 2, Appendix G.

Thomson, Jr., James C., Peter W. Stanley, and John Curtis Perry. *Sentimental Imperialists: The American Experience in East Asia*. New York: Harper & Row, 1981.

Tiempo, E.K. *Watch in the Night*. Manila: Archipelago Publishing House, 1953.

Tolentino, Rolando. *National/Transnational: Subject Formation and Media in and on the Philippines*. Quezon City: Ateneo de Manila University Press, 2001.

Tourjée, Eben. *A Plea for Vocal Music in Public Schools*. Boston: Mudge, 1871.

Tsukahara, Yasuko. 19-*seiki no Nihon ni okeru Seiyo Ongaku no Juyo* [*Reception of Western Music in Japan in the Nineteenth Century*]. Tokyo: Taga-shuppan, 1993.

United States War Department. *Ninth Annual Report of the Philippine Commission, 1908*. Washington: Government Printing Office, 1909.

Valenzuela, Pio. "The Memoirs of Pio Valenzuela" (1914), trans. Luis Serrano. Appendix A. In *Minutes of the Katipunan*. Manila: National Historical Institute, 1978a.

———. "Testimony of Dr. Pio Valenzuela in the Case of Vicente Sotto" (1917), trans. Luis Serrano. Appendix W. In *Minutes of the Katipunan*. Manila: National Historical Institute, 1978b.

Vanoverbergh, Morice. "Isneg Songs." *Anthropos* 55 (1960): 463–824.

———. "Kankanay Songs." *Asian Folklore Studies* 37, 2 (1978): 1–104.

Waterman, Christofer. "Our Tradition is a Very Modern Tradition: Popular Music and the Construction of the Pan-Yoruba Identity." *Ethnomusicology* 34, 2 (1990): 367–79.

Wheeler-Bennett, J.W. "Thirty Years of American-Filipino Relations, 1899–1929." *Journal of the Royal Institute of International Affairs* 8 (1929): 503–21.

White, Richard. "Creative Misunderstandings and New Understandings." *William and Mary Quarterly* 63, 1 (2006): 9–14.

Wielenga, Frison. "An Inability to Mourn? The German Federal Republic and the Nazi Past." *European Review* 2, 4 (2003): 551–72.

Williams, Daniel R. *The Odyssey of the Philippine Commission*. Chicago: A.C. McClurg & Co., 1913.

Williams, William Appleman. *The Tragedy of American Diplomacy*. Cleveland: World Publishing Co., 1959.

Wilson, Lawrence L. *Apayao Life and Legends*. [Baguio], 1947; Manila: Bookman, 1967.

Wilson, Woodrow. "Democracy and Efficiency." *The Atlantic Monthly* 87 (March 1901): 289–99.

Worcester, Dean C. "The Non-Christian Tribes of Northern Luzon." *Philippine Journal of Science* 1, 8 (1906): 791–875.

Yamaori, Tetsuo. *Folklore of Death: Japanese Perspectives on Life and Death and the Funeral Rites* [*Shi no Minzokugaku: Nipponjin no Shiseikan to Sousougirei*]. Tokyo: Iwanami Shoten, 2002.

Yang, Eun-sik. "Korean Women of America: From Subordination to Partnership, 1903–1930." *Amerasia Journal* 11 (1984): 1–28.

Yasuda, Hiroshi. *Shoka to Jujika* [*Shoka and the Cross*]. Tokyo: Ongaku no Tomo-sha, 1993.

Yeoh, Brenda, and Louisa-May Khoo. "Home, Work and Community: Skilled International Migration and Expatriate Women in Singapore." *International Migration* 36, 2 (1998): 159–86.

Yoshida, Yutaka. *Showa Tenno no Shusen-shi* [*Showa Tenno and His End-of-War History*]. Tokyo: Iwanami Shoten, 1992.

Yoshikawa, Yoko. "Jose M. Tagawa and the Japanese Commercial Sector in Manila, 1898–1920." *Philippine Studies* 46 (1998): 162–94.

Young, Louise. *Japan's Total Empire: Manchuria and the Culture of Wartime Imperialism*. Berkeley: University of California Press, 1999.

Yu-Jose, Lydia N. "Japanese OCW's to the Philippines, 1903–1917." *Philippine Studies* 45 (1997): 108–23.

———. *Japan Views the Philippines, 1900–1944*. Quezon City: Ateneo de Manila University Press, 1999.

Zaide, Gregorio. *Political and Cultural History of the Philippines*, rev. ed. Manila: Philippine Education Co., 1957.

Zapanta, P.A. "The Lapiang Malaya Story: Tragedy of the Deluded." *The Sunday Times Magazine,* June 4, 1967, p. 13.

Newspapers, Websites and Speeches

"22-nenme no Taimen (3) [The Reunion after 22 Years (3)]." *Minami Nippon Shimbun,* December 26, 1967, p. 9.

"22-nenme no Taimen (6) [The Reunion after 22 Years (6)]." *Minami Nippon Shimbun,* December 29, 1967, p. 9.

"Aguinaldo, 94, Dies; Led Filipino Revolts." *New York Times,* February 6, 1964, p. 26.

"Casualty Toll Hits 60 in R.P. Battle: Report Blames Fanatics' Leaders." *Pacific Stars and Stripes,* May 24, 1967, p. 7.

"Commander of Armies That Turned Back Japan Led a Brigade in World War I." *New York Times,* April 6, 1964, p. 26.

Constitution of Japan. Available at <http://www.solon.org/Constitutions/Japan/English>.

Dowd, Maureen. "Hypocrisy and Apple Pie." *New York Times,* April 30, 2003, Section A, Column 2, Editorial Desk, p. 27.

Go, Fusako. "Rizoto 'Kankodori' Ryoko-gyosha Kankan [Nobody at Resort: Tourist Industry Enraged]." *Asahi Shimbun,* January 8, 2001, p. 8.

"Hanase Annual Memorial 03/27/2004_01 Ringing the Bell," Available at <http://jp.youtube.com/watch?v=nG8w7V2ou5M>.

"Hanase Annual Memorial 03/27/2004_03 Shinto Ritual (1)" Available at <http://jp.youtube.com/watch?v=JBnw4T0uT4o>.

"Hanase Annual Memorial 03/27/2004 _09 P3C Prayer & End," Available at <http://jp.youtube.com/watch?v=iKRLvVDNtwg>.

"Japan Apologizes over Battle of Manila." *Manila Bulletin.* February 19, 2006. Available at <http://www.highbeam.com/doc/1G1-142249584.html>.

"Japanese Girl Visits Father's Grave." *Manila Times,* December 8, 1967, B2-A.

Japanese Ministry of Justice. "Table 5. Foreign New Entrants Based on Nationality and Visa," 2006. Available at <http://www.moj.go.jp/>.

Japanese Ministry of Justice. "Table 6. Foreign New Entrants Based on Nationality and Visa," 2007. Available at <http:// http://www.e-stat.go.jp/SG1/estat/List.do?lid=000001029660/>.

Jin, Naoko. "Bridge for Peace: Objective." Available at <http://bridgeforpeace.jp/objective.html>.

Johnson, Brett. "Yoshihiko Amino's Contentious History: Emperor and Outcastes in Medieval Japan." *The Journal of the International*

Institute 4, 1 (Fall 1996). Available at <http://hdl.handle.net/2027/spo.4750978.0004.109>.

"Kaigai Senchi no Ireihi Jittai wo Chosa: Hokai Sunzen no Hi mo [State of Overseas Battle Site Memorials are to be Investigated: Some of Them About to Collapse]." *Asahi Shimbun*, July 4, 2004, p.15.

"Kyouri no Tsuchi ni Yasuraka ni [Rest in Peace at Home]." *Minami Nippon Shimbun*, April 21, 1968, p. 12.

Mohacek, Bozi. "Ca 1910: De Dion-Bouton Busses and Lorries for Baguio City in the Philippines," 2003a. Available at <http://www.svvs.org/philippines1.shtml>.

———. "Stanley Steamers and Yorkshire Steam Wagons in 1908 Philippines," 2003b. Available at <http://www.svvs.org/philippines2.shtml>.

Nagano, Yoshiko. "Transcultural Battlefield: Recent Japanese Translations of Philippine History." UCLA Center for Southeast Asian Studies Occasional Papers, 2006. Available at <http://repositories.cdlib.org/international/uclacseas/op/Nagano>.

Petras, James. "Modernity and Twentieth Century Holocausts: Empire-Building and Mass Murder," 2006. Available at <http://www.axisoflogic.com/artman/publish/printer_22549.shtml>.

Recto, Claro M. "Our Lingering Colonial Complex." Speech delivered before the Baguio Press Club, June 24, 1951.

Reid, Lawrence. "Dancing and Music: Notes from Guinaang, Bontoc, Mountain Province, Philippines." 1961[2009]. Available at <www2.Hawaii.edu/~reid/combined%20Files/A2,%201961%20Dancing%20and%20Music.pdf>.

Reischauer, Edwin O. "Memorandum on Policy towards Japan," 2000. Available at <http://www.iwanami.co.jp/sekai/2000/03/146.html>.

"Remarks by H.E. Ambassador Ryuichiro Yamazaki on the Occasion of the 61st Anniversary of the Battle for the Liberation of Manila." Intramuros, Manila, February 18, 2006.

Stolberg, Sheryl Gay, and Shaila Dewan. "In Memphis, Two Heads of Government Visit the Home of Rock 'n' Roll Royality." July 1, 2006. Available at <http://www.nytimes.com/2006/07/01/washington/01bush.html>.

Toshi Kushu [City Raids]. Available at <http://www.asahi-net.or.jp/~un3k-mn/kusyu.htm> .

Wikipedia. "Aung San." Available at <http://en.wikipedia.org/wiki/Aung_San>.

Contributors

Patricia O. AFABLE is Research Associate in the Department of Anthropology, National Museum of Natural History at the Smithsonian Institution, Washington DC. She edited *Japanese Pioneers in the Northern Philippine Highlands, A Centennial Tribute, 1903–2003* (Baguio City: Filipino-Japanese Foundation of Northern Luzon, 2004) and her published articles include "Journeys from Bontoc to the Western Fairs, 1904–1915: The 'Nikimalika' and Their Interpreters," *Philippine Studies* 52, 4 (2004).

Oscar CAMPOMANES is Assistant Professor in the Department of English, Ateneo de Manila University. His publications include "*La Revolución Filipina* in the Age of Empire," *Japanese Journal of American Studies* 18 (2007), and "Images of Filipino Racialization in the Anthropological Laboratories of the American Empire: The Case of Daniel Folkmar," *PMLA* [*Publications of the Modern Language Association of America*] 123, 5 (2008).

Augusto ESPIRITU is Associate Professor in the History Department, University of Illinois at Urbana-Champaign. He is the author of *Five Faces of Exile: The Nation and Filipino American Intellectuals* (Palo Alto, CA: Stanford University Press, 2005) and "Transnationalism and Filipino American Historiography," *Journal of Asian American Studies* 11, 2 (2008).

Kiichi FUJIWARA is Professor of International Politics at the Graduate Schools of Law and Politics, University of Tokyo. His published works include "Between Terror and Empire: Japan's Response and the Post-9/11 Order," in *Japanese Responses to Globalization: Politics, Security, Economics and Business*, eds. Glenn D. Hook and Harukiyo Hasegawa (Basingstoke, Hampshire: Palgrave Macmillan, 2006); and most recently, *Shinpen: Heiwa no Realism* [*A Realist Proposal for Peace*], new edition (Tokyo: Iwanami Shoten, 2010).

Julian GO is Associate Professor of Sociology at Boston University. His most recent publication is *American Empire and the Politics of Meaning: Elite Political Cultures in the Philippines and Puerto Rico during U.S. Colonialism* (Durham, NC: Duke University Press, 2008).

Reynaldo C. ILETO is Professor in the Southeast Asian Studies Program, National University of Singapore. He has authored *Filipinos and their Revolution: Event, Discourse, and Historiography* (Quezon City: Ateneo de Manila University, 3rd printing, 2003) and *Pasyon and Revolution: Popular Movements in the Philippines, 1840–1910* (Quezon City: Ateneo de Manila University, 8th printing, 2008).

Yoshiko NAGANO is Professor of International Relations and Asian Studies, Kanagawa University in Yokohama. Her works include *Firipin Ginkoshi Kenkyu: Shukuminichi-taisei to Kinyu* [*Philippine Banking History: Colonial State and Finance*] (Tokyo: Ochanomizu Shobo, 2003), and most recently, "The Philippine Currency System during the American Colonial Period: Transformation from Gold Exchange Standard to the Dollar Exchange Standard," *International Journal of Asian Studies* 7, 1 (2010).

Satoshi NAKANO is Professor of History at the Graduate School of Social Sciences, Hitotsubashi University. Among his numerous publications are "Gabriel L. Kaplan and U.S. Involvement in

Philippine Electoral Democracy: A Tale of Two Democracies," *Philippine Studies* 52, 2 (2004) and "South to South across the Pacific: Ernest E. Neal and Community Development Efforts in the American South and the Philippines," *Japanese Journal of American Studies* 16 (2005).

Floro C. QUIBUYEN is a retired Associate Professor of Philippine Studies at the Asian Center, University of the Philippines. His publications include "Towards Community in a Doomed World: Rediscovering Rizal's Prophetic Vision in the Age of Peak Oil and Global Warming," *Asian Studies* 41, 1 (2005/2008) and *A Nation Aborted: Rizal, American Hegemony and Philippine Nationalism*, revised, 2nd edition (Quezon City: Ateneo de Manila University Press, 2009).

Temario C. RIVERA is Professor of Politics and International Relations at the International Christian University of Tokyo. His major works are *Landlords and Capitalists: Class, Family and State in Philippine Manufacturing* (Quezon City: University of the Philippines Press, 1994) and "The Struggle of the Muslim People in the Southern Philippines: Independence or Regional Autonomy?" *Asian Cultural Studies* 15 (2006).

Hiromu SHIMIZU is Professor of Anthropology at the Center for Southeast Asian Studies, Kyoto University. He is the author of *The Orphans of Pinatubo: Ayta Struggle for Existence* (Manila: Solidaridad Publishing House, 2001), and most recently, "Reorganizing Regional Networks in the Global Age: Possibilities for Long Distance Environmentalism," in *In Search of Sustainable Humanosphere: A New Paradigm for Humanity, Biosphere and Geosphere*, eds. Kaoru Sugihara, *et al.* (Kyoto: Kyoto University Press, 2010).

Nobue SUZUKI is Professor of Anthropology in the Faculty of Letters at Chiba University. She has written and published numerous articles such as "Outlawed Children: Japanese Filipino Children, Legal Defiance, and Ambivalent Citizenships,"

Pacific Affairs 83, 1 (2010) and "'*Japayuki*,' or Spectacles for the Transnational Middle-Class," *Positions* (forthcoming).

Michiyo YONENO-REYES is Assistant Professor at the Graduate School of Asian Studies, University of the Philippines. Her publications include "Under Attack: Impact of Mass Media Technology on Indigenous Musical Practice in the Cordillera in the Philippines," in *Global Goes Local: Popular Culture in Asia*, eds. T. Craig and R. King (Vancouver: University of British Columbia Press, 2002) and "Salidummay's Hybridity and 'Congregational Singing,'" *Humanities Diliman* 7, 1 (2010).

Index